Freedom or Serfdom?

The Case for Limited, Constitutional Government and Against Statism

By

Hal Lillywhite

For questions or permission to use parts of this work email
hlillywh@juno.com

Published in conjunction with createspace.com

Table of Contents

Acknowledgments

I could not create a work of this length in a vacuum. Many people contributed to the ideas herein, some unaware that they were doing so. Among the latter are many posters on the newsgroup oregon.politics. Discussions there helped find problems with how I was expressing my ideas and sharpen my thinking. Particularly valuable were those with viewpoints opposed to my own.

I greatly appreciate my wife, Merlene, who read the manuscript on top of putting up with me and the time I spent working on this book.

I especially thank my daughter, Rebecca Bogardus. In spite of raising a family, home schooling her children, church work, and teaching music, she found time to review the entire manuscript and make valuable suggestions. Her efforts greatly improved this book. Any remaining problems, however, are mine and mine alone.

Chapter 1, Twenty-first Century Serfdom?

Oh Lord, protect me from those who would protect me from myself.
(Anonymous)

In the United States of America, the people have more freedom than almost anywhere else on earth, and even the poor have more of this world's goods than the middle class in many countries. Why, then, do some want to exchange our system of freedom for a statist government similar to that in countries lacking those advantages?

Intentions.

Actions.

Results.

Do results match intentions? That is the big question, particularly with government.

Government intended to eliminate poverty. Poverty has increased.[1]

Government intended to make health care more accessible. The cost of health insurance for most people has increased.[2]

Government intended to make it easier for the poor to buy houses. Many of those low-income home buyers lost both their homes and their credit ratings.[3]

---

1   Discussed in Chapter 8 of this book.
2   Likewise discussed in Chapter 8
3   Discussed in Chapter 26

Our government set out to help us, in many cases to protect us from ourselves. A bigger, more powerful government now meddles more and more in our lives. It approaches a statist, collectivist system, a system having much in common with serfdom. Yet it seldom reaches the goals used to justify that government power. The problem is results, not intentions.

The statists see some children with little food. They see a huge gap between rich and poor. They see too many minorities incarcerated. They want to do something about it so they pass laws and make bureaucratic rules and regulations. The intentions are good, but what of the results?

Statism assumes that the central planner, hundreds of miles away from the action, can decide more wisely than the person on the scene. In practice, that results in one-size-fits-all regulations that really fit nowhere.

Statism assumes that government functionaries can effectively manage the entire economy. In practice, that economy is so complex that effective central management is impossible.

Statism constructs wonderful, self-consistent theories and applies them to the people, be those people in agreement or not. In practice, those theories make shipwreck on the rocks of reality – but statists ignore the shipwrecks and insist that their theories are still good.

Statism demands unlimited power to do what it claims will help us. In practice, that power is turned against the citizens for the benefit of the powerful.

Statism requires experts in the bureaucracy, empowered to make regulations for the rest of us. In practice, that creates conflicting and burdensome rules, harmful to both freedom and the economy.

Statism promises security, food, clothing, medical care, housing, and on and on. In practice someone must create those things and government must take from the productive for the benefit of the recipients. That eviscerates incentive, and the productive become less productive.

Statism promises freedom. In practice, bureaucrats and others force their decisions on the people.

Statism promises benign rulers who will act in the best interest of the people. In practice, it provides opportunity for the power-hungry, even psychopaths, to rule.

Statism promises that government-controlled property will provide for all. In practice, that common property is either allowed to deteriorate or is exploited for the benefit of the ruling class.

Statism promises democracy – until that democracy goes against the wishes of the powerful, whereupon it finds a way around the will of the people.

Statism promises security, but delivers the security of the serf or slave. And even that can be revoked at the will of the rulers.

The promises of statism/collectivism are myriad – and only marginally related to what it actually delivers. It does, however, deliver serfdom-like bondage.

Serfdom, 1639

An emissary from the lord of the manor! John shudders, stops threshing his grain and hopes that the man on the black stallion will not thresh him. Did someone overhear his complaint yesterday?

This serf, whom we shall call John I, lives in Western Europe. His one advantage is that he cannot be fired. Neither can he quit and seek employment elsewhere. His sons will follow in his footsteps. His daughters, if they grow up pretty, may be taken into the manor as servants – and unofficial concubines.

Britannica Online defines serfdom:

> [The] condition in medieval Europe in which a tenant farmer was bound to a hereditary plot of land and to the will of his landlord. The vast majority of serfs in medieval Europe obtained their subsistence by cultivating a plot of land that was owned by a lord.... A proportion of the grain the serf grew on his holding had to be given to his lord. The lord could also compel the serf to cultivate that portion of the lord's land that was not held by other tenants (called demesne land). The serf also had to use his lord's grain mills and no others.[4]

Why should John's problems concern us? We are not bound to the land, but do other parts of that definition apply to us? Do we fit a description of modern serfdom?

Freedom – United States of America, 1895

"Whoa!" John's descendant, John II, stops the horses and looks back at the row of sheaves behind the reaper-binder. What an invention! Between John and his boss they will have the harvest done in half the time it took last year with a crew of 10. Across the field he sees his son Jim, bringing in the cows. Jim likes farming and will follow his father. His other son, Bill, is in town, apprenticed to the blacksmith. Daughter Betsy is studying to be admitted to normal school and become a teacher. John has only one nagging worry: his savings are approaching

---

4   http://www.britannica.com/EBchecked/topic/535485/serfdom

what he needs to buy his own farm. Does he really want that risk and responsibility? Does he want to leave George, who is both employer and friend? His ancestor would have been delighted to face such worries.

John II and his family cannot be jailed for criticizing their employers or the government. They work hard, but they are free and life is generally good. If they decide they don't like their current situation, they can move away and seek better opportunities elsewhere.

How did John II end up so much better off than his ancestor? What forces brought about freedom for John II, and what forces are destroying that freedom today? Chapter 6 will discuss that question, but now let's look in on yet another John.

Today – Diminishing Freedom

John III is a descendent of the other two Johns. He leaves his office, looking forward to watching his favorite football team on his big-screen TV. Technology is so much a part of his life that he doesn't even think about it. He does think about the silly restrictions the city puts on the taxi business. John put himself through college as a cabbie and tried to start his own taxi company. The city denied his request for a license, claiming that the existing company provided enough taxis; there was no public need for another company in that business. John's contention that taxi service was poor and overpriced fell on deaf ears. In fact they threw him out of the office when he mentioned that the mayor's cousin owns the existing taxi company.

John III faces some features of serfdom. Depending on where he lives, he may pay over half his middle class income in taxes and fees. Government forces him to buy approved health insurance. An unholy alliance of government and business restricts competition with established businesses, such as the existing taxi company. The businesses thus protected love that protection; customers and potential competitors do not. Like serfs forced to grind their grain only at the lord's mill, customers pay inflated prices for poor service while would-be competitors remain frozen out.

John's friend Bill wants to be a barber. The problem? He lives in Oregon where the state requires 1100 hours of training before he can put up his barber's pole. That is more training time than what it takes to become an EMT! The reason? Crony capitalism. Barbers already licensed do not want competitors, and cosmetology schools want more students. The seven-member Oregon Board of Cosmetology establishes requirements for getting a barber's license, and its rules have the force of law. As I write this, six of the seven board members are either in the barbering business or teaching those who want licenses. They have a vested interest in making it difficult to become a barber. Another serfdom-like requirement, directing business to favored enterprises.

John's cousin Bill in Tennessee faced a similar problem. When his neighbor died, the widow was forced to buy a casket at an inflated price. Jim saw an opportunity to help the bereaved while establishing a good business for himself. He would sell caskets and other funeral supplies, undercutting the ridiculous prices funeral parlors demanded. Not so fast! The state shut down the business and fined him; it was illegal for anyone but a licensed funeral director to sell funeral supplies. Eventually a court overturned that (*Craigmiles v. Giles)*, but for years that law gouged the bereaved. The citizens were again "serfs," forced to do business only with state approved casket vendors.[5]

Even worse is what John's niece Betty faces in Louisiana. She enjoys making floral arrangements and everybody loves her work. Clearly she should go into business.

Sorry Betty. Louisiana protects customers from "dangerous" flower arrangers. Only licensed arrangers are allowed to work and that license required a written and practical test, given four times per year, usually in Baton Rouge. The practical test was graded by licensed arrangers, the very people who didn't want competition from people like Betty. Surprise! Most people taking the test failed, even experienced arrangers who had been successful in other states. Finally the court struck that down in *Chauvin v. Strain* but, as far as I can determine, the written test is still required. Getting married? Need flowers for a funeral? Do you want flower arrangements for a party? You will pay the monopoly prices the state approved flower arrangers demand. And Betty is still not allowed to sell her arrangements; she is dyslexic and cannot pass the written test.

Governments often create monopolies or oligopolies by such things as limiting the number of licenses available. They protect established businesses, but at the expense of fewer choices for customers. Serfdom-like crony capitalism leads to higher prices and poor service; and it shuts out would-be entrepreneurs like John III.

---

5   http://www.ij.org/tennessee-caskets-background

Freedom of Speech?

At least John III has freedom of speech – or does he? What if he needs a business license, but the powers that be don't like his opinions? Think they won't retaliate? Think again. Shortly before this writing, several local governments tried to keep a restaurant chain out of their jurisdictions. What made those restaurants so dangerous? The owner had the temerity to disagree with city politicians on same-sex marriage.[6] The thought police made a frontal assault on freedom of speech and of religion.

Nor is restriction on free speech limited to profit-making businesses. Some jurisdictions control internet advice about diet and exercise, even if the advice is free. They claim that giving such advice is an "occupational activity" requiring a license.[7] How long until they start prosecuting people who give friendly advice over the back fence? The only real difference is that current technology makes it easy for government to notice what happens on the internet. What if that changes and they can monitor what you say over the back fence? Do you think that your neighbor should exercise more, or that his family should include more vegetables in their meals? Maybe you better get licensed before you make any such suggestions.

We have not yet sunk to serfdom, but we have lost many freedoms.

---

6   http://newsfeed.time.com/2012/07/23/boston-mayor-blocks-chick-fil-a-franchise-from-city-over-homophobic-attitude/

7   http://www.huffingtonpost.com/2012/08/08/unlicensed-diet-blogger-steve-cooksey_n_1757695.html (And other sources. Though Huffington may not be the most reliable source, it does lean significantly to the statist side. It is significant that this problem is so bad that a statist source publicizes it.)

The Future -What Will it Hold?

What about the descendent of the other Johns, John IV who will see the next century? What will his life be like? Surely technology will have changed, but what about his freedom and the economy in which he lives? That will depend on what we do today, on how we restrict or fail to restrict government power. Maybe he will be as free as John II, but with technological advantages we cannot even dream of. Or maybe government will use that technology to control his life, just as the lord of the manor controlled his ancestor.

If we allow government to control how we earn our living, what beliefs we are allowed to express, where we live, we will face a modern form of serfdom. That serfdom will rule, not because people of ill-will want to enslave us, but because of well-intentioned efforts to improve our lives. The danger is not an external tyrant; rather it is that we will gradually allow government to do more and more for us. Every added benefit hands over more power, control, and tax money to government. That restricts freedom, harms the economy, and creates the dependency of a modern serfdom.

We decide which way we will go. Then, as surely as going south from Detroit takes us to Canada, we will reach the destination at the end of our path. Will that destination be freedom or serfdom?

And yes, going south from Detroit does take us to Canada. Action leads to results, be those results expected or not. Likewise increase of government power will take us to its inevitable destination, be that destination what we expect or not.

Serfdom in Your Life?

Your car gets worse gas mileage than it should, and you pay more for food than you should. Why? By government edict, nearly all the gasoline you buy contains alcohol, manufactured from corn. That rule was established to reduce fossil fuel consumption and carbon dioxide emissions. Does it work? Probably not. It takes energy to grow that corn and extract the alcohol. There is probably no net gain, but the rule remains.

The federal government tries to mandate what shall be in school lunches, whether the kids like it or not. Much of that tax-subsidized food goes into the garbage.

The National Security Agency probably has a record of your phone calls and emails.

If a "special" student disrupts your child's class, learning suffers. School personnel cannot apply normal discipline, nor can they easily remove the disruptive student from that class.

Government created those problems. Worse, it continues to create problems. Our freedoms, hard won since the time of serfdom, are in retreat.

Worse Than a Crossroads

> *Multitudes, multitudes in the valley of decision.*
> *(Holy Bible, Joel 3:14)*

We are building, today, the future for ourselves, our children, our grandchildren, and beyond. Will government functionaries decide how we earn our living, what medical care we shall receive, where we will be allowed to live, and every other aspect of our lives? Or will freedom once again reign in this land? We decide.

This is not a crossroads, it is much more difficult. At a crossroads we could decide once and for all, then get on with our lives. Instead we face a decision we must make every day. We travel the poorly marked path of freedom through the morass of statism/collectivism/serfdom. The temptations to deviate from the path are attractive and frequent. Yielding to those temptations will cost both freedom and prosperity.

With every election, every opportunity to influence voters or representatives, we defend freedom or move toward statism. I am so bold as to say that this is the most important decision we face as a nation: *Will we be serfs, bought and paid for with our own tax money; or will we be free men and women?*

The Parable of the Pigs

It started with a few loose nails. A sow knocked a board loose and a few small pigs squeezed through. Then a boar knocked another board off the fence and the entire herd escaped. Next morning the farmer got about half of his animals back before other duties called. The remaining hogs fled to a swampy area. They did what comes naturally and soon multiplied into a valuable quantity of pork on the hoof. Hunters and trappers, anxious for easy money, converged. The pigs refused to cooperate and the hunters gave up.

Then a stranger came to town. He got a local lad to show him where the hogs lived, then went to a trucking company and reserved its largest cattle truck for two months hence. Everybody laughed. If he wanted to lose his deposit on the truck, that was his problem.

For two months the stranger mostly lounged around town, leaving once a day for reasons unknown. Then the truck he had reserved made three trips, each time returning packed with pigs. Farmers in the area bought the younger pigs, the larger hogs went straight to the slaughter house.

As the stranger celebrated with a pork roast, someone asked him how he did it. "Easy," he responded. "I just gave them a free lunch for a while. I put some corn on the ground, near where they lived. They were suspicious, the first couple of days some sniffed at my corn but none would eat. Then one small pig helped himself to a few bites. Next day, several young pigs joined in. Every more and more joined the feast until they were all enjoying my corn. They were nervous at first, ready to run if I got close. That didn't last long though.

"Then I started putting posts around my 'lunch counter.' The older hogs didn't like that, but soon they ignored the posts. In fact, some of them ignored me.

"Next I started putting poles between the posts, low at first and then building a fence higher and higher. I left only an opening for the gate. After a few days I had a fence high enough that the hogs couldn't get over it. I let them eat for a couple of days, then closed the gate and got the truck. I put some corn in the truck and they charged right up the loading ramp. My biggest problem was stopping them when the truck got full."

The application to our dependence on government is obvious. That dependence will lead to a serf-like existence, to government ownership of our lives.

Modern Serfdom?

For our purposes here, "serfdom" means government control of nearly all aspects of life, similar to what medieval serfs faced but without the agricultural connection. The opposite we shall call freedom.

Government is necessary of course. It can build roads, maintain police and fire departments, provide national defense and perform a myriad of functions not feasible for the private sector (see Chapter 16). Indeed, in the absence of official government, the biggest bully on the block will impose a de facto government. The question is not unlimited government or no government. Rather it is a question of just how much power government should have and how to limit that power. Will we allow continued expansion of government power? Or will we realize that every increase in rules, regulations, "entitlements," etc. is a step away from freedom and towards serfdom?

Government can be a good servant but a fearful master. How do we, in a changing world, keep it as a servant and not let it become our master?

Freedom, Serfdom, and Change

Societal changes affect our freedom. We have technology undreamed of only a few years ago – technology that may soon allow government and others to track our every move. Do you think that is not a risk? Wait until you get to Chapter 26 in this book.

Those changes will affect our lives, but we should be careful *how* we allow them to affect us. We can sit back and let them control us, or we can stand up like men and women, limiting their power and controlling them as we choose. The first course is easy; we just let things happen and suffer the consequences. The second is more difficult; it requires that we remain alert and fight for our freedom. One course leads to a serf-like existence, the other to freedom.

Advancing technology is a two-edged sword. On the plus side, computerized communication destroys the near monopoly of a few news sources. It is now difficult for government, or a few news organizations, to control available information. The other edge of the sword cuts through our privacy; we are approaching a time when government can become the all-knowing "Big Brother" depicted in Orwell's novel, *1984.* As I write this, there is a major controversy about how much citizen information the National Security Agency is collecting, and what the government will do with that information. Will it simply use it to protect us from criminals or foreign enemies? Or will it use that information to eliminate opposition to powerful politicians? Uncontrolled, the technology that gives us nearly unlimited information also threatens our privacy and even our freedom.

How will we decide? Will we stand up, think for ourselves, and accept responsibility for our own lives? Or are we mere recipients of orders and handouts, waiting for someone else to take over our responsibilities? Is this the land of the free and the home of the brave? Or is it the land of the sycophant and the home of the bootlicker?

Will we act, or will we be acted upon?

A Warning from the Past

I write to warn of the danger from an ever-growing government. This book is loosely patterned on a previous warning, F. A. Hayek's book *The Road to*

Serfdom.[8] That book describes many of the evils of increasing government power, how the well-intentioned can lead us into bondage. Written during World War II, it is prophetic. Much of the free world is traveling the road to serfdom he describes. That book is a warning, a sometimes frightening warning.

Hayek describes how the U.S. and especially the United Kingdom were following many of the same trends that led to Nazism in Germany, albeit years behind and moving more slowly than did Germany. We have not instituted the concentration camps and gas chambers of Hitler's Germany, but we do face a growing government power: a power that slowly strangles our freedom. We must understand the forces driving us in that direction lest they drive us to a modern serfdom.

Hayek had a close-up view of the rise of Nazism in Germany. Though he moved to London before Hitler came to power, his time in Austria and his familiarity with the German language and culture gave him unusual insight into that country. He saw how Nazism rose to become one of the most heinous tyrannies in history. That allowed him to spot parallels with some of the movements in the British and U.S. governments of the time. Living in different countries allows a person to see the how one country is repeating the follies of the other.

---

8   Quotes and references to Hayek's *The Road to Serfdom* are taken from the 2007 University of Chicago Press edition, edited by Bruce Caldwell, which that publisher calls "The Definitive Edition." Pagination may differ in other printings.

We Are an Aberration

The freedoms we have had in much of the western world are rare on this earth. For most of history mankind has been subject to kings, emperors, caliphs, lords of the manor, and other absolute rulers. Many have been tyrants. Even today, most of mankind lives with restrictions similar to those faced by our John I. Throughout most of history, the only thing limiting tyranny was the limitations on the ability of rulers. Until recently, they lacked the technology to really control their people. That technology is now available. We cannot depend on voluntary restraint; governments that voluntarily restrict their own power are as rare as zebras galloping through Central Park. Freedom comes only through limited government. Only relatively recently have constitutional limitations on government power protected people from tyranny. Even those limitations protect only a minority of earth's residents, and only as long as those residents remain vigilant in defense of freedom.

The ideas expressed in the U.S. Constitution and Declaration of Independence were radical when written. They remain unusual today. China, North Korea, Russia and its possessions, much of the Islamic world, and others, all lack the freedoms that we take for granted in the U.S. Our task is to avoid regression to the statism that still dominates most of the planet. That will take effort; we cannot depend on the words of the constitution. Just look at Article 34 of the Constitution of the USSR. "Citizens of the USSR are equal before the law, without distinction of ... *attitude to religion...*"[9] (emphasis mine) Under communism, Russian citizens were constitutionally guaranteed freedom of

---

9   http://www.departments.bucknell.edu/russian/const/77cons02.html

religion. Nice words, but in practice the openly religious Soviet citizen risked the gulag.

Without citizen vigilance, constitutional protections are mere words on paper. Those in power can ignore the words or twist them into meaninglessness. Our freedoms can become as ephemeral as was freedom of religion in the USSR.

The rarity of our freedom indicates that it is abnormal, an aberration, out of the ordinary. Aberrations are unstable. Without conscious effort in their defense, they regress to the norm. In the case of freedom, that defense must come from citizens who value liberty, who are willing to make the effort and sacrifice necessary to protect it. We must remain alert and work to defend our freedom, lest we regress to the statist norm that dominates most of the world.

Where Are We Going

The future: what does it hold for us and for our John IV? Will we progress toward the freedom John II enjoyed, or regress toward the serfdom of John I? Our society has forces driving us both directions.

On one hand, we have a tradition of freedom, and people mostly capable of reading. A literate and engaged electorate, valuing freedom, is the best defense against creeping tyranny, especially if that electorate has learned critical thinking. On the other hand, any astute observer knows that government tends to become increasingly powerful and almost never gives up any power once acquired. "Nothing is so permanent a temporary government program."[10]

---

10 http://www.goodreads.com/quotes/138790-nothing-is-so-permanent-as-a-temporary-government-program (Milton Friedman)

So how can we maintain our freedoms? The first step is clear communication about the issues.

Vocabulary

"Words do not convey meanings, they call them forth."[11] Therein lies much confusion, both deliberate and inadvertent. Words mean different things to different people. To a Democrat in the United States today, the word "liberal" means big, unlimited government providing largesse to the masses. To someone with Hayek's background it means limited government that does not unduly interfere with the lives of the citizens.

Clear communication requires that we all understand words in the same way. The meaning that a word calls forth for you as a reader must be the same meaning it calls forth for me as author. Only when that happens will we communicate clearly.

Furthermore, the enemies of freedom deliberately hide and twist word meanings, and they use words that sound good but really say nothing. That is a common and very effective way to mislead people. "There's so many people who can talk and talk and talk and just say nothing, or nearly nothing."[12]

Saul Alinsky even wrote a book of advice on how to overthrow the status quo and impose statist ideas on the country. His advice includes the recommendation to use general phrases: liberty, equality, fraternity, common welfare, pursuit of happiness, bread and peace.[13] Such language sounds good, but

---

11 Attributed to David O. McKay
12 From "One Note Samba" by Antonio Carlos Jobim
13 Saul D. Alinsky, *Rules for Radicals*, Vintage Books, 1973, 1989, p45

is so flexible as to be meaningless. That is precisely what Alinsky intends. He wants his followers to disguise their intentions and lead us down the path to collectivism. Freedom lovers must never do that. We must communicate clearly, with precise language that conveys our meaning.

If we are to avoid confusion, we must be careful about the words we use.[14] Use of the terms "liberalism" and "liberal" in the U.S today would cause confusion so I shall try to avoid them. Likewise "conservative" has a meaning so flexible that it would cause confusion. Similarly, "right" and "left" in political terms can be confusing.

I shall use the words "freedom," "free," and "free men" (men in the generic sense applying to both sexes), to describe people and ideas that support limited government, individual choice and accountability. I shall use the words "central planning" (or just "planning"), "statist," "statism," or "collectivism" or "serfdom" to describe increasing government power. This will cause less confusion than the more commonly used words. It also avoids arguments about questions such as if the likes of Stalin and Putin, Pol Pot, Hitler, and the Kim family in North Korea are on the left or right; conservative or liberal. They have been accused of being in all those camps. However, we can agree that they are or were statists, believing in central planning and collectivism. They certainly never supported freedom.

This book is not just about socialism and communism versus capitalism. It is about freedom versus statism. Use of these words will free us from confusion. For example, at this writing the so-called Patient Protection and Affordable Care Act, Obamacare, is taking effect. There is controversy about if it is socialized medicine or a step in that direction. However we can avoid that argument by

---

14 See for example my book, *A Dictionary of Polspeak, What Politicians Really Mean.*

agreeing that it is clearly a statist, central planning program. Obamacare moves us toward government control of our lives, of that there is no doubt.

The Statist Life

Statist systems are all repressive, though in different ways. Communism and socialism attempt to control the means and distribution of production. A pure dictatorship such as Haiti under the Duvaliers gives power and riches to the dictator. Statist systems may differ one from another, but all deprive people of freedom. Those ordinary people become both oppressed and poor.

Even the statist systems often regarded as good examples oppress their people. For example, Sweden is often presented as an example of a model socialist country with a great socialized medicine program. Yet that country not only refused a multiple sclerosis patient medication expected to help his condition, it would not even allow him to pay for and obtain the prescription himself. The bureaucrats said it would set a bad precedent by allowing unequal access to treatment.[15]

And what is the effect of prohibiting or discouraging unusual medical treatment? All advances, medical or otherwise, are unusual when first tried. There can hardly be anything more unusual than something done for the first time. Everything from antibiotics to brain surgery was once new and novel. Had collectivist restrictions such as those in Sweden been in place, modern treatments might have never become available. Our medical system would continue to be one-size-fits-all, no new treatments allowed.

---

15 http://townhall.com/columnists/walterewilliams/2009/03/04/swedens_government_
health_care/page/full

Fortunately Sweden seems to be backing away from the central planning model. Many Swedes are even getting private health insurance, often paid by employers who want their people at work, not standing in line until the medical system gets around to treating them.[16]

It is no accident that the lion's share of medical advances are developed in the United States.[17] Freedom allows progress, statism inhibits it.

Exceptions to the Rule?

China is attempting to become an exception to the statist norm. That country intends to allow at least some capitalism but maintain tight control otherwise. The people are to be free to do business and make money, but not allowed freedom of speech or other freedoms. They want their people to be John II economically but John I in other ways. It will be interesting to see how that experiment plays out, but I doubt it will work. Economic progress depends on information – but that information brings information about the freedoms available elsewhere. What will happen when the Chinese develop a desire for the freedom they see in other parts of the world? Their government will be forced either to crack down on all freedoms, or to start allowing individual freedoms.

What about the opposite of what China is attempting? That is, countries with collectivist economies but great individual freedom? That may work in the initial stages, but it does not last, and in later chapters we shall see why. Briefly, the power necessary to enforce central planning can suppress individual freedom

---

16   http://www.thelocal.se/20140117/hospital-queues-tied-to-insurance-trend

17   http://www.forbes.com/sites/matthewherper/2011/03/23/the-most-innovative-countries-in-biology-and-medicine/

as well. Powerful people do not like criticism, and suppression of opposition can be an irresistible temptation. The natural "progress" is to more and more restrictions on freedom as government acquires more power and the rulers defend that power. As we shall see in Chapter 22, power migrates to those of dictatorial mindset.

A Call to Action

John III and John IV await our help. Will we stand up and provide them the freedom all men and women deserve? Only if free men win the battle can we enjoy liberty. We must hold the standard of independence high, even in the face of statist opposition. The fate of the world depends on our success.

This book is intended to slow or reverse our march toward statism, toward a serf-like existence. And I have a favor to ask of readers. My fear is that readers will say that this was an interesting book and leave it at that. Please, go beyond intellectual assent! This is a call to action! I ask that you read to understand, and think carefully about the differences between statism and freedom, then act! Every time a proposal for more government power or largesse is submitted, I hope that you will ask what it will cost in terms of both money and freedom. Then spread the word and do what you can to oppose advancing statism.

Chapter 2, What Went Wrong?

What has always made the state a hell on earth has been precisely that man has tried to make it his heaven. (Johann Christian Friedrich Holderlin)

Politics is the art of looking for trouble, finding it everywhere, diagnosing it incorrectly and applying the wrong remedies. (Groucho Marx)

Our John III enjoys his car, big screen TV, computer and other inventions his ancestors could not even imagine. He does not enjoy the fact that his inflation-adjusted income is declining, and that his freedom is clearly less than what John II enjoyed. That lack of freedom threatens his economic situation – and yours and mine. What caused those problems?

Control of Our Problems?

For decades we expected continual improvement of the U.S. economy. Except for brief downturns and the Great Depression, each generation had it better than the last. Most of us today work fewer hours than did either John II or John I, yet we earn more. That is changing. For many, pay is not even keeping up with inflation. The loss of freedom that began decades ago is strangling our economy.

Graduates of high school or even college live with their parents, work at fast food restaurants or do not work at all. Young people no longer expect a sound economic future, and their elders fear pink slips. The unemployment rate, under 6% in mid 2008, has since shot up to double digits. The number has since declined, but mostly because many have dropped out of the workforce and are no longer counted as unemployed.[18] Others work part-time or in jobs far below their qualifications.[19] Our actual employment problem is far worse than the numbers show. Why? And why is our freedom slowly vanishing?

False Accusations

Theories abound. Blame is thrown at everything from alpha males to omega fatty acids, from Wall Street greed to poor education. However, our current problems are almost certainly not the result of one or even a few superficial causes. It is more likely that the problems were caused by fundamental changes in our society. We need to look at what has changed – and what has not.

Wall Street has always been greedy; so has pretty much the entire human race. That has not changed. Greed, in spite of the damage it can do, is not our prime suspect.

Education is likewise not the sole source of our economic difficulties. True, many schools fail to educate, but we have always had some in our country who fail to get educated. Our primary problem is not lack of educated people, but lack of good jobs for those educated people. Education shares the blame, but not for failure to teach core subjects (though they have been guilty of that). Rather the educators' main crime is counterproductive teaching, encouraging an entitlement mindset and an unjustified self-esteem.[20] A generation taught that it is wonderful regardless of accomplishment is unlikely to work hard. A generation taught that it is entitled to this world's goods will seldom make much effort to earn those goods.

18 http://www.heritage.org/research/reports/2014/09/not-looking-for-work-why-labor-force-participation-has-fallen-during-the-recovery
19 http://stateofworkingamerica.org/charts/number-of-underemployed/
20 http://aspeneducation.crchealth.com/articles/article-entitlement/

No, we cannot blame greed, education, or other simple causes for our current problems. Failure to understand the causes, or blaming the wrong cause, will guarantee continued problems.

So what did go wrong?

Malevolence or Mistakes?

I submit that the most significant change was a migration from individualism and freedom to statism and centralized decision making. That change directly affected our freedoms and harmed the economy. At the same time we suffered a change in attitude, especially among some who influence our national thinking: the politicians, celebrities, and others who get a lot of exposure in the news (see Chapter 27). Instead of urging independence and self-help, they now preach a gospel of blame, entitlement, and class warfare. For example many of them, including President Obama, blame the rich, what they call the "1%," for the country's problems. Some of those people casting blame are probably honest if misled. Others are demagogues who have found a wonderfully useful tool for their purpose, an accusation that gives them triple duty:

They have a scapegoat to blame

They create class warfare to divide and conquer, and

They justify more power to redistribute what that 1% has.

The blame game is an invitation to disaster. Anyone who blames his problems on society, racism, evil corporations etc. will not prepare himself for productive employment, nor will he run the risk of entrepreneurship. Instead he will think society owes him a living; he will take what he can from government programs. On the other hand, someone who believes in individual responsibility will stand up on his hind legs like a man, take control of his own life, and become a productive and happy citizen. Sadly, we have too many casting blame and too few taking responsibility for their own lives. That is the result of mostly well-intentioned but misguided teachings and actions.

It is still true that the road to Hell is paved with good intentions. It was not the intentions but the results that caused our problems. Only when we recognize those past errors can we make corrections and improve our future. Unfortunately, admitting error is a foul fish to fry. In Hayek's words:

> When the course of civilization takes an unexpected turn – when, instead of the continuous progress which we have come to expect, we find ourselves threatened by evils associated by us with past ages of barbarism – we naturally blame anything but ourselves. Have we not all striven according to our best lights and have not many of our finest minds incessantly worked to make this a better world? ….
>
> We are ready to accept almost any explanation of the present crisis of our civilization except one: that the present state of the world may be the result of genuine error on our own part and that the pursuit of some of our most cherished ideals has apparently produced results utterly different from those which we expected.[21]

Errors are nothing new. Our race has made mistakes, often spectacular mistakes, for as long as it has existed. The problem arises when we persist in our errors. It has been wisely said that when you find yourself in a hole, the first thing you should do is stop digging. Unfortunately, some think that when we are in a hole we should dig faster. If powerful government created problems, they expect an even more powerful government to solve those problems. For example, both Obamacare and the Veterans' Department have serious problems. Some suggest

---

21   Hayek, op cit, pp65-66

that we just haven't gone far enough, that the solution is socialized medicine [22] (for which they use the euphemism "single payer health care"). They claim that a government incapable of running the Veterans' Administration will somehow do better at running a medical system many times the size of the Veterans' Department. I confess that I cannot understand such thinking.

There are some mistakes we clearly make and should correct. Let's look at a few.

Where We Went Wrong

We engage in stage one thinking. We look only at the immediate results we expect, ignoring side effects and other unintended consequences. For example, we have placed well-intentioned restrictions on productive businesses without considering the harm those restrictions can do to our economy and to the people who lose their jobs. (See Chapter 7.)

We listen to politicians' words and ignore their actions. Talk is cheap and politicians are famous for broken promises. If a politician says one thing and does something else, believe the action and ignore the words. If his actions contradict his words, consider him a liar and do not trust him at all. For example, President Obama and powerful members of Congress promised that under "Obamacare" everyone would be able to keep their doctors and health plans if they wanted to.

---

22 Cf http://time.com/2954306/after-hobby-lobby-a-single-payer-health-care-solution/, http://www.nytimes.com/roomfordebate/2013/05/29/is-obamacare-too-complicated-to-succeed/a-single-payer-system-would-be-better-than-obamacare. Other sources are easily available with an on-line search.

That was false and they knew it [23] Every politician who made that promise showed himself to be a liar, not to be trusted.

We ignore the results of our actions. We assume that government action will accomplish the ends intended. We create programs and fail to evaluate their effects. Poverty, declining before the Kennedy/Johnson War on Poverty, has since increased. Yet almost nobody will consider that government action may have worsened the problem it was intended to solve. (See Chapter 8.)

We regard government as having some special wisdom. Even the Supreme Court, when failing to overturn "Obamacare," indicated that congressional action should be generally not questioned. Yet there is no reason to believe that government is any wiser or more moral than you or I. (See Chapter 9.)

We look at proposed actions in isolation. We cannot afford all good programs, to say nothing of expensive programs that are not worthwhile, yet we fail to prioritize. Instead we spend and borrow as if there were no tomorrow, piling program upon program. We also ignore interactions between programs, and the fact that a program helpful in one area may cause problems elsewhere. (See Chapter 11.)

Related to the lack of prioritization, *we create numerous quasi-independent ruling bodies* such as the aforementioned Oregon Board of Cosmetology. Each rules in isolation and there is no overall authority either to limit the number of rules, or to make sure they do not work against each other. Those bureaucracies

---

23   http://www.usatoday.com/story/news/politics/2013/11/11/fact-check-keeping-your-health-plan/3500187/ Of course that lie is well-known as has been documented in many places.

are essentially accountable to nobody, but have the power to impose their will on the public. We shall discuss this further in Chapter 12.

We create programs with concentrated benefits and diffused costs. The beneficiaries of those programs persuade authorities to fund them, regardless of value to the country. However the cost is so diffuse that the average taxpayer has little incentive to protest. As further discussed in Chapter 13, this aids and abets the piling of program upon program, leaving the taxpayer with a large aggregate bill.

We create "entitlements" leading people to believe that they have a right to what others have produced. This diverts resources and destroys incentive. See Chapter 14.

Too often we have "government by decibel;" the loudest special interests get what they want. Hard-working citizens lack the time to make that much noise, so the non-productive who have time to protest have undue influence. One example was the "occupy Wall Street" movement that started in 2011 and spread to occupations of other areas. Meanwhile people with jobs had to go to work. The protestors, who were visible and loud, had political power beyond their numbers.

The creation of government programs is a one-way street. We establish them. We allow them to grow. Almost never do we shrink them. A program once instituted is difficult or impossible to kill, or even to cut back. Its beneficiaries fight for it, even if a majority of citizens think it not worth the cost. For example, over 50 years ago the US started subsidizing wool and mohair as strategic fibers.

The subsidies continue, even though the military says there is no need for them.[74]
The producers of wool and mohair fight any attempt to shrink their gravy train.

Cotton farmers also benefit from an obsolete program. In 1933 the Agricultural Adjustment Act was enacted to help farmers during the Great Depression. The program continues today, giving about $2.5 billion per year to mostly corporate farms. Brazil complained that the subsidy constituted unfair trade. The World Trade Organization agreed and decreed that Brazil could impose trade sanctions against the U.S., including suspension of intellectual property rights. That would mean that innocent businesses would lose control of license fees for movies and music. Then Congress acted: it bought off the Brazilian cotton farmers with a tax-funded bribe of about $147 million per year.[25]

Other programs have similar defenses; their beneficiaries fight to keep them regardless of cost or value to the country.

We think of government as Santa Claus. We ignore the fact that we pay for government benefits with our own money. Too often we vote for the politician who buys our votes with our own money. I once talked to a county commissioner about wasteful spending of some federal grant money. He agreed it was wasteful, but said that he regarded it as his duty to get as much federal money into the county as he could, even if it was wasted. That commissioner was regarded as a fiscally conservative Republican.

---

24   http://www.jonathanrauch.com/jrauch_articles/wool_and_mohair_
        the_golden_fleece/
25   Philip K. Howard, *The Rule of Nobody, Saving America from Dead Laws and Broken Government,* W. W. Norton and Company, 2014, pp123-124

We refuse to recognize that taxpayer resources are limited. We are heavily in debt, including money owed to tyrannical regimes not friendly to us. Yet we continue to commit to more programs and spending.

We allow politicians and unelected bureaucrats to make too many decisions for us. Government decisions are invariably made by third parties, far removed from the problem. The person making the decision neither pays the cost nor receives the benefits. He does not suffer the consequences of his decision. Chapter 15 discusses the evils that causes.

We have instituted so many rules that it is often impossible to do what should be done. Bureaucracies require endless layers of approval to take action. Almost any group can sue to block major projects; all they need do is claim that some procedure was not properly followed, it matters not if the project meets the ostensible goals of the law. Procedure reigns at the expense of rationality. Much of this is rooted in well-intentioned attempts to bloc corruption, but the effect is to consider public employees corrupt at the outset, block good actions, and allow corruption by those who know how to work the system.[26] While no upstanding citizen would approve of corruption, we have gone so far in attempts to prevent it that the cost of prevention exceeds the cost of some corruption. This slavery to procedure costs not only tax money for all the layers of approval, but costs in terms of obstruction of what ought to be done. A multitude of regulations, reaching into every aspect of our lives and work, has created legal lockjaw, paralyzing much of our effort.

---

26 Ibid, the whole book. See also Howard's earlier book, *The Death of Common Sense, How Law is Suffocating America,* Random House Paperbacks, 1994, 2011

We allow name calling to replace rational discussion. For example, rather than openly discuss government involvement in health care, one side calls the other socialists and communists, while that other side calls its opponents racists and anarchists. There is little discussion of the actual merits or constitutionality of that law. Worse, as described in Chapter 16, many of us accept the name calling as truth without bothering to check the facts.

Too many educators excuse failure to learn. Instead they preach the apostate gospel of self esteem and entitlement.[27] [28] This gives us citizens unable to think critically or logically, but with enough false self esteem that they think they deserve what they have not earned. Too few graduates have the true self esteem that would come from being able to solve a tough math problem, or to deconstruct sophisticated political propaganda. Those poorly educated "graduates" are the demagogue's natural prey. Fortunately this may be changing as some educators recognize the value of rigor in education.[29] Students expected to actually learn will be far ahead of those with only self-esteem – and what better for their self-esteem than to know that they can solve a difficult math or logic problem.

Group identity too often trumps qualifications. Many people voted for Barrack Obama because they thought, "It's time we had a black president." Others voted for Hillary Clinton because they thought it was time we had a woman president. Those are terrible reasons to vote for anybody. That is not to say

---

27 http://www.educationworld.com/a_curr/shore/shore059.shtml

28 http://www.thewagnerreview.org/2012/11/teach-children-a-sense-of-entitlement/

29 http://www.washingtonpost.com/local/education/in-schools-self-esteem-boosting-is-losing-favor-to-rigor-finer-tuned-praise/2012/01/11/gIQAXFnF1P_story.html

anything about the qualifications of either, it is only to say that skin color and gender neither qualify nor disqualify anyone for office. We need office holders of integrity and wisdom, and who support our constitutional government. Martin Luther King, Jr. had it right when he asked that we judge people by the content of their character rather than by the color of their skin.[30]

Too many ignore evidence, instead jumping to conclusions based on emotion and identity politics. Shortly before I wrote this, a white policeman in Ferguson, Missouri shot and killed a young black man. That led to riots as people claimed that the cop was racist, only wanting to kill Blacks. Schools allowed students time off to protest, and even the president implied that the shooting was racially motivated. All that ignored the evidence. While not solidly proven, it is highly probable that the young black man attacked the policeman, punched and injured him, and tried to take his gun. The preponderance of evidence, both forensic and from witnesses, indicates that the officer was defending himself. Yet many, even federal officials, are demanding that investigation continue.[31] It is almost certain that they will not be satisfied until the officer is convicted, evidence be damned.

All those mistakes created our problems of today. Those problems will remain until we take appropriate action, based on a sound understanding of their causes, and of possible solutions. They will harm our freedom and our ability to live comfortably in this world.

---

30 http://www.brainyquote.com/quotes/quotes/m/martinluth115056.html

31 http://www.nytimes.com/interactive/2014/08/13/us/ferguson-missouri-town-under-siege-after-police-shooting.html?_r=0

Chapter 3, Economics, Freedom, and Life

The control of the production of wealth is the control of human life itself. (Hilaire Belloc)

Economics: dull, boring, a subject for eggheads right? Maybe not. Just maybe it is central to the way we live, and not as difficult to understand as we think. And it just might be key to other parts of life. In fact, as Belloc's quote indicates, economics controls most of our lives. By controlling the economy, statists take over everything.

Conjoined Triplets

Family and friends, freedom, and finances. Those human concerns are all tied up together. Freedom enhances economic well-being and economic well-being enhances freedom. Freedom and a good financial situation give us time to spend with family and friends, and good relationships with others help us financially. Like conjoined triplets, those human concerns depend on each other, and no surgeon knows how to separate them. Yes, that means that economics is a very human concern, important to all aspects of our lives. We need not become experts, but we should all have a basic knowledge of how economies work and which systems enhance our freedom, finances and friendships. Even if we do not aspire to be filthy rich, we do need enough to live, preferably enough to live comfortably.

So just what do we mean by economics?

Economics: A Working Definition

Is economics about money? Not really. It is about resources, goods, and services. Economics is about the food we eat, the clothes we wear, the work of the mechanic fixing our car, and all the other services and goods we use. Money is only a convenient way to track and exchange those items. Thomas Sowell defines economics as *the study of limited resources that have alternate uses*. Human time and talent, beachfront property, easily accessible petroleum, anything we want or need.

This is officially called *the economic problem*. "All societies face the economic problem, which is the problem of how to make the best use of limited, or scarce, resources. The economic problem exists because, although the needs and wants of people are endless, the resources available to satisfy needs and wants are limited.*"[32]* John III wants a nice house on the beach, maybe you do too. Beachfront property, however, is limited, and that house does not build itself. Someone must cut the logs, saw them into lumber, haul that lumber to the site, cut the boards to the right sizes, nail them together, install the plumbing and electrical wiring, finish the interior, and perform a myriad of other tasks. Those materials and land, and that labor could be used to build a hotel or school instead of John's house. Not everyone who wants such a house can have one.

How about food? Most of us want our food to be tasty and nutritious, and we want enough of it to satisfy our hunger. However there is not enough steak for everybody. Like the house on the beach, food requires effort to grow, harvest, transport, and prepare. We cannot all have prime rib and cherry pie every day.

---

32 http://www.economicsonline.co.uk/Competitive_markets/
   The_economic_problem.html

Then there is the very human problem of health care. We all want the best possible treatment when we have medical problems, but what does that take? The typical physician in the U.S. spends four years as an undergraduate, four more in medical school, and then more time in internship or residency. Meanwhile he needs food, a place to live, clothing to wear, and money to pay the university and hospitals where he studies. Producing a physician requires a tremendous amount of resources. Then he needs office space, equipment and supplies, access to a hospital, nurses and other resources, all of which could be put to other uses. Medical care is a limited resource.

We could go on and on. Nearly every aspect of life requires limited resources that could be used for something else.

For purposes of this book, we define economics as: *The manner in which we allocate resources, including human time and talent, natural resources, and resources we create ourselves.*

Yes, we can create some resources, but inevitably at the expense of others. You probably spend only a small fraction of your income on food, leaving the rest of your money for such things as housing and recreation. It was not always so. Two hundred years ago most of our people had to work on farms to grow enough food to feed the country. Then entrepreneurs invested time, talent, and natural resources to improve agricultural productivity. People no longer needed on farms are now producing cars, computers, carpets, or other goods and services.

Other human talent improved medical care, communication technology, transportation, etc. Such efforts created new resources for all of us, but those resources were not free. Like beachfront property, talent used in one endeavor is no longer available for other uses. For the good of mankind we should seek economic systems that direct talent and other resources toward their most beneficial uses. Which system does best at that? The answer may surprise some people.

Resource Allocation

How do we allocate resources? There are two opposite methods. At one extreme is the collectivist, central planning model exemplified by the various incarnations of socialism. At the opposite pole we find freedom and capitalism. Of course there is a continuum between the extremes, with many attempts to combine some central planning with some free enterprise.

John I lived in a world of statism and central planning. His serf masters decided what to plant, how to divide the results of the harvest, who got the castle and who got the hovel. John II on the other hand was able to use his earnings pretty much as he wanted. He could save for the farm he hoped to own, spend on fancy clothing for his wife, or otherwise make his own decisions. You and I, along with John III, again fall in between. We have many options at the store, but government limits the cars we drive, which taxi or bus companies we use, and many other choices that John II could make for himself.

What will John IV's life be like? Will he, and our grandchildren, be able to decide for themselves how to use their earnings? Or will an all-powerful government make decisions for them? Will they have the economic resources to live as they choose, or will a collective take whatever it wants from their production, allowing them only a subsistence life style? That will depend on our actions today. We can allow government to run amok, or we can limit its power.

Economics and Individual Well being

Life, on and off the job, depends on economics. If we have the resources, we can eat a good diet, live in a comfortable home, and get good medical attention. Then we may still have time and money to enjoy the company of family and friends, attend concerts or sports events, and otherwise enjoy life. We can even help with causes we believe in.

John III coaches his son's little league team and volunteers at a food bank. His wife volunteers at school and serves in their church. They donate money to the church and to a scholarship fund for inner city kids. Yet they still have the time and money to go skiing several times a year. Meanwhile, the person with scant economic resources will have none of John III's opportunities. His home, clothing, and diet will be undesirable. He will have little if any recreation. He will have to work long hours, leaving little time for family and friends, and probably nothing for charitable endeavors.

I have lived in three different third-world countries, not as a tourist but among the people. I became well acquainted with the various socioeconomic classes in those countries. While the middle and upper classes have leisure and the ability to do things they enjoy, the poor spend their time scrambling to survive. Should those poor people get sick or injured, they get bad medical attention if they get any at all. In contrast, a study conducted in 2011 showed that of U.S. households that the government considers poor:

80% had air conditioning.

92% had a microwave oven.

Nearly three-fourths had a car or truck, and 31% had two or more cars or trucks.

Nearly two thirds had cable or satellite TV.

Two-thirds had at least one DVD player, and 70% had a VCR.

Half had a personal computer, and one in seven had two or more computers.

More than half of poor families with children had a video game system.

43% had internet access.

One-third had a wide-screen plasma or LCD TV

One forth had a digital video recorder.[33]

Why are most of the "poor" in the U.S. so well off compared to the rest of the world? It is not because of natural resources or the talent and diligence of the people. Those third-world countries have great natural resources and hard-working people. What they lack is a good economy, an economy that allows people to earn a reasonable living.

Good economies are rare. Most of the world's population is worse off than even the poor in the United States. Why has our system been so kind to the average citizen? Along with many economists, I believe that our major advantages are greater freedom and less corruption. People in a free economy work harder and produce more than those in controlled economies.[34] And they produce what

---

33 Robert Rector and Rachel Sheffield, "Understanding Poverty in the United States: Surprising Facts About America's Poor" available at http://www.heritage.org/research/reports/2011/09/understanding-poverty-in-the-united-states-surprising-facts-about-americas-poor

34 Milton Friedman, Walter Williams, Thomas Sowell and other economists have

people want and need. Controlled economics produce (or attempt to produce) what some bureaucrat orders them to produce. Then, because statist power abets corruption, officials divert much of that production to their own ends. Chapter 22 discusses the type of people likely to rise to the top in a statist system and why they tend to be corrupt.

Just how beneficial is economic freedom compared to a controlled economy? We can learn from an inadvertent experiment. In the Soviet Union, workers on government farms were allowed small private plots to grow crops and raise animals. Those private plots totaled less than one percent of the agricultural land, yet they produced nearly one third of the total farm output for the entire country.[35] It was those private plots that prevented even more mass starvation in the Soviet system.

Economic freedom serves the citizens. Statism serves the rulers. Chapters 6 and 18 treat that in greater detail.

Economics and Freedom

Can we have personal freedom without economic freedom? The answer is a resounding "no;" it just won't work. Not everybody will voluntarily cooperate with the collective, so authorities must force the recalcitrant to join the system. Any government powerful enough to force people into collectivism is powerful enough to destroy personal freedom. Then government officials, being human, defend their power and authority at the expense of the people. Contrary

---

written extensively on this.
[35] Milton and Rose Friedman, *Free to Choose,* Avon Books, 1980, 1979, page 2

viewpoints and other freedoms will go the way of the passenger pigeon. Control of jobs will include control of income and everything associated with that income.

When government controls the economy, officials have the power to give good jobs to the favored and to assign those out of favor to the worst jobs. An excellent example (well actually an atrocious example) it the persecution of the Jews in Germany. Paraphrasing Hayek a bit:

> It is well known that the Nazis in Germany resented the Jews. What is less well known is that this resentment was a direct result of the anticapitalism on which the entire Nazi movement was based. It was in fact quite similar to the resentment toward the Kulaks[36] in Communist Russia.
>
> In Germany and Austria the Jew had come to be regarded as a representative of capitalism. That was because large classes of the population in those countries had a traditional dislike for commercial pursuits. That left those pursuits readily available to groups like the Jews who were excluded from more highly esteemed occupations. It is the old story of the alien race being admitted only to the less respected trades, then being hated still more for practicing those trades.
>
> The fact that German anti-Semitism and anticapitalism sprang from the same root is of great importance. It helps us understand what happened there. However foreign observers rarely grasped that point.[37]

Such outcasts are probably necessary to statism; they become scapegoats. The statist government can then exclude both opponents and scapegoats from the better jobs, just as many European countries excluded Jews from the more

---

36 The Kulaks were prosperous landed peasants in Czarist Russia. The communists classified them as exploiters and eventually deported most to remote locations or arrested them and confiscated their property.

37   Hayek, op cit, p161

desirable occupations. Express the wrong opinion, belong to the wrong church, or have the wrong ancestors and you get to be the garbage collector instead of the college professor. Freedom of speech, press, or religion will not exist in such an economy. Indeed neither will freedom of association; anyone who associates with the outcasts risks becoming an outcast himself.

Chapter 26 discusses scapegoats in more detail.

Planning vs. Choice

Like an overprotective parent, collectivism controls not only jobs, but other choices in our lives. To see why, let's look at our spending decisions. Unless you are Bill Gates, Warren Buffet or someone similar, you can't have it all. You have to decide what fits your budget, then use the available money for what is important to you. You may want a boat; your neighbor may prefer a big-screen TV; your cousin may decide to use his money for skis and a season lift ticket. Each spends on what is important to him, at least in a free society.

But what happens in a fully planned economy? Bureaucrats determine types of housing available, recreational facilities and equipment produced, and all other uses of time, talent, and natural resources. The planners, by deciding where economic resources shall be used, control essentially every aspect of your life. The bigger and more powerful the state, the more areas fall under its control and the less choice is left to citizens. The planners decide which goods and services are available, and at what prices. Well, actually they decide what they think should be available. In practice, there is a wide gap between plan and reality. However that gap seldom extends to making available what citizens want instead of what the planners think they should want. They may decide not to make boats or TVs bigger than a certain size. They may decide to reduce injuries by making only cross-country skis; no downhill skis will be available.

And what of your employment? In a free society you can choose your occupation, subject to talent and opportunity. If opportunity or talent is lacking, you may even sacrifice, study harder and prepare for the job that suits you. Not so in a planned society. The planners will decide how many school teachers are needed, how many welders, electricians, accountants etc. It might even become like what I faced in the army. Military bureaucrats decided how many infantrymen, radio operators, military police, etc. were needed, then simply informed each soldier what his job would be.

If planners assign you to a particular job, that will affect every aspect of your life. It will determine who you associate with. It will determine where you live, thus affecting family relationships, friends, and recreation opportunities. It will even have a major effect on your health, both physical and mental.

Our economic system determines our freedom – in all areas of our lives. But what about the other direction? What does freedom do for the economy?

Freedom and the Economy

As a good economy enhances freedom, a free society enhances economic well-being. Free men and women start companies, invent things, create artwork and engage in other activities that bring them satisfaction. Their motivation may be personal gain, but the road to prosperity crosses the chasm of failure on a bridge of satisfied customers. That bridge is built with goods or services, available at a price customers are willing to pay. Free men and women create jobs, goods and services, even tax money.

Cyrus McCormick's reaper was partly the result of a free society. He and his father invented a better way of harvesting grain – and reaped not only wheat but also the financial rewards of that invention.[38] Other inventors also created things we all enjoy, and many got rich off their inventions. The freedom we enjoy, along with patent protection, encouraged everyone from Edison to the inventors of television. The United States became the invention factory of the world.

On the other hand, a centrally planned society removes incentives to individual enterprise. As discussed in Chapter 5, the very term "individualism" is anathema in such a society. There are few incentives to take risks, to try new ideas. Innovation grinds to a halt.

The Stifling Effect of Central Planning

Another problem with a planned economy is that the planners can never be perfect. They cannot know everything, but their mistakes can even be deadly. For example in 1962, Khrushchev announced an increase in the price of meat and butter, effective throughout the Soviet Union. The same day a planner announced a pay cut for workers at the Electric Locomotive Works in Novocherkassk. Higher prices plus smaller paychecks meant hunger. Workers went on strike and protested. Troops sent to quell the "rebellion" shot many residents,[39] all because planners, far from the scene, made decisions for the people affected.

We shall treat these topics throughout the book, after we look at a common economic misconception.

---

38 cf http://www.american-inventor.com/cyrus-mccormick.aspx
39   Aleksandr Solzhenitsyn, *The Gulag Archipelago,* Vol three, Harper and Row, 1976 pp507-514

A Zero-sum Game?

Two children are building snowmen in the park. One has six snowballs, he can build two snowmen. The other has only one snowball, not even enough for one snowman. How can we best help the second child? We could step in and just take two snowballs from the first child and give them to the other little guy. Or we could encourage the other child to make more snowballs so he could build one or even two snowmen. We might even help him make his snowballs. The first method is a version of statism, the second an example of freedom.

Statists often claim that the only way to help the disadvantaged is to take from the rich. They imply that economics is a zero-sum game; in other words they believe that there is a fixed amount of economic resources available, and that the only question is how do divide it up ("distribution" is the word they use). In their mind, whenever one person gets more, someone else must have less. That is clearly untrue. Every useful invention, every successful production endeavor, every increase in organizational efficiency, produces resources previously unavailable. That allows improvement in the economic situation of some people, maybe even everybody, without taking anything from anyone else. The "poor" child with only one snowball can create more, just as the entrepreneur can create more economic resources.

On the other hand, every restriction or tax on production reduces the resources available to everyone. It is possible to create new resources, but also to destroy or reduce available resources. For example, the tax on medical devices imposed to support "Obamacare" takes resources away from medical device makers. Those companies now have less money to use for research and development. They also have less incentive to invent, since government will take a chunk of any return on that investment. Those devices, which now may never be invented, would improve quality of life for people who need them.

Gambling is a zero-sum game. It only changes resource ownership from one person to another. However industry and labor are not zero-sum; they create or destroy resources. In fact creation of resources allowed the United States and other advanced countries to improve the lot of essentially all their citizens.

The big question is: How can we continue that improvement?

If we destroy the system that brought us these benefits, we will lose the benefits along with the system. Recent years give us reason to be concerned.

A better understanding of economic forces would help us make good decisions about our economy. That would allow us to preserve the system that has given us so much. If we decide unwisely, our economy will decline and the laws of economics will not care why.

The system that brought us so many good things is free market capitalism.

Capitalism

The statists have few economic successes, but they do have one big accomplishment: they have made capitalism into a dirty word. They point out that capitalists are often greedy and sometimes harm the average person. That is nothing new; Adam Smith, the patron saint of capitalism, described it centuries ago. The advantage of free market capitalism lies not with the capitalist managers, but with the competition that keeps their greed in check. Yet it is the statists who are most anxious to remove that competitive check on the greedy. It is the statists who are most likely to replace free market capitalism with crony capitalism or other forms of monopoly.

There is a big difference between the free market and cronyism. In the free market, a company will either serve customers at an acceptable price or face a bankruptcy judge. In crony capitalism, the company will demand and receive special protection or tax money regardless of how effectively it serves customers. In the effort to "help the deserving," government officials pick the winners. Surprise! Those winners are often cronies of the officials: the mayor's brother-in-law, the companies that contribute heavily to congressional or presidential campaigns, the college friends of powerful officials. Somehow all those people seem to be running enterprises deserving of our tax money. That distorts competition and limits freedom.

Nor are the beneficiaries limited to companies in the U.S. The Export-Import Bank makes loans at artificially low rates to foreign companies, especially to foreign airlines. For example Emirates, an airline owed by Dubai, already has the advantage of that country's oil money. Yet the Export-Import Bank provided loan guarantees that saved that airline $20 million in the purchase of wide-body airliners. That transaction benefited Boeing, but harmed domestic airlines that compete with Emirates.[40]

This difference between the free market and crony capitalism is central to our topic. Free market capitalism allows citizens to make their own choices and to be responsible for those choices. Crony capitalism, on the other hand, puts choice in the hands of the authorities. Those authorities decide not only who gets

---

40 http://aviationweek.com/commercial-aviation/opinion-ex-im-bank-
    subsidizing-my-competitors

government contracts, but who is licensed to do business with the public. Crony capitalism has all the charms of the lord of the manor who forced his serfs to take their grain to his own mill and no other. It is in fact related to socialism/communism in that it is a statist economy, controlled by government officials. The socialist, the communist, the fascist, the crony capitalist. All transfer decision making from individuals to government with its bureaucratic controls and misguided incentives.

Rewarding Empathy

And capitalism rewards empathy, a virtue that the statists claim is important. For example, several years ago a Japanese businessman took his family to the beach. Teenagers playing boom boxes at high volume disturbed the experience for his family and nearly everyone else. How to solve that problem? The statist solution would be strict limits on music volume in that area, maybe even prohibit music altogether. Put a few music police in place and everything would be fine. However that businessman had a capitalistic solution, one growing out of his empathy for both the teens and the people they were disturbing. Akio Morita invented the Walkman.[41] Teens could have their music without disturbing others.

Is empathy unusual in a successful businessman? Hardly, it is in fact nearly mandatory. Success in business depends on providing what people want. You cannot provide what they want unless you know what it is that they want. In the case of the Walkman, Mr. Morita provided something people didn't even realize

---

41 Dinesh D'Souza, *America, Imagine a World Without Her, Regnery Publishing, 2014* p365

they wanted until it became available. Other business people also succeed by understanding their customers, their wants and needs. While the statists often preach about the importance of empathy, it is business people who practice it most successfully. It is business that depends on knowing the desires of customers. Statists, on the other hand, want to force their ideas on the people, regardless of what those people want.

Impersonal Forces

Maybe we don't like the laws of economics. Too bad; those laws are quite as fixed as those of nuclear physics, albeit not as well understood. They care not why we act as we do, any more than gravity cares why a man fell or jumped from a cliff. Gravity propels that man downward, economic forces propel us to the inevitable result of our decisions. Like any law of nature, action determines outcome. It is folly to claim that economics should give a different result, just as it would be folly to insist that the law of gravity make exceptions for those who fall off cliffs through no fault of their own. We can whine, rage, pass laws, or complain however else we want to. Gravity will still pull downward anyone who falls off a cliff, and the laws of economics will still produce their inevitable results. No amount of human desire, lawmaking or other effort will change that.

That is the bad news. The good news is that, with a modicum of understanding, we can use the laws of Nature to our advantage. Understanding the law of gravity has facilitated everything from the construction of robust buildings to putting men on the moon. We do that, not by demanding that the law of gravity be changed, but by considering that law when we design buildings and rockets. Likewise we cannot change the laws of economics, but we can use them to our advantage. We can wisely consider them in designing our legal and economic system; and history shows that free market economics is the best system for meeting our needs.

Of course we should not demand more from economic laws than they are capable of providing. No rational person would demand that the law of gravity provide him with beautiful music. Yet there are those who reject capitalism because it does not provide what they regard as an acceptable philosophy. Why should it? Gravity does not provide music, capitalism does not provide philosophy. Capitalism provides goods and services and, if used wisely, gives humans the time to create philosophy.

Nor do we need a detailed understanding of economics to benefit from its laws. Mankind used gravity to advantage for millennia before Newton formulated his law. Even today most people know nothing about Newton's equation – yet they know better than to go jumping off cliffs. Likewise we do not need to understand economics at the PhD level to realize that creating a collectivist state is the economic equivalent of jumping off a cliff. All we have to do is look at the shortages and lack of freedom in collectivist countries compared to the surpluses that we often have in the United States. Chapter 17 discusses that further, but first let's look at how people fool themselves into believing that statism will help.

Chapter 4, Information Immunity

Theory without empirical evidence is mere speculation. Empirical evidence without theory is simply a collection of facts. Theory supported by empirical evidence is science.

The Road to Statism

How is this for an opportunity? You want to move to a new country but there is a ten to twenty year wait to get a visa. Or you can reach that country by taking a dangerous and unpleasant trip, across rivers and deserts, guided by unsavory characters who will probably demand extra money at the end of the trip and who believe that part of their fee is the right to rape any women they are guiding. At the end of your journey? You find a country that many claim is not as well-governed as where you are now. Yet millions wait years for visas, or make that dangerous trip, to enter the United States. If our country is so terrible, why do so many want to move here?

I have friends who risked everything to reach the United States. Yet many of the so-called elite denigrate our country. They claim that we should copy Europe or other systems. Those elitists want a statist system, similar to what my friends fled. Even some who flee to this country want to make us into a copy of the tyrannies they left. Why? Almost certainly because they accept the nice theories and ignore the evidence. They never ask what makes this country so attractive that people risk their lives to get here.

To the credit of my immigrant friends, I've never known even one who would not change his mind when I pointed out his inconsistency. Our native statists, on the other hand, seem immune to such reasoning. They reject the limited government our founders gave us, the standard of freedom that was widely accepted only a few decades ago. Why the difference? The immigrants have seen statism in action. The natives, on the other hand, have only a theoretical idea of what it is like. They pay attention to words, not results. Contrary information bounces off them like a ball off a wall.

One notable exception was Eldridge Cleaver who metamorphosed from violent socialist to conservative Republican. He spent time in Cuba, saw what it was really like, then rejected the statist ideology. Of course he realized that the U.S. is not perfect, but he also found that the grass is not always greener on the other side of the fence. Not so most native-born statists. They reject the freedom our John II enjoyed, preferring the restrictions placed on John III, even desiring to strengthen those restrictions.

How can people, often smart people, be so blind to the evidence? I attribute it to three factors, three kinds of information immunity:

> First, such people seldom see information contrary to their preconceived belief. They get their news only from sources that support the statist ideology. I have friends who refuse to even open a book or web site if they think it will present a viewpoint contrary to their belief system. In this the news media is complicit, as we discuss in Chapter 27.

> Second, when presented with evidence of collectivism's problems, those people deny that it can be that bad. For example, they become justifiably angry about Hitler's atrocities, yet they refuse to believe the truth about Cuba under Castro or Venezuela under Chavez. The information ball bounces off their wall of preconceptions.

> Third, many fall for a "grass is greener" syndrome. They see the problems we have and assume that other systems will be better. I even had a friend claim that our slums were the world's worst. Anyone who has seen the slums in other countries, as I have, knows better. Yes we have problems;

nobody in his right mind would deny that. However that does not mean that other systems are better.

There is, in many circles, an unquestioned and unquestionable belief that government power is good, that we must trust government and reject constitutional limitations on that government. It is time to question that unquestionable belief. We, as free men and women, must question the news media, politicians, and especially educators. We must ask them appropriate questions and provide well-documented information to counteract the statist claims. Only when freedom lovers ask questions or present facts will we begin to turn the tide. And the statists will fight back, often unfairly with lies and accusations. We must not allow their anger or accusations to deter us. Instead we must aggressively strive to educate anybody who will listen. Publicize the truth, the whole truth, in spite of pressures to the contrary. Partial information is dangerous.

The Parable of Partial Information

Witnesses still have nightmares about the accident. The taxi screeching around the corner. The awful thump as it knocked Eunice out of the crosswalk. Eunice flying through the air. The horrid crack of her head on the pavement.

Eunice was a delightful lady, the neighborhood grandma who told stories and gave cookies to all the children. She never regained consciousness.

Nobody got a license number, but witnesses assured investigators that the taxi was blue. There was only one blue taxi in town. Just to be certain, the detectives had the witnesses watch as taxis drove past the scene. They were 100% accurate identifying the colors of the taxis.

Police quickly arrested Albert, the driver of the blue taxi. No other vehicle in town remotely resembled his cab and the prosecutor looked forward to an easy day in court. As popular as Eunice was, Albert was lucky that the days of the lynch mob were over.

He was even luckier that his dispatcher remembered something. In a town about 40 miles away there were three blue taxis. She called their dispatcher. Bingo! One of their blue taxis had dropped a fare within a quarter mile of the accident, just before Eunice was hit. A detective found that the driver of that taxi had gone to a body shop, paying with his own money. After a little questioning, that driver confessed. New information completely turned the case around.

Similar things happen regularly. Initial information appears definitive, then more facts come to light and we find that we were wrong, sometimes very wrong. We should not only remain open to new information, we should actively seek such information.

Similar problems affect our beliefs about freedom and economics. The statists easily point to individuals their programs helped or might help. Then a wider view often shows that those programs do a great deal of harm, but that harm is less visible than the benefits. It is easy to point out the job that a black person got because of "affirmative action." It is more difficult to find the white man denied that job, or to show how a less qualified employee harms the economy. It is easy to find minority students admitted to top universities to "achieve racial balance." It is more difficult to track down the minority students who flunked out but who would have done well in a less prestigious school. It is easy to claim that government help kept a company such as General Motors in business. It is more difficult to determine the damage done by taking all that money out of the rest of the economy, or what alternative measures might have saved the company without putting that burden on the taxpayers.

Only when we look at all available information can we hope to reach correct conclusions. That is a problem with politicians of all stripes. They pay attention only to information that supports what they want to do. Then they pass a law and we find that they have created problems – or the problems they created remain hidden.

The Source of Current Beliefs

Why has statism destroyed freedom so rapidly? Has there been any factual change in the way the world works? Any scientific reason to believe that we must change the values that made the U.S. what it is? Of course not. Yet today we drift toward collectivism. We ignore the lessons of history in favor of unproven theory and wishful thinking.

We change our actions, but fail to foresee the results of those changes. We ignore evidence from countries where the "new" ideas failed. Our problems are not as serious as those in Europe only because we lag behind them in pursuit of statism/collectivism. In parts of Europe, employees cannot be fired and are guaranteed early, lucrative retirement. That sounds attractive – if only it were possible without creating other problems. Sadly, in that part of the world obligations exceed resources, people refuse to recognize facts, and politicians refuse to stand up for the obvious. Greece, for example, continues to increase government spending even as the country sinks deeper into economic disaster.[42,43]

---

42 http://www.americanthinker.com/2012/05/never_call_socialism_by_its_ right_name.html.
43 http://www.forbes.com/sites/timworstall/2012/11/28/eurozone-how-they-

Any serious attempt to reduce their unaffordable largesse triggers riots. Under pressure from the European Union, the Greek government finally cut back on public sector employment. That triggered the expected turmoil.[44]

We are not there yet, but we are drifting in that direction. And the main theory doing the damage is belief in entitlements, a belief that amounts to a refusal to face the facts, both economic and moral.

"Entitlements"

Is anybody entitled to what somebody else produced? Yet the European model of protected jobs and early, lucrative retirement is just that. It is an entitlement divorced from production. Some think that their very existence obligates "the system" to provide them with the necessities and niceties of life.

Too many, even in the U.S., expect rewards unrelated to production, indeed unrelated to availability of those rewards. They regard government as Santa Claus, able and obligated to give citizens whatever they claim they need. They give no thought to the source of those benefits. That is especially true in Europe. Keep a job for a couple of decades even though you are not productive? Fine, it is illegal to fire you. Retire at 55 with a pension equal to the paycheck you had while working? Who wouldn't want such a deal? There is only one slight problem: Who will produce what that pension or paycheck is expected to buy?

This takes us right back to what economics is all about: goods and services, not money. If such non-production becomes common, people will be "entitled" to

really-solved-the-greek-debt-problem/
44 http://articles.latimes.com/2013/jul/17/world/la-fg-wn-greece-public-employees-20130717

a lot of things that are just not available. The only source of goods and services available to the non-productive is to take from the productive. Once that becomes common, the productive have no incentive to produce. Once the productive stop producing, there will not be enough to go around. The entitlement society is a manifestation of the reverse mob effect discussed in Chapter 6.

Any society where consumption exceeds production is headed for trouble. Inflation will make money less valuable; or some people will have to work harder and longer; or someone will have to make the decision to reduce benefits. Then what happens? People think they are being denied what is theirs by right. Those people react unpredictably, often violently. They may riot, or they may find scapegoats and attack them. Or sometimes a dictator will take over and impose the equivalent of serfdom.

Refusal to face the facts about transfer of wealth is an act of willful ignorance. Entitlements unearned are a weapon of national suicide.

Chapter 5, The Individual and the Collective

This is the issue ... Whether we believe in our capacity for self-government or whether we abandon the American Revolution and confess that a little intellectual elite in a far-distant capitol can plan our lives for us better than we can plan them ourselves. (Ronald Reagan)

Now this is the Law of the Jungle –
as old and as true as the sky;
And the Wolf that shall keep it may prosper,
but the Wolf that shall break it must die.

As the creeper that girdles the tree-trunk
the Law runneth forward and back –
For the strength of the Pack is the Wolf
and the strength of the Wolf is the Pack.

*("The Law of the Jungle," from Kipling's **The Jungle Book**)*

The Denigration of Individualism

Are you an individual, a man or woman who enjoys life, family and friends on your own terms? Or is your sole purpose to serve a collective? Do you have value as an individual human being, or are you worth only what you contribute to the group? Statism and freedom have very different attitudes about those questions.

Aleksandr Solzhenitsyn tells us what an individual is worth in a collectivist state. In the USSR, a person was worth only what he produced for the benefit of the collective – an idea enforced in the gulags. Anyone even suspected of disloyalty could be arrested and sentenced to slave labor. Authorities even went so far as to practice "preventative law enforcement," arresting people because they *might* break the law. That "preventative detention" was especially useful when they needed more workers in the prison camps. Once there, inmates had essentially no value because the state could always arrest someone else to replace them. Even people outside the gulags, people who were not officially prisoners, were mere cogs in a machine, valued only for what they produced. The individual mattered not at all.[45]

Not so freedom. In a free society, any group exists for the benefit of individuals and for no other purpose. Be that group religious, recreational, government or business, it has no value apart from the individuals it serves. As Jefferson said in the Declaration of Independence, "That to secure these rights, Governments are instituted among Men, deriving their just powers from the consent of the governed." The rights mentioned are individual rights. Government exists for the governed, not for its own sake. Nor do the governed exist for the benefit of government.

Now let us be clear, the individualism at issue is not egotism or selfishness. Rather, it is right to live one's own life, to decide for himself, subject only to not interfering with the rights of others. Individualism allows us to be fully human, to have our own lives, beliefs, preferences. The individualist is not just a cog in a social machine. He is himself; he has value as a person, and individual differences provide a wonderful variety in this world.

Of course the statists do not openly disparage the individual. Instead they disparage the right of individuals to decide for themselves, to live as they see fit.

---

45 Solzhenitsyn., *The Gulag Archipelgo,* op cit, information scattered throughout the three volumes of that work

For example, "Obamacare" not only determines that every individual shall have health insurance but mandates what that insurance must include. It treats citizens as though they were all identical. Cogs in a machine again, all forced into the same mold.

Our John I was not regarded as an individual, he was part of his lord's property just like the fields and the sheep. In contrast, John II had status as an individual human. John III again falls between his two ancestors. Will John IV be a human or a cog in a statist machine? That depends on our efforts today. Will we control government, or will we allow it to control us?

Individual Responsibility

Does an individualist society mean lack of rules? Nothing could be farther from the truth. Individualism includes not only the right to make one's own decisions, but the duty to accept the consequences of those decisions and to not impose on others without good reason. The individual is responsible for his own livelihood and to live a law-abiding life. Should he break the law, he and he alone is accountable. Should he fail to educate himself (or should he educate himself in a field with little opportunity), he and he alone lives a life of poverty.

Nor does individualism ignore the less fortunate. Many individualists are quite generous with their time and money, volunteering for community projects and donating to charity. The individualist does this of his own volition and with good will. Do you want someone to donate money to a good cause? Help in a soup kitchen? Give directions to a stranger? Look for a free man; he is more likely to help than is a statist.[46] Meanwhile, the collectivist expects "society" to take care of the problem.

Nor does individualism imply isolation. Individualists form families; they play on sports teams; they cooperate in businesses and volunteer work. Some even work in government. Each brings his own talent and knowledge to enhance the whole, and does so of his own free will.

Loss of Individualism – the Price We Pay

George Washington, Thomas Edison, Martin Luther King Jr., John Bardeen,[47] Abraham Lincoln. They and many others made a positive difference. Where would we be without them? Nobody told them what to do, they decided for themselves, then did it. They were individuals, acting on their own volition, sometimes in the face of danger. Such people grow best in the soil of freedom with the fertilizer of adversity, as we shall discuss below.

But what happens when the collective absorbs the individual? When citizens are told that government is responsible for their livelihood? They lose motivation to help themselves. They remain trapped in poverty with government as an enabler, providing them enough to get by and to destroy incentive. And those who consume without producing reduce the resources and freedom available to everyone. So do those in charge who take from the productive to give to the unproductive. They suck our national resources dry.

---

46   Arthur C. Brooks, *Who Really Cares,* Basic Books, New York, 2006.
            Documents the fact that so-called "conservatives" are more generous
            than those calling themselves "liberals."

47 John Bardeen was one of the inventors of the transistor, the active component
    of the chips that enable today's technology.

The Census Bureau reports that, as of 2011, U.S welfare recipients outnumbered people working full-time.[48, 49] That denies us the potential productivity and creativity of millions of people. Worse, it denies those welfare recipients the dignity and humanity that comes from being productive citizens. Of course some are disabled or otherwise unable to earn a living, but many are capable of doing useful work.

And what does the able-bodied welfare recipient do with all the time on his hands? Some of course become couch potatoes, watching TV all day; but what of those who want to burn off some energy? They cannot do it by working, at least not legally; that would reduce their welfare benefits. Some play sports and find other harmless diversions. Some supplement their benefits with anything from under the table work to armed robbery. If the collective is responsible for everything, a man's conscience need not bother him if he steals his neighbor's car or TV. Society should provide him with as much as his neighbor has, should it not? As we shall see, collectivism militates against individual responsibility and enables crime.

---

48   http://cnsnews.com/news/article/terence-p-jeffrey/census-bureau-means-tested-govt-benefit-recipients-outnumber-full

49 Many on the statist side dispute that statistic. However those who dispute it leave out some critical information. For example, they count as welfare recipients only the adults who receive the money, ignoring the fact that the money is often intended for children. By not counting those children who receive welfare, they undercount people being assisted. They also tend to ignore the fact that the workers in that statistic are those working full-time, year around. It is true that there are part time and temporary workers. Adding them to the employed would of course change the conclusion, but that is not what is claimed. The claim is simply that welfare recipients outnumber full time workers.

And collectivism tends to treat people, not as individuals, but as simply members of a group.

Getting into a Rut

Do you think you can classify people by race, gender and other obvious characteristics? Allow me to introduce you to two real people, one a statist and the other a strong supporter of freedom. See if you can guess which is which. The first is a black woman. She is an excellent musician and has been deeply involved in government. Call her Jean. The second is a white man, very militaristic and a strong advocate of patriotism. Call him Joe. What is your impression of those two, which is the statist and which the freedom lover?

Jean? She is actually Condoleezza Rice, famous for her support of freedom. Joe? Joseph Stalin, one of history's nastiest statists. Skin color, gender, and patriotism do not determine support for or opposition to freedom. That is a major problem with collectivism; it considers people by group, ignoring individual characteristics. For example, many just assume that black people will be democrats and support the welfare state. Some even claim that black "conservatives" are not "authentic Blacks." That attitude pressures people to engage in groupthink rather than use their own intelligence. Likewise, group identity encourages bias for or against certain groups. I have encountered people who claim that minorities cannot be racist and that all "conservatives" are racist. Neither is true of course. There are racists and non-racists, hard workers and goof-offs, in every large group of people. Only by treating them as individuals can we determine who is and who is not racist, lazy, smart, etc. Individual characteristics should trump group identity.

Lumping people into groups makes mischief in many ways. Among others, it creates excessive deference to those perceived as underdogs.

Protected Groups – the Underdogs

I write this after watching a few football games. Like many sports fans, I was rooting for the underdog (none of them won on this day). The team that knocks off a heavy favorite, the guy who comes out of the ghetto to become a success in entertainment or business, the nerdy kid who stands up to the bully. Don't you just love such turnarounds (unless of course that underdog beats your favorite team)? They not only tug at our heart strings, they give us hope. David beats Goliath, the coal miner's daughter becomes a superstar, the unheralded team knocks off the champion. If they can do that, maybe we can overcome the obstacles in our own lives.

Rooting for the downtrodden is great – but we can take it too far. That is especially true if we paint the underdog with an undeserved patina of righteousness to the detriment of others more deserving. Underdogs may be downtrodden, severely abused, and deserving of our sympathy. On the other hand they may be abusers themselves, playing on our sympathy to their benefit. Nowhere is this more evident than in race relations. Some automatically look at skin color instead of the individual when trying to assign guilt.

This is a turn-around from the Jim Crow days when an accused black man in the south would automatically be considered guilty and might be lynched. That was wrong, many innocent men died or spent years in prison. It is just as wrong to do it the other way around. Fortunately lynching seems to be a thing of the past and we seldom falsely imprison people today, but that is not for lack of trying. A few examples come to mind.

First is the case of Tawana Brawley, a fifteen year old black girl, who claimed that six white men kidnapped and raped her, then smeared her body with feces. The response was immediate, with a wide-spread assumption that the accused were guilty. It became a national scandal that such a thing could still happen in this country. Even today Al Sharpton, who helped enable the scandal, defends the accusation. The whole thing was a lie, probably an attempt to escape punishment for running away from home. Both physical evidence and at least one witness prove that the alleged crime never happened.[50, 51] The problem is not that a girl made a false accusation; it is that so many people accepted that accusation before the facts were in, so many neglected the individuals involved and instead looked only at group identity.

A second example is the shooting of Trayvon Martin, a black teenager. This was a sad case; any time a young person loses his life is an unhappy time. That, however, should not have been the legal issue. The real question is if George Zimmerman, the shooter, was acting in justifiable self-defense. I doubt we will ever know, there is simply not enough evidence. Yet this case became a cause célèbre, with many in the news and elsewhere assuming that Zimmerman was racist and guilty. When jurors found him not guilty, there were screams of injustice.[52]

---

50 http://blackamericaweb.com/2013/08/05/commentary-its-time-for-reverend-al-sharpton-to-step-up-again-for-tawana-brawley/

51 http://nypost.com/2013/08/04/pay-up-time-for-brawley-87-rape-hoaxer-finally-shells-out-for-slander/

52 http://www.cnn.com/2013/06/05/us/trayvon-martin-shooting-fast-facts/

Neither Martin nor Zimmerman was as "squeaky clean" as initially depicted. However, criminal cases should be decided on the basis of evidence of specific crimes, not who is nicest. In this country the burden of proof is supposed to be on the accuser, who must provide proof of guilt beyond reasonable doubt. The prosecutor did not even come close to meeting that standard. Another case of judging on the basis of who is in which ethnic group, rather than looking at the individuals and the facts.

Another example is from Ferguson, Missouri where as mentioned a police officer shot Michael Brown, a black teenager. Again we lack good information, but there was no indictment, much less a conviction – at least a conviction in a court of law. Not so in the minds of those who judge by group identity. They have the cop convicted and spread their group politics by inflicting punishment on anyone in the area not belonging to their own group. They are rioted, smashed windows, stole merchandise and otherwise made mayhem. They punished the white man by stealing big screen televisions from merchants who were completely uninvolved in the incident. To them, skin color trumps evidence.

Judgment by ethnicity is dangerous and counterproductive, it perpetuates racial animosity and causes miscarriage of justice. Assigning blame on the basis of ethnicity is akin to a bill of attainder; it convicts on the basis of who people are, not what they do.

Yes, some white men have murdered black men. In fact in the Jim Crow days that was all too common. That, however, does not mean that all black deaths at the hands of whites are bigoted murder; sometimes it was a matter of genuine self defense. Some powerful groups have oppressed minorities, but sometimes the minority, such as Hamas in Gaza, is trying to murder the supposed oppressors.

Again, we should avoid a rush to judgment and look at the evidence. Being an underdog carries neither special virtue nor special guilt. We must determine guilt or innocence on the basis of facts, not skin color or other irrelevancies.

One more example, but I must warn you: unless you have a strong stomach, you may want to skip the next three paragraphs.

Rotherham, Yorkshire, United Kingdom Men rove the streets, picking up young girls who become sex slaves, victims of gang rape. In many cases fathers and their sons, along with their friends, rape the same girl. There are at least 1400 victims, many of whom later self-harm or commit suicide. Police find one twelve year old girl, previously gang raped, in a house with several abusers so they take action. They arrest the girl for being drunk and disorderly; her abusers go free.[53] In another case, two fathers find where their daughters are held and try to rescue them. Police arrest the fathers and release the rapists.[54]

Why protect the criminals? Because they are Pakistani Muslims, brown-skinned and of a minority religion. The authorities are more concerned with avoiding the appearance of racism than with protecting the girls. It seems that among that group of Pakistanis, gang rape of little girls is considered normal and even expected.[55] We can't interfere with the culture of minorities now, can we? Group identity trumps reason.

---

53 http://www.telegraph.co.uk/news/uknews/crime/11059138/Rotherham-In-the-face-of-such-evil-who-is-the-racist-now.html
54 http://www.breitbart.com/Breitbart-London/2014/08/27/Muslim-gang-rapists-are-springing-up-everywhere-Why-can-t-we-be-honest-about-it
55 Ibid

Yes, that is sick, so sick that I can barely stand to write it and I apologize for putting it in front of my readers. However, we must understand just how far some will go to protect the allegedly downtrodden.

Sometimes the underdog deserves a licking. Sometimes the top dog deserves a licking. Until we look at evidence, and at individuals instead of group characteristics, we will never have a just, peaceful world.

The Fully Human Individual

The worst effect of denigration of the individual? It militates against our becoming fully human, against becoming all we can and should be. If we are just cogs in a big machine, why make the effort to develop our talents? Why engage in serious critical thinking? Indeed, group pressure discourages individual effort and improvement. It is reminiscent of crabs in a bucket. If there is only one crab, it will escape. However if we put several crabs there, as soon as one starts to climb out, the others will pull him back. Likewise, collectivism pulls us back into the bucket of groupthink.

We should be humans, not crabs. C.S. Lewis sums this up in "Screwtape Proposes a Toast," the appendix to his delightful book, *The Screwtape Letters.* His devilish protagonist explains how "democracy" can be used as an incantation against anyone with the temerity to be different, to fully develop his abilities. "Under the influence of this incantation those who are in any or every way inferior can labour more wholeheartedly and successfully than ever before to pull down everyone else to their own level. But that is not all. Under the same influence, those who come, or could come, nearer to a full humanity, actually draw back from fear of being undemocratic."

That devil even claims, "All is summed up in the prayer which a young female human is said to have uttered recently: 'O God, make me a normal twentieth century girl!' Thanks to our labours, this will mean increasingly: 'Make me a minx, a moron, and a parasite.'"[56]

This is sometimes called "tall poppy syndrome" after the accounts of some ancient rulers who demonstrated how to control the people. They cut off the tops of the tallest poppies in their gardens to demonstrate how to handle anyone who stood out. That is an effective technique for the tyrant; just eliminate those who stand out. Get rid of anyone who insists on being an individual instead of a cog in a machine. If you allow people to be fully human, they just might think for themselves. Freedom, however, encourages us to be individuals, individuals who live tour own lives and make our own decisions.

Individualism and Decision Making

Collectivism by its very nature imposes third-party decisions on the entire country. Officials and bureaucrats issue decrees, often from hundreds of miles away. They determine hiring qualifications, what products should be manufactured, and a host of other decisions. Then the new work rules cause shoddy product, the people hired turn out to be unqualified or unmotivated, the product is not what people want. However those who made the centralized decisions are seldom held accountable. In Chapter 15 we will discuss third-party decision making and its odious outcomes.

---

56   The book has been published several times, so page numbers may not agree. However this quote can be found on line at http://screwtapeblogs.wordpress.com/2009/06/30/screwtape-proposes-a-toast/

There are worse problems. Collectivism induces groupthink. People go along with what the group wants, or with what they think the group wants. They suppress their own opinions. The "yes man," the sycophant, rises to the top. Information and analysis is excluded. In some cases everyone goes along with what they secretly oppose because nobody has the courage to speak up.

Irving Janis in his book, *Victims of Groupthink,* describes some of the problems this creates. For example, as described in Chapter 2 of that book, groupthink was a major factor in the Bay of Pigs fiasco during the Kennedy Administration. The U.S. supported some Cubans who tried to overthrow the Castro regime. Officials believed they could hide our involvement, and that Castro's forces would rebel. They ignored readily available information to the contrary, leading to one of the worst foreign policy debacles in U.S. history. The whole story is well worth reading.

Our John I and his fellow serfs had no choice but to engage in groupthink. The master was automatically right and any contrary opinions had to be wrong. John II, on the other hand, was free to express his own ideas. John III has some restrictions, but is still able to think for himself. What about John IV? Will he and his associates be able to discuss things openly? Or will they be inhibited in expressing their ideas?

Allowing, even encouraging, individualism can stop groupthink. And it is one of the best defenses against institutionalized idiocy and evil.

Individualism vs. Evil

How does a society become fully and completely evil? A horror like Nazi Germany, like Cambodia under Pol Pot, or North Korea with the Kim family in charge? How does it create the hell that Solzhenitsyn describes in *The Gulag Archipelago?* In such societies, torture is not limited to a few sociopaths; it becomes the norm, an accepted means of reaching state goals. The state then rewards the torturers and punishes those who oppose their methods. How do such societies develop?

The answer is that ideology trumps the value of the individual. In a free society, there will be ideology, but it will be aimed at serving the individuals in that society. The Declaration of Independence, for example, expresses an ideology that all men, as individuals, have the right to life, liberty, and the pursuit of happiness. We have benefited greatly from trying to reach that ideal. On the other hand, Nazi Germany, Cambodia under Pol Pot, Cuba under Castro and others put ideology above people and created hells on earth.

Once the individual becomes subordinate to ideology, all restraint is removed. Will a false accusation advance the ideology? By all means, make that false accusation. A conviction with no evidence? If it advances the cause, do it. Send the supposed offender to a concentration camp or gas chamber? Certainly, if that will move the ideology forward. Do you suspect someone of disloyalty to the cause? Throw him in the gulag, no sense taking chances. After all, you can't make an omelet without breaking eggs,[57] and what does one person matter anyway?

When the omelet of ideology reigns, the individual has no more value than an egg. He is simply a one cog in the machine, to be used, replaced, or mistreated as the authorities deem proper. Be that ideology collectivism, racial superiority, or anything else, the result is dehumanization of individuals.

---

57 Attributed to Stalin though probably used earlier in the French Revolution and maybe even earlier than that.

That ideological mindset justifies lying, torture, false accusations and more. Even normal people justify heinous actions in the service of ideology, or more likely those normal people do not even think about the magnitude of their crimes. Solzhenitsyn himself wonders if he would have become a torturer instead of the tortured if he had that opportunity.[58]

An ideology that specifically values the individual can never justify such crimes. However in a society where individuals have no value, those abominations are inevitable.

The Importance of Strong Individuals

Sam Walter Foss expressed the poetic wish,

Bring me men to match my mountains,
Bring me men to match my plains,
Men with empires in their purpose,
And new eras in their brains[59]

His wish has been granted by men and women who matched the mountains of war, bigotry, disease, science and technology, and other challenges our citizens have surmounted. We still have mountains to conquer, but those people gave us a good start. They did that by taking action, not by waiting for "somebody" to solve the problem.

We need such people today. We need real men and women in all walks of life, including in the home and neighborhood. We still face bigotry, poor education, crime and a host of other problems. We need men (and women) to match those mountains. Where will we get them if we denigrate individualism?

---

58 Op Cit, Solzhenitsyn, Volume 1 Chapter 4
59 Sam Walter Foss, "The Coming American," 1894

As described in the anonymous story below, we could delegate all our problems to Nobody.

"This is a story about four people named Everybody, Somebody, Anybody and Nobody. There was an important job to do and Everybody was asked to do it. Everybody was sure Somebody would do it. Anybody could have done it, but Nobody did it. Somebody got angry because it was Everybody's job. Everybody thought Anybody would do it, but Nobody realized that Everybody wouldn't do it. It ended up that Everybody blamed Somebody when Nobody did what Anybody could have done."[60] Collectivism, by removing individual responsibility, assigns action to "Everybody." As a result, we can guess who will act. That's right: Nobody. Every successful business manager, every competent business or military leader knows that nothing happens until he assigns the task to a specific individual. Assigning something to a group, even to government, guarantees poor performance.

Daniel Hannan describes how the welfare state has eviscerated self reliance and neighborly aid in Europe. "It wasn't so long ago that any adult, seeing a child out of school during term, would stop him and say, 'Why aren't you in class?' Now this is seen as the state's duty. It wasn't so long ago that we all kept an eye out for elderly neighbors, and looked to see that they were still collecting their milk bottles each morning. Now this too is seen as the government's responsibility. When unusually heavy snow carpeted Europe at the end of 2009, people

---

60 Charles Swindoll in his book, *Strengthening Your Grip* (though this has been repeated so many times that the original authorship is uncertain.)

complained because the authorities were slow to clear their driveways and pavements. Their grandparents simply would have taken out their shovels."[61]

Where will we get the Thomas Edisons, the Clara Bartons, the George Washingtons of the future? Where will we get the neighbors who assist the widow or the elderly couple unable to keep up with yard or house? Where will we even get citizens who are willing and able to take care of themselves in a storm or disaster? I fear that a developing nanny state will produce "sheeple," sheep-like excuses for humans who wait for Somebody to solve their problems. Instead we should be producing men and women who stand up on their hind legs and take action.

That is one of the biggest problems with government-provided health care and other largesse. We cannot grow independence by fostering dependence. We cannot develop men and women of action by molly-coddling our citizens. No, the independent thinker, the person willing and able to advance both himself and his fellow man, must be grown in the crucible of self-reliance and difficulty. Only thus can people develop the courage, the guts to preserve our freedoms.

Opposition breeds strength, dependence breeds weakness. Statist rulers love dependence and weakness; it makes us easy to control.

The Hatching of Chickens

Imagine that you are visiting a friend who raises chickens. You notice that an egg is starting to hatch, but the chick inside is having an awful struggle. It pecks at the shell, then stops for a while before pecking a little more. The poor

---

61   Daniel Hannan, *The New Road to Serfdom,* Harper Collins, 2010, p100

little thing, you kindly help it out of the shell. You just killed it. Baby chicks need the exercise they get from their battle to escape the shell. Without it, they will be so weak that they are unlikely to survive.

Humans likewise must struggle to fully develop. Without opposition, we become weak and dependent. Worse, we might go looking for mischief to relieve the boredom, maybe even follow the footsteps of a terrorist like Mohammed Bouyeri whom we shall discuss shortly.

Guts!

What does it take to be all we can be, to meet the obstacles life will surely throw at us? Laurence Gonzales wrote a valuable book called *Deep Survival*, a book with applications far beyond the tragic circumstances his protagonists faced. He describes people who overcame great odds to stay alive. His survivors demonstrate what it takes to make a positive difference in our family, public, or business life. Those people take charge of their own lives. If trapped in a mountain accident, they take action to protect or rescue themselves. If shipwrecked, they take the lead in solving the problem. If stranded by aircraft or automotive problems, they do all that is possible, more that we would think possible, to get themselves out of the problem.

The main determinant of who lives and who dies is not what's in his pack. It is not even what is in his head. It is what is in his heart. It is what athletes call guts. A team behind as time runs out is said to face a gut check, a chance to see if they can dig down and find that extra something that will pull out a victory. Those who survive disaster face a similar gut check. They have to dig down inside themselves and produce that extra effort to defeat the Grim Reaper.

We face similar needs in every aspect of our lives. Be it a death threat such as an earthquake, or something as simple as a misbehaving child, we need the ability to do whatever it takes.

Consider the remaining bigotry in our country. The easy part of that battle is done; the Jim Crow laws and similar restraints are no more. Now we face the task of changing minds and hearts, something we cannot legislate. What do we do about that? We can sit back and say "Somebody should do something. Then Somebody will delegate that job to Nobody. However, if we have the courage to confront the bigots, to befriend those others regard as inferior, we will become men and women who match the mountain of bigotry.

That may require that we risk alienation from friends, family, even employers. We may even risk having our property vandalized or our persons harmed. It will take courage, courage that must come from individuals – individuals with guts.

That is the courage that allows a soldier to dig down inside for what he needs to fight the terrorists a little harder. It is the courage that allows a government or business employee to risk his job and expose corruption. It is the courage a parent needs to care for a disabled child or to discipline a child who is starting to engage in unacceptable behavior. It is the courage, the guts, this country needs to preserve our freedom and continue to improve our lives. It is the courage we will not develop as wards of a nanny state.

The Devil's Workshop

But what about the flip side? If we fail to grow those heroes, we may well create monsters, nurtured in the devil's workshop of an idle mind. The nanny state provides thousands of people with enough to eat but no pressing business to keep them out of trouble. Some will use their free time to commit crimes or engage in terrorism. Some of those will even resent the hand that feeds them.

The world has already seen Muslims in Europe use their idle time to attack, even murder the citizens of their host countries. For example, in November of 2004 Mohammed Bouyeri, a Moroccan living in Holland, shot filmmaker Theo Van Gogh in the neck, then sliced him open with a machete. As he walked away he screamed, "Now you know what you people can expect in the future."[62] Bouyeri might have become such an animal in any case, but the protection he received from the government of Holland abetted his crime. The system provided several steppingstones to fanatic crime:

> First, time to listen to fanatic recruiters, and to think and plan. People with jobs seldom have time to get involved in the type of grandiose schemes the Islamic fanatics like.

> Second, boredom. Some bored people watch TV, others seek action.

> Third, protection. For fear of being labeled racist, most western governments are reluctant to gather information about minorities or to prosecute those minorities vigorously.

Of course those potential steppingstones to fanaticism are not sufficient to create a Bouyeri. Millions in similar situations remain law-abiding, some engage in other types of crime, some even do good. However the welfare state did make it easier for Bouyeri to become a dangerous fanatic.

Nor can such antisocial actions be blamed on poverty or other such alleged causes. Muslims in Britain were loyal citizens during the First World War, even

---

62 Ibid, p106

fighting against Islamic countries. It was only with the advent of the welfare state, and when British elites began speaking against patriotism, that the Islamic minority started its campaign of violence.[63]

Lack of Individual Freedom

It is disheartening to see how, after the struggle to obtain them, our freedoms have ebbed away. Decision-making power, together with economic control and responsibility, migrated from the individual to the central planners. That destroys freedom and militates against the development of strong individuals. We are in danger of becoming a nation of sheeple, not of fully developed men and women. Statism destroys both humanity and freedom.

---

63   Ibid, p107-113

Chapter 6, Freedom and Statism

Disregarding the lessons of history there has been a disposition to revert to the methods of tyranny in order to meet the problems of democracy. Intent on some immediate exigency, and with slight consideration of larger issues, we create autocratic power.... We should know by this time that arbitrariness is quite as likely to proceed from an unrestrained administrative officer of the republic reigning by the grace of an indefinite statute as by the personal government of a despotic king. (Charles Evans Hughes)

The Birth of Freedom – Where We Came From and Where We Are Going

It happens nearly every presidential election; movie stars threaten to leave the country if the Republican wins the White House.[64] Then if the Republican does win? They develop "public laryngitis" and remain in the country without another word about leaving. It seems that they prefer to live here, even under a republican president, than in any other country. For one thing, in the United States they have the freedom to speak their minds, and to make the movies they want to make. In countries like Cuba or Venezuela, expressing certain opinions can bring an appointment with the judge – or late night "visitors" who take you away. Even Canada lacks the freedom of expression we have in the United States.[65] The Canadian definition of hate speech includes church ministers saying that homosexual actions are sinful.[66]

---

64 http://www.snopes.com/inboxer/outrage/leave.asp
65 http://www.parl.gc.ca/content/lop/researchpublications/2010-31-e.htm
66 http://www.cbc.ca/news/politics/top-court-upholds-key-part-of-sask-anti-hate-

How did the U.S. and a few other countries develop the freedom and economic advantages we enjoy? Not all that long ago, rigid hierarchies governed the known world. The king or emperor was at the top. Below him were princes, dukes, and counts, right on down to the lord of the manor and his serfs. These were very statist societies; each aristocrat made decisions for everyone below him. The king even claimed that he ruled by divine right.

That aristocratic organization was often coupled with a guild system. Each craft had its guild, and if you wanted to be a shoe maker, blacksmith or other craftsman, you joined the guild and followed its rules. The guilds did teach the craft and assure competence, but they also restricted competition and kept prices high. Guild power came from charters granted by local authorities, and did vary with time and location. In some cases the guild would control both trade and manufacture; in other cases only manufacture leaving trade free; and in yet other cases they had minimal control over either.[67] In all cases however, the guild had monopoly powers.

Agricultural land was in the hands of a hereditary aristocracy, and the guilds controlled most of the rest of the economy. That economic stagnation restricted freedom. Disobey those with economic power and you could get mighty hungry.

It was a controlled, stable society, but that kind of stability seldom coexists with freedom and progress.

---

law-1.1068276

67 http://www.socsci.uci.edu/~garyr/papers/Richardson_2004_Explorations-in-Economic-History.pdf

The Birth of Freedom

From the serfdom of John I to the freedom of John II, what drove the change? Certainly not the kings and aristocracy; they preferred to keep their power. No, the forces of freedom and progress arose elsewhere. A complete history would take volumes, so what follows is admittedly sketchy, just to give an idea of how freedom came about and how we can lose it.

The journey from serfdom to freedom was long, slow, and torturous. In fact many of those initially advancing the cause had no idea that they were doing so; they sought their own economic benefits, freedom for the masses was a side effect. Only later did people like the founders of the United States work deliberately to attain and preserve freedom.

Prologue to Freedom

Freedom means the right to choose, a right that is meaningless without knowledge. Control of information is control of people, a fact not lost on today's statists. John I and the other serfs lacked freedom not only because of their political status, but because they were illiterate. Nor would literacy have helped much since few books were available; why go to the trouble of becoming literate when there was nothing available to read? That started to change after about 1439 when Gutenberg invented movable type. As his invention spread, so did books and other printed material.

Gutenberg's invention was half of the solution to the information problem. The other half came when Protestantism emphasized individual Bible study and encouraged its adherents to learn to read,[68] Once literate, they did not stop with the Bible. Newspapers, almanacs, history books and all manner of other printed material appeared. The amount of information available to the common man exploded, and with it the knowledge necessary to make wise choices.

Meanwhile, other changes were reducing the power of the aristocracy.

Freedom: the Beginnings

Two key developments came out of what is now Italy: expanded maritime commerce, and innovations in banking.[69] Of course commerce had been important to civilization for centuries, especially in the eastern Mediterranean. What the Italian cities did was expand shipping throughout the known world – and eventually expand that known world. They enriched themselves as their ships traded throughout the Mediterranean and eventually beyond. Even Columbus was an Italian, born in Genoa. His opening of the New World was effectively an extension of the trade that the Italians pioneered. Queen Isabella and King Ferdinand sponsored his voyages in an attempt to acquire a profitable trade route to the Far East.

Banking grew in tandem with maritime commerce and boosted both economics and freedom. The Italian innovations provided enforceable loan collection.[70] Merchants and others could put money in the bank and that bank could then make loans to people who needed it to finance businesses.

---

68 http://www.ecu.edu/cs-educ/TQP/upload/tqpTheReformationAug2014.pdf, p 4
69 http://www.researchgate.net/publication/4768694_Italian_city-states_and_financial_evolution
70 Ibid

Entrepreneurs could acquire ships, start manufacturing enterprises, and otherwise develop businesses not dependent on the limited land available.

Imagine that you want to start a business, say using a better loom to weave cloth. You have the skill and drive, but you lack money for start-up costs. Before the banking innovations you had to go around to a few money lenders and try to convince them to support your enterprise. You might have had to convince several of them before you had enough to get started. After those banking innovations, you just had to convince the banker to get your financing. Plus the depositors were more willing to put their money in the bank; they gtt it back with interest. That gave you the freedom to leave your old job, and it gave your potential employees a choice of employment. And, as discussed in Chapter 3, that economic freedom spawns freedom in other areas.

Competition Rises, Aristocracy Falls

The commerce and banking innovations spread, reaching the Low Countries and the British Isles. Trade expanded, eventually to other parts of the world. No longer was wealth dependent on land ownership; commerce provided opportunity for any young man of ambition and ability. And maritime advances soon opened a whole new continent to the Europeans. No aristocracy controlled land in the Americas; agriculture there did not depend on the lord of the manor. Limits on creation and acquisition of wealth vanished – as did much of the power of the aristocrats. Unable to control the economy, they lost their ability to control other aspects of society.

No longer did everybody depend on the prices set by the guilds or the king. They could buy cotton from Egypt or the southern part of what became the United

States, spices from India, sugar from the Caribbean, manufactured cloth from any of several sources. The force of competition provided widespread opportunity as it broke the economic stranglehold of the aristocracy and guilds. Thus was the stage set for the reduction of the power of the British king, and eventually for the U.S. Declaration of Independence.

The new economic world gave men a sense of power over their own fates. No longer did everyone depend on the king, the prince, the count or the lord of the manor. Instead they could go off and seek better employment wherever they could find it, or even establish some enterprise of their own. That was the original – and successful - "power to the people" movement. Power migrated from the aristocracy to the more ambitious and able of the common people.

As commerce and manufacturing expanded, people noticed that individual actions, not controlled by "higher authority," were capable of producing complex social and economic systems. Eventually this phenomenon was described in such works as Adam Smith's *Wealth of Nations* and Leonard Read's more accessible (and fun) essay "I Pencil," the latter now readily available on the internet. Both describe how the actions of individuals seeking their own interests can spontaneously create economic structures that benefit everybody. By serving customers at an acceptable price, those individuals not only enrich themselves but also provide for the needs of others. As Smith describes it, "It is not from the benevolence of the butcher, the brewer, or the baker that we expect our dinner, but from their regard to their own self-interest."[71]

---

71 http://www.goodreads.com/quotes/68664-it-is-not-from-the-benevolence-of-the-butcher-the

Competition Produces Freedom

As society became freer, citizens could engage in whatever occupations they liked, subject only to ability and demand for their services. Competition forced business people to hire the best employees they could find, improve their products, and reduce their prices. People were freed to seek employment where they preferred, and to buy what and where they preferred.

With economic freedom came other freedoms. Eventually the United States, the United Kingdom and a few other countries reached what Hayek calls the liberal state, what in this book we call freedom. Our John II could seek employment wherever he preferred. His son could become a blacksmith and his daughter a teacher, all without seeking permission from any employer or government authority. They could even criticize their government.

Serfdom died, murdered by cold-blooded competition.

Special Cases Where Competition Does Not Work Well

Though competition is great, there are a few cases for which it is at present not feasible. The prime example is utilities that require pipes or wires. Each such utility carries a cost of installation, and there would be an extra cost for each competitor selling natural gas, electricity, or land line phone service. Worse, those pipes and wires take up right-of-way space and may require digging up public streets. Can you imagine the mess if ten or twenty companies all ran pipes or wires to our homes? It is therefore reasonable to grant monopoly status to some utility companies and to regulate how they do business.

Fortunately, some of those services have become competitive. Telephone land lines are no longer necessary; most people can choose among several cell phone providers. Even the users of land lines may chose between the traditional phone company or the cable TV company in their area. The cable TV company in turn faces competition from satellite companies and the internet, with the internet service available through the phone company, via wireless connection, or even the cable company. That competition benefits consumers greatly and we can hope that it will expand. However, electricity and natural gas still require pipes or wires to our homes, so it makes sense to regulate them.

So how do we regulate monopoly utilities? One problem is that government is tempted to own them. Since only one gas or electric company is going to serve the city, why not have the city own and manage that gas or electric company? That may work reasonably well on a small scale, at the city or county level. However, even there the monopoly tries to protect its own interests. On a larger scale, any government monopoly and its ability to protect itself discourages innovation and progress. Suppose there had been a nation-wide government-owned telephone monopoly before the advent of cell phones. Could the cell phone have ever developed, or at least developed as fast as it did? Almost certainly not. That monopoly would have had both the incentive and the power to suppress potential competitors, but no incentive to pursue the new technologies. Likewise, a government-owned cable TV company would suppress the development of competing technologies.

The better model is already used in much of the country. State or local governments license monopoly utility companies, then regulate them to see that they serve the people well without (we hope) excess prices. That somewhat separates government power from utility profits and reduces temptation to protect the utility from new technologies. Not as effective as competition, but probably the best we can do when competition is not feasible.

It is clearly better to have as much competition as feasible, and to limit government power to those functions where private business is ineffective. However, of late we are going the other direction. Why? We shall discuss that later, but for now let's return to the development of freedom.

Taming the King

Freedom had a long history in the British Isles, going back before the Norman Conquest. It was the Normans who imposed a dictatorial king on the British, after which the English oscillated between freedom and regal power for centuries. By the time of the American Revolution, Englishmen in their home country were the freest people in the world. The colonists' problem was that they lacked the freedom available in England. A full discussion is beyond the scope of this book, but Daniel Hannan gives a good account of this part of history in his book, *Inventing Freedom.*[72]

We continue to fight a major aspect of the rule of kings even today. The British kings and their supporters tried to increase their power by royal proclamations. They claimed that Parliament moved too slowly, so the king and his representatives needed power to make rules without consent of Parliament. That royal power is a precursor to the power of bureaucracies today, which we discuss in Chapter 12.[73]

---

72 Daniel Hannan, *Inventing Freedom*, Broadside (Imprint of Harper-Collins Publishers), 2013
73 Hamburger, op cit. The entire book is devoted to bureaucracies and their rule-

"Ambitious crown lawyers under Elizabeth pressed for royal legislation outside Parliament. With their eyes on the Crown's authority and their own advancement, they urged paths that went outside and above the law, and they now found a propitious climate for their absolutist claims."[74] Eventually parliament won and the king's power was restricted. Then, as we shall discuss in Chapter 10, the U.S. Constitution guaranteed freedom and limited government.

Progressives and Liberals?

How did we get from the limited government our founders gave us to the current concentration of power in Washington, D.C.? Obviously some influential people preferred the collectivist model, but how did they persuade so many voters to go along with their program? Not by openly advocating loss of freedom! We discuss elsewhere how they gradually increased federal power, but why did the voters fail to realize where those changes were leading? One reason is that statists hijacked two words: "liberal" and "progressive." They led the unthinking to pay more attention to high-sounding words than to the actual programs behind the words.

In the past, liberal meant well, liberal. Live and let live. No unnecessary restrictions on business or personal life. Another meaning was generosity with one's own resources. Today in the U.S. "liberal" has a meaning exactly opposite of its historic meaning. It refers to someone who supports big government, lots of regulation, and tax-supported welfare.

---

making.
74 Ibid, p40

Likewise "progressive" has taken on a new meaning, becoming essentially a synonym for the statist use of liberal. That is convenient for the statists; when one word falls into disrepute they switch and use the other, still hiding their intent. What are they "progressing" towards? If we look at the actions behind the words, they are going right back to big, all-powerful government. They want federal rules to determine how many sidewalks local jurisdictions shall have and to otherwise engage in centralized decision-making. They are regressing to a system of centralized government like the one we rebelled against in 1776, a system in which the rulers are all-powerful and regarded as always right. The "progressives" are really reactionaries, in spite of the accusations they throw at freedom lovers.

Is Freedom "Conservative" or "Anti-Government?

You've heard the accusations. "Conservatives want no change and hate all government." That is demonstrably false and one reason I avoid the term "conservative." It is an artifact of the mislabeling of political positions. Because freedom advocates are often called "conservative," it is easy to assume that those "conservatives" oppose change. Not so! The goal is *freedom*. That includes freedom to change. And it allows others the same freedom. What we do oppose is unnecessary government restrictions.

And statists sometimes accuse freedom lovers of wanting to abolish all government; they push the false choice of no government or unlimited government. Free men realize that those are not the only options. We need not have government controlling every aspect of our lives.

We might compare the statists to a gardener who wants to control the growth of the plant. Free men, on the other hand, are like a gardener who controls the conditions and allows the plant to do the growing. The free man wants government to be confined to its own legitimate sphere and to leave people alone otherwise.

The Legitimate Sphere of Government

Just what is the legitimate sphere of government? Let's look at a few examples:

> You go on vacation, driving on an interstate highway built under government direction.

> The fire department responds to your neighbor's house fire.

> Burglars would break into your cousin's apartment, except the police caught them during a previous crime and they are now in jail.

> A foreign tyrant looks enviously at Alaskan oil, but leaves it alone when he sees the ability of our military.

> Your nephew lives downstream from a factory that might pollute the river if it were not for the laws against that pollution.

Those represent legitimate functions of government. They provide what economists call *external costs and benefits,* or *externalities*. Externalities are defined as costs or benefits accruing to someone not directly involved in the transaction. Your cousin is not involved in the burglars' "business" but he would pay if government didn't enforce the law. As citizens we are not involved in the tyrant's "business," but we lose if government fails to defend the country. Individually, you paid next to nothing to build that freeway, but many people travel on it. Those are all externalities. Externalities and nothing else are the properly the domain of government.

However that does not mean that government should automatically meddle with all external costs and benefits. It should determine if a proposed action is really worth doing, fair, and worth the cost. For example, it should not build the new road that primarily benefits the mayor's cousin, nor should it build a fancy stadium that brings minimal benefit to the people. Government should also avoid actions that unduly restrict freedom, even if those actions fall within the sphere of external benefits. Some would claim that government should do things like dictate the colors houses should be painted. Free men, however, would object on the grounds that people should make their own choices in such matters, not force their idea of beauty on others. We should remain free unless there are strong and compelling reasons to impose a restriction.

Freedom allows us to make our own choices. And it has economic advantages as well.

Advantages of Competition

What has freedom done for us economically? Plenty. For example, I remember when a long distance telephone call was a very big deal. Those calls were expensive and the sound quality often poor. As children, we would be kept very quiet so Mom or Dad could hear the weak voice on the line. There was also a time before answering machines and voice mail became available; if you weren't home, you just missed the call.

Compare that with the telephone service today. My cell phone gives me unlimited calling all over the United States, plus voice mail, books equivalent to a small library, music, even access to the internet. For all that, I pay an inflation-adjusted price less than what my parents paid for their land-line telephone. Why do we have that advantage? Mostly because businesses, competing with each other, sought better ways to serve us and attract our business.

Freedom and competition are a boon to consumers. Our automobiles often provide GPS navigation systems, great sound systems, air conditioning etc. My digital camera takes great pictures that I don't even have to send out to be developed – and I can send those pictures to friends and family instantly at essentially no cost. Most homes in the U.S. today have at least one computer with more capability than the computers that helped put a man on the moon. And those examples hardly scratch the surface of what competition has provided to consumers.

Yet there are people who oppose competition.

Forces Against Competition

Competition benefits consumers. It does not always benefit the companies forced to compete. For decades Kodak was almost synonymous with photography – until that company failed to keep up with the change from film to digital and was forced into bankruptcy. It only recently emerged with an entirely different business model. Foreign competition forced the "big three" auto makers to improve their products. Smith Corona was once a major manufacturer of typewriters and mechanical calculators, devices some readers may have seen only in a museum. That company was wiser than Kodak, switching its business model as computers displaced the typewriter and the mechanical calculator.

With such a history, it is no surprise when businesses want to limit what they call "cut-throat competition." That would make their life easier, just as the old guild system made life easier for the shoe maker. However, competition forces them to serve their customers better.

The statists often ask, "If businesses want to be regulated, shouldn't we listen to them? After all, they know their business better than anyone else." However they fail to ask the follow-up questions: "Who benefits from this regulation?" "How will it affect the country in general, those businesses, their customers, and competitors?" In most cases the beneficiaries of regulation are the same businesses that support the regulation. Those regulations may limit competition, or they may mandate features customers really don't want. That allows some businesses to improve their bottom line at the expense of customers. They support some regulations for the same reason a burglar would support laws against watchdogs.

For example, in my area there was a push for a law requiring grocery stores to charge customers for the bags they use. The grocery stores all supported the measure, but a bit of thought shows why. They would be able to charge their customers for the bags and not have to worry about a competitor giving them away free. The proposal would have restricted competition and harmed customers for the benefit of the stores.

Businesses have long sought regulation to protect themselves, what economists call "rent seeking." Back in the 18th century Adam Smith pointed out that, "To widen the market and to narrow the competition is always in the interest of the dealers... The proposal of any new law or regulation which comes from this order, ought always to be listened to with great precaution, and ought never to be adopted, till after having been long and carefully examined, not only with the most scrupulous, but with the most suspicious attention. It comes from an order of men, whose interest is never exactly the same with that of the public."[75]

The first regulatory agency in the U.S. provides an example. The Interstate Commerce Commission was established in 1887 to oversee railroads. All the railroads supported the idea because they expected to use it to for "trickery and evasion," and they wanted the public to have to complain to that commission instead of appealing directly to the courts.[76] We shall discuss bureaucratic problems further in Chapter 12.

Of course, the people involved in any business do have knowledge and insights the rest of us lack, but we should carefully examine the claims of those who want regulation. Many companies and politicians employ spokespeople, "hired guns," very adept at convincing people to support their viewpoint. We should evaluate their claims carefully and avoid "government by the silver tongue." If we are not careful, companies will regulate themselves into monopoly or oligopoly status, creating a form of state capitalism. Should that happen, we will lose the freedom we might otherwise enjoy, along with the benefits competition provides to consumers.

In fact Roosevelt's attempt to deal with the Great Depression did create a form of state capitalism. The National Industrial Recovery Act (NIRA, later shortened to National Recovery Act, NRA) encouraged some industries to collaborate and fix prices. Those companies could form cartels and effectively

---

75 This quote from Adam Smith's *The Wealth of Nations* can be found in several sources, including https://www.marxists.org/reference/archive/smith-adam/works/wealth-of-nations/book01/ch11c-3.htm

76 Hamburger, Philip, *Is Administrative Law Unlawful?* The University of Chicago Press, 2014, footnote p453

make laws restricting competition. That law protected some powerful businesses, but it harmed both the common people and smaller, competing businesses. In fact one major cause of that Depression was lack of money in circulation. The higher prices those cartels imposed exacerbated the problem. The Depression continued.[77] Competition is messy and unpredictable. It can drive business managers bonkers. Fine, let them live with the problems it gives them. In most cases it provides great benefits for consumers so let's encourage competition.

Creating a Climate for Competition

So what should government do to foster competition and economic growth? There are several good externalities, ways government can foster "conditions for growth." One of the most important is a sound legal system. We need enforceable contracts for everything from home rental to business deals. We need title to property. As the Italian innovators discovered, we need enforceable loans. We need enforcement of laws against fraud, theft, violence etc. All of that is in the province of government.

It is important that the legal environment be stable and understandable. If the rules change from day to day, nobody will know what is allowed and not allowed. Even worse would be rules that change after the fact and apply retroactively, ex post facto laws. How could a person or business remain law abiding if a law made today applies to what happened yesterday?

That is one of the problems with judge made law. Nobody can predict how a court will rule. Furthermore, those rulings are ex post facto; they apply to actions

---

77 Folsom, Burton Jr., *New Deal or Raw Deal* 2008 Threshold Editions (Davison of Simon & Schuster), Chapter 4

that occurred before the ruling. For example in Ferebee v Chevron Chemical Co., the court ruled that an EPA mandated label for the herbicide paraquat was insufficient. The court held the company liable for damages caused when a worker ignored instructions on the label.[78] That ruling was an ex post facto rule which company officials could not have known until they had already violated it.

A stable, understandable legal system is necessary for economic success. It also helps if that legal system is friendly to business while providing appropriate protection for citizens. Providing that legal system is the business of government.

The Monetary System

Almost as important as the legal system is the monetary system, a concept that has freed mankind from the necessity of bartering. The carpenter who builds a house for the butcher gets paid in currency instead of meat. He can then use that currency to buy anything from avocados to zucchini. A stable currency also encourages saving for everything from retirement to a down payment on a house. However, that money saved loses value if the government creates inflation. Inflation distorts the economy as businesses must take measures to compensate. It harms people whose savings lose value. I remember a coworker who retired, then had to return to work because inflation had devalued her savings. I doubt she was the only retiree facing that problem.

Governments are always tempted to increase the money supply by borrowing or printing more money. That gives them a way to spend more without raising taxes. The problem is that money is quite as subject to the law of supply and demand as is anything else. If the money supply increases excessively, people

---

78 http://openjurist.org/736/f2d/1529

will have more to spend and will be willing to pay higher prices. That creates inflation. An excellent book on this problem is *Money Mischief* by the late Milton Friedman. That author, a Nobel Memorial Prize laureate, explains inflation and its causes in simple yet entertaining terms.

Money is another externality that is in the legitimate province of government.

Freedom and Inequality

Likewise, government can legitimately work for equality of opportunity. It should not, however, concern itself with equality of outcome. Under freedom and individualism, some have more of this world's goods than others – and often it is luck as much as effort that brought them that wealth. Bill Gates helped found Microsoft and as a result became one of the richest men in the world. Even he would probably admit that luck had a great deal to do with his success. The market happened to be anxious for what Gates offered just when he made it available. Without that, his success would have been less spectacular.

Does Bill Gates really deserve his billions? That is the wrong question. A better question is, "do consumers benefit from his software?" That shifts the discussion from merit and jealousy to the question of what buying public wants. Merit is a rather nebulous term, and jealousy is hardly a good reason to change policy. However, we do know that Gates' company produces something that customers regard as worth buying.

How many other companies created good software but failed to reach Gates' success? We have no way of knowing, nor is it important to the average consumer. What we do know is that Gates' company provides products that serve customers at prices they are willing to pay. There are valid reasons to criticize Microsoft, but we must admit that the company has played a big part in making useable computers available to millions of people.

It is no coincidence that Microsoft was created and grew under a system of free enterprise. A collectivist society would have removed incentives and controlled the software development. The company would never have reached its current size, nor would it have helped put computers in so many homes and schools. The same can be said of its major competitor, Apple. They and other companies in the free world have succeeded wildly by giving customers what they want. Collectivist countries cannot boast such successes.

Competition helps us in many ways, but providing equality of outcome is not and should not be among them.

The Great Divide

We want freedom!

We want equality!

We want freedom!

We want equality!

That argument will never be settled as long as the people demanding equality think of it as equality of outcome. We can have freedom and equal opportunity, but equality of outcome is incompatible with freedom. Indeed it is probably incompatible with human nature; the ruling class always ends up "more equal than others." As long as people are free, some will acquire more than others. That may be the result of intelligence, hard work, dumb luck or a combination of the three, but it will happen. Only statism can force anything resembling equality of outcome, and statism achieves that goal much better in theory than it does in practice.

No human creation has ever achieved perfection, nor has any human creation ever helped all people equally. Though freedom has helped all economic classes, there are still some who are regarded as poor.

I am writing this as Barrack Obama begins his fifth year as president of the United States. He and his followers make a lot of noise about income differences. In fact, he has taken steps aimed at reducing that inequality. The intention may be good, but what of the results? Income inequality has increased.[79]

And nobody seems to be asking the president the simple question: How much inequality do you think we should allow? If the answer is "none," we are back to making sure everyone has the same income and wealth, regardless of talent or diligence. That reduces wealth for everybody. If we are to allow only some specific difference, more nasty questions arise. Exactly how much difference is acceptable? Will that vary with the jobs people do? If so, who will decide which jobs are worth more than others? Will it vary with needs? Who will decide on those needs? Will people be allowed to save for a rainy day or something special they want? If so, what will happen when those people end up with more than their neighbors? And finally, how will we enforce that limited inequality? Then, once we unleash the power of forced equality, who will control it (or attempt to control it)? Who do we trust with such power? In Chapter 22 we

---

79 http://www.huffingtonpost.com/2012/04/11/income-inequality-obama-bush_n_1419008.html
(And other sources. Though Huffington may not be the most reliable source, it does lean significantly to the statist side. It is significant that this problem is so bad that a statist source publicizes it.)

will discuss the reasons why, especially in a collectivist society, potential tyrants rise to the top.

Is it really more important to eliminate inequality than it is to provide wealth for everybody? If, as is the case in the United States, even the poor have more than they did a few decades ago, why should they be upset that the rich have more?

Many ignore the general improvement that we have under freedom. They focus instead on the fact that some have less than others. Starting in the last century, various varieties of statism began attacking the foundations of our free society, especially the fact that wealth is not spread equally. Statists believe that freedom is insufficient; a more intelligent direction is required. They want deliberate direction and they assume that it is possible to have it without causing worse problems. Again, they ignore the question of whom we should trust with the power they advocate.

The battle of ideas today is between the collectivist and individualist world views. That spills over to an argument about income inequality, an argument that ignores what freedom has done for us, economically and otherwise. All too often, we miss the lessons of history. We ignore the evidence and, as in the following parable, we try to find a better way.

The Parable of the Pelts

With winters among the coldest on the planet, martens developed the thickest, warmest fur known to man. Trappers converged, anxious to enrich themselves. The martens refused to cooperate. About a dozen pelts per winter, that was all a trapper could expect – except for Old Billy. Year after year Billy brought in hundreds of prime pelts.

His bank account soared and finally Billy decided to spend winters in the tropics. His knowledge and skill? What a shame to waste that; he took a young man as an apprentice and showed his pupil all the tricks. Submerge some traps under the ice, in freezing water; put others in odd and hard to reach sites; treat them all carefully to avoid leaving human scent. None of that was easy, but it worked. Billy showed it all to the young man, then headed south.

Come spring, Billy returned and asked the understudy how it went.

"Oh it was an awful year, only about 20 pelts all winter."

"What? What happened? Did you do what I showed you?"

"Oh no. I found a better way."

That "better way" caught few martens.

If we find a "better way" to manage our country and our economy, we should be sure that we are "catching martens." Our constitutional, limited government "caught martens" more effectively than any other form of government in history. We created a thriving middle class, an educated populace, and a free people. However the "better way" tried in the last few decades reversed that momentum. Our middle class is in trouble. Our freedoms are threatened. Our schools give us "graduates" who cannot read and students incapable of critical thinking. We should return to the old way that actually worked.

But why do so many swallow the "better way" that doesn't work? Maybe because they accept a theory, a vision of the world, that does not correspond with reality. Unless a theory actually works in the real world, we should reject it. Let's look at two opposite visions of the world.

Visions of the World

Thomas Sowell's book, *A Conflict of Visions* describes two different mindsets which he calls the constrained and the unconstrained visions. The unconstrained vision is based on the assumption that people, at least the elite, are both wise enough and moral enough to manage all aspects of life – their own lives and those of everybody else. That is an attractive theory, especially if you are one of the "elite" with the power to make those decisions for everybody. And it is a vision that supports statism.

The constrained vision, on the other hand, assumes that humans are neither perfectly moral nor perfectly wise. Those with this view believe that each person is likely to know more about his or her own life and work than some elite ruler far away. They want to devolve decision-making to the smallest practical group. They believe that the mechanic in his garage or the farmer in his field knows more about his business than does a political functionary in a government office. That is true even though the government functionary may have scored higher on an IQ test. The constrained vision supports freedom.

Most, if not all, of the divide between freedom and statism is related to this difference in visions. The unconstrained vision sounds wonderful in theory but fails in practice. Its proponents seldom go beyond what is called stage one thinking. The constrained vision, on the other hand, supports not only freedom but individual decision-making. It creates fewer problems than does the unconstrained vision, and it does not impose third-party decisions on the citizens.

The constrained vision requires looking at human limitations, what is and is not reasonable for us to attempt. Thus it encourages deeper thinking, going beyond stage one.

Chapter 7 Stage One Thinking

Each of those changes flowed, in large measure, from the decisions of men who saw themselves as reformers. But their reforms showed an uncanny ability to take bad situations and make them worse. (William Stuntz)

The unofficial barracks chess championship was on the line – and I had my opponent on the ropes. He should have resigned, but since he didn't I would just trap him and nail him. It would be easy.

I trapped too well. He could not make a move without putting himself in check. By the rules of chess, the game ended in a stalemate, a tie. We became unofficial co-champions.

My mistake was stage one thinking. I made a move without thinking out its consequences, without asking the simple question: what next? Had I done so, I would have seen that my move was not as good as it first appeared. That is a common human error – and not only in chess. In stage one thinking we fail to look beyond the immediate result. We do not ask, "What next?"

Who among us has not made some mistake we could have avoided by just a little more thought? Maybe we took advantage of a "great bargain," only to learn that the merchandise was defective or not what we really needed. Maybe we decided on a field of study that really intrigued us, then learned that job prospects were terrible. Maybe we married on the basis of looks or personality, only to learn that the spouse was unfaithful, a spendthrift, or a control freak.

Stuntz's quote above refers to reforms in the criminal justice system. He was talking about reforms that led to increased crime, especially to more minorities being murdered and robbed. However the same thing happens in much of life; well-intentioned actions backfire.

Thinking beyond stage one helps avoid problems, including mistakes much more serious than buying the wrong car or even marrying the wrong person. What if our stage one thinking affects a whole country? And if the consequences last for generations? Such mistakes are a major cause of our current path toward modern serfdom. Good intentions, bad results.

A "Fifty-cent Word"

As a missionary, I was called to the hospital where a young mother faced death. Her husband watched their three children in the lobby while her mother and grandmother looked on hopelessly. I believe we were able to give some comfort to the family, but the woman still died. The cause of her death? She reacted badly to prescribed medication. The medical profession calls such problems "*iatrogenic*," created by the treatment. Though the word is not widely used, the concept applies everywhere.

Humans are imperfect, we make mistakes. Efforts to solve a problem may worsen that problem or create new problems. However clear thinking, and going beyond stage one, can reduce our iatrogenic problems.

Digging Deeper

We engage in too much stage one thinking. We too often look only at the immediate results of our actions, ignoring what may follow. We place well-intentioned restrictions on productive businesses, schools, and families; but do we consider the harm those restrictions might cause? Perhaps no example is more fitting than the de facto quotas created by affirmative action. Anyone who thinks such quotas do not exist need only talk to a hiring manager in any large company. A friend of mine was refused permission to hire the best applicant for a job. That applicant had a problem: he was white and male. The company's human resources department decreed that my friend needed more women and minorities to meet the quota. His department became less effective than it could have been. We can call that an iatrogenic problem, a problem created by a supposed remedy.

Stage one thinking looks only at the help we think such quotas give minorities. Beyond stage one we would ask: what does that do to the person not hired, to our society and economy, and even to the person hired for such reasons?

Perhaps one of the best examples of how quotas adversely affect our society comes from a case in which the courts actually overturned the quota. In New Haven, Connecticut, several white firefighters and one Hispanic were denied promotions for which they had qualified. The reason? Blacks had not done as well on a test as did others. The city decided to invalidate the whole test, even though it had been carefully designed to be race-neutral and to measure abilities important for fire department commanders. Nobody got promoted, and the fire department was left without the number of officers it really needed.

In the ensuing case of *Ricci v. DeStefano,* the Supreme Court said that New Haven was wrong to deny promotions on that basis. Of course that led to the usual accusations and hand-wringing. Stage one thinking said that the decision would be bad for minorities, but was it? Who really won in that case?

The typical headline was that the white firefighters won. They did, but they were hardly the only winners. I would argue that nearly everyone in the U.S., black, white, or any other skin color is a winner, and that there are few if any real losers. True, there were many who complained about loss of what they see as a deserved "helping hand" to the oppressed, but what is the long term effect of that "helping hand"? Could it actually be counterproductive and create iatrogenic problems? Let's look at the winners.

The first winner is anyone who might need help from a fire department – maybe you or me. What if you are trapped in a burning house or a wrecked car? Do you care about the skin color of the firefighters and their officers, or do you care about their competence? As a result of this decision, you have more assurance that the fire department commander will be competent. The firefighters will be better organized and trained than they would be under a less-qualified officer. You will benefit directly from that improvement. This applies not only to New Haven, but across the country. Going beyond stage one, asking "what next?" we see that this decision provides a benefit for the public. We can also ask "What happens next if we give preference to less qualified candidates of any race?" The firefighters will be less competent at their jobs – to the detriment of both those firefighters and the public they serve.

Second, millions of young people, maybe you or your son or daughter, have greater assurance that diligent study will pay off. The New Haven ruling says that qualification, not skin color, should determine hiring and promotion. This decision strikes a blow against the quota system that has come to exist in this country.

Other firefighters in that department are also winners. Fighting fires is dangerous work, with safety dependent on teamwork among competent officers and co-workers. With officers selected on the basis of qualifications rather than skin color, it is more likely that those firefighters will work safely and effectively, helping each other and going home to their families at the end of their shifts.

Third, minorities will benefit in at least two ways. First, hiring and promotion will become more merit based. There will be less suspicion that the minority employees got their jobs because of skin color. Many competent minorities have been tarred with the same brush as the quota hires. Those competent and dedicated employees will be more respected as the system of preferences dies off.

The second way minorities will benefit is that they will be encouraged to develop their natural talents instead of relying on preferences – and those preferences do real harm. I recall a secretary in our department many years ago. She had the skills to be an excellent employee. Instead she did not apply herself and would say in effect, "You can't fire me, I'm a black woman and you need me for the numbers." Eventually she left the company, taking her attitude with her. I later saw her picture in the paper, sentenced to jail for dealing drugs. Did her attitude at work contribute to her descent into crime? It is impossible to say, but that does appear likely. Such people easily develop a belief that the world owes them something; that they should have special immunities. Did her attitude, enabled by the discrimination called affirmative action, help her in the long run? Almost certainly not. Very probably it harmed her, creating an iatrogenic problem, an attitude of entitlement that stage one thinking enabled.

"But wait," someone says. "What about the minority firefighters denied promotion? Weren't they harmed?" I would say that they were not, at least in the long run. It is true that they had less money than they would have had had they been promoted. However money is not the only, or necessarily the most important, consideration in job satisfaction. Most people like to feel that they are productive in their employment.[80] Preferential employment militates against that. A person who got a job because of his skin color is unlikely to have the same job satisfaction as someone hired and promoted because he does great work.

If an employee thinks he can get promoted because of his skin color, he is likely to depend on that skin. However if he is confident that promotions are merit-based, he is likely to work and study to become more qualified. That will increase satisfaction with his job and his life. For that reason, I maintain that the firefighters who did poorly on the test also will benefit in the long run. They cannot change their skin color, but they can change how they work and how they study for the next promotional exam.

Minorities who depend on the quota system fail to become what they can and should become. The *Ricci v. DeStefano* decision will help alleviate those problems.

Affirmative Action Damage

But am I just theorizing or is there real, documented damage from affirmative action? There is. John Lott Jr. did a study of minority and female police officers. There are some clear advantages, such as having a rape or domestic abuse victim work with a female officer. However looking at the overall data he concluded:

> I find that more black and minority police officers increase crime rates. This arises because lower hiring standards involved in recruiting more minority officers reduce the quality of both minority and non-minority officers. The most adverse effects of these hiring policies have occurred in

---

80 http://smallbusiness.chron.com/causes-job-satisfaction-23514.html

the most heavily black populated areas. The additional annual victim cost for all categories of crimes was at least $5.4 billion.[81]

In an effort to help minorities, somebody failed to go beyond stage one thinking. They forced police departments to hire more minorities. That caused a reduction in standards, leading to poor police work, and more crime. Most victims of that extra crime were the very minorities the change was supposed to help. Too much attention to poorly thought-out theory, no attention to results. We shall discuss that further in the next chapter.

It is true that many minorities have suffered discrimination and economic problems. Indeed discrimination has been pervasive throughout human history, from the Israelites held as slaves in ancient Egypt to various immigrants such as the Irish and Chinese in the U.S. However, history shows that minorities who overcome such problems do so by struggle, hard work, and education. Preferential treatment enables failure. It discourages the hard work and education necessary for advancement.

The affirmative action requirement for quotas sounded like a good idea. However, when we go beyond stage one in our thinking, the flaws become apparent. If we ask "what next?" we see that it creates other problems. We have less competent people in many jobs and we keep minorities down by not expecting them to be the best they can be.

Other examples of stage one thinking include rent controls that discourage building of adequate housing, laws to help the handicapped now being interpreted as requiring such things as expensive machines in every swimming pool to move people in and out of the water, etc. Real thought as to their complete

---

81 http://www.law.uchicago.edu/files/files/56.Lott_.Police.pdf

consequences would have prevented institution of most of those rules. Sadly, that was not the case and we have many serfdom-like regulations. Some of those rules are discussed throughout this book.

Chapter 8 Results? What Results?

After all is said and done, more is said than done. (Attributed to Aesop)

One of the scariest aspects of our times is how seldom either people or policies are judged by their track record. (Thomas Sowell)

We've all done it. We spend money or give instructions, but fail to follow up. Then we find ourselves disappointed, often in difficulty because of unexpected results, or no results.

Your ten-year old did the dishes last week, but neglected to mention that he broke a nice bowl. Now Mom needs that bowl for the party that starts in half an hour.

The employee assigned to deposit yesterday's receipts got sick and left the deposit locked in his desk.

We told a teenage son to put gas in the car. Now we're nearly late for a meeting and the needle points to "empty."

The contractor we hired to paint the conference room promised that it would be done today. The room is a mess and he now says it will be done next week. Where can we meet with that important customer due in this afternoon?

Such things happen when we expect results without follow-through. Government does more of that than anyone. It throws laws and money at a problem, then moves on to something else. Nobody checks to see if the laws or money actually did any good.

We ignore the results of our actions We assume that once a government program is in place it will actually accomplish the ends for which it was created.

At the same time we ignore side effects and iatrogenic problems. For example, poverty was declining before the Kennedy/Johnson War on Poverty threw billions of dollars at the problem. It has since increased.[82] Yet almost nobody asks the questions: Did that program actually help the poor? Might it in fact have harmed them? If we ask those questions we find that a government dole fosters dependence, and dependence fosters poverty.

Likewise government-mandated sex education is correlated with an increase in teen-age pregnancy and venereal disease; and changes in the criminal justice system have led to more crime and recidivism.[83] Hardly anyone looks at the results of those programs.

Plans and Actions are not Results

Neither plans made nor instructions given assure the desired outcome, and that goes double for government.

Government programs abound. They cost money, and interfere with our economy and freedom. Yet they never seem to die, regardless of how effective they may or may not be.

Why does this happen? Part of the problem is stage one thinking, but there is more. It is easy to think that we solve problems by giving orders, making rules, and spending money. Then we fail to follow up; we fail to assure that what we did was actually effective. Government is especially subject to action without results, or with counterproductive results. Congress generates lots of publicity by passing

---

82 Thomas Sowell, *The Vision of the Anointed, Self-Congratulaton as a Basis for Social Policy,* Basic Books, 1995, pp 9-15
83 Ibid, pp 15-21

laws, but when is the last time you saw a front page article on how effective those programs are?

This causes a confusion of ends and means. The rules, laws, funding etc. become the goal rather than a means to reach the goal. There is no system in place to evaluate the effectiveness of those laws, or to check for unintended consequences. In addition, representative government has a bias toward action, or at least the appearance of action. Any politician who advocates ignoring an alleged problem will be called a do-nothing and probably not re-elected. That gives us a myriad of laws that succeed only in interfering with life and the economy.

Indeed, sometimes even proponents of a law agree that it would not solve the problem, yet they advocate for it anyway. As I write this, there is a push for gun control laws. That is largely because of a few mass shootings, yet even some proponents of those laws agree that the proposed legislation would not have stopped the shootings. For example after one such shooting a senator manifested that bias toward action saying, "nobody here, not one of us in this great capital of ours in good conscience could sit by and not try to prevent a day like that from happening again." However, senate aides admit that the proposed legislation would not have stopped that shooting, nor would it stop similar shootings in the future.

> "They are expanding on a broken system that we know will fail," says the aide.

> Under this law, I'm told, Adam Lanza would still have been able to steal the so-called assault weapon that his mother legally owned—and use it to shoot up the school.

But what about a similar sort of massacre, I ask. Is there anything in the bill that would prevent that?

"No," said the aide, who has reviewed all the details released of the bill (but not the bill itself—since it has not yet been released). "Nothing in the bill."

So how does one explain the legislation? "It's clearly—Congress wanted to do something after what happened at Sandy Hook," the aide explains. "They wanted to do something."[84]

That is a common problem. Do something, even if it's wrong, even if it makes things worse. Too many people are unwilling to consider that inaction may at times be preferable to action.

Another example is the institution of "Obamacare," the Affordable Care Act. This was supposed to solve the problem of people not having health insurance. At this writing, it appears that more people have lost health insurance than have gained it as a result of that law.[85] Are supporters of that law working to fix the problems it caused? Of course not, they are defending their "baby" against all criticism. To modify it would be an admission that the law is flawed. In spite of the evidence, proponents continue to claim that Obamacare works. They point to the number of people who have signed up (many of whom have yet to pay so they remain uninsured) and ignore those who lost insurance.

The Program Failed? Then Expand It

In fact, some are claiming that the problem is that "Obamacare" doesn't go far enough, that we should go all the way to "single payer health care," which is

---

84 http://www.weeklystandard.com/blogs/senate-aide-gun-law-wouldnt-have-stopped-newtown-massacre_716215.html

85 http://dailycaller.com/2014/01/01/its-official-obamacare-debuts-with-more-cancelled-plans-than-enrollments/

nothing but a euphemism for socialized medicine. The response should be, "Let me get this straight, you agree that our government has not been able to manage either Obamacare or the associated web site, nor has it been able to manage the Veterans' Administration medical system very well. Why do you think it will do any better at managing a system that would be much bigger and more complicated? That makes no sense at all."

The same government that runs "Obamacare" and the Veterans' Administration would be running socialized medicine, a much bigger and more complicated program. Why would anyone expect that government to do any better with a more difficult undertaking?

Head Start Stalls

As a final example let's look at Head Start, the program started in 1965 and expanded in 1981. Head start was intended to help low-income children do better in school. Has it achieved that end? Anyone familiar with the effectiveness of government programs can probably guess. For this one the federal government, wonder of wonders, did evaluate results with a randomized study. They even released that study – in 2010, 45 years after the program started and 29 years after it was expanded. There were a few statistical gains in early childhood, but those gains did not last. "Looking across the full study period, from the beginning of Head Start through 3rd grade, the evidence is clear that access to Head Start improved children's preschool outcomes across developmental domains, but had few impacts on children in kindergarten through 3rd grade. There was little evidence of systematic differences in children's elementary school experiences through 3rd grade, between children provided access to Head Start and their counterparts in the control group."[86]

What that government gobbledygook amounts to is that any gains from Head Start disappeared by the end of third grade. Lots of money spent, but no positive results. Is anyone proposing elimination of that program? Of course not!

Government especially has a tendency to not evaluate results. Even in those cases where evaluation is done, politicians almost never use that evaluation to change the law.

If It Ain't Broke, Fix It Anyway

Beyond problems not solved, government likes to attack problems that are minor if they exist at all. All it takes is a few people calling attention to the alleged problem. If they can get enough publicity, politicians will act. For example, many want restrictions on political campaign spending. They want to solve the problem that "money buys elections." That does sound good; we know that politicians and advocates of all stripes spend amazing amounts of money on political advertising. Almost nobody bothers to ask, "How effective is that spending?" The answer: it is almost totally ineffective. A typical winning candidate could cut his spending in half and lose only 1% of the vote. If a typical losing candidate had doubled his spending, he would have increased his vote total

---

86 Third Grade Follow Up to the Impact Study, OPRE Report 2012-45, October 2010 page xvi available on line at http://www.acf.hhs.gov/sites/default/files/opre/head_start_report.pdf

by only 1%.[87] Donating lots of money to a candidate may buy access after the election, but it is unlikely to buy the election.

The motto for medical personnel is, "first, do no harm." That means be careful to not create problems with your actions; avoid iatrogenic problems. However the politicians' motto seems to be, "first, do something, no matter how much harm it causes. Then, whatever you do, never look at the results."

When government sets out to solve a problem we can be certain of two things: taxpayer money will be spent, and rules or laws will be written. We will move away from the freedom our John II enjoyed, toward the controlled life of John I. Will the problem be solved or even ameliorated? Probably not, but officials will claim credit for fixing it. And those officials are smarter than we are, aren't they?

---

87 Steven D. Levitt and Stephen J. Dubner, *Freakonomics, a Rogue Economist Explains the Hidden Side of Everything,* William Morrow, 2005 p11

Chapter 9 Big Brother is *Not* Always Right

Blind obedience to authority is dangerous, whether that authority occupies a pulpit or a government office.

Adolph Hitler, Jim Jones, Joseph Stalin, David Koresh. All those and more destroyed the lives of their followers, and of others. All demanded strict obedience, which is the very definition of tyranny. Why then should we think that any government, or any government program, is exempt from questioning? Yet I have known people who insist that we must obey government without question. Believe it or not, they actually claim that once something is the "settled law of the land" we no longer have any right to oppose it.

Too often we regard government as always right.

Some have "progressed" from an unsubstantiated belief that the majority is always right to an even sillier belief that our leaders are always right. I have had many conversations with statists who insist that we must defer to government in all things. Most recently, they defend "Obamacare," saying that it is the settled law of the land and therefore nobody should oppose it. That demand for blind obedience is the essence of statism.

Implicit in statism is a belief that government is somehow both wiser and more moral than the average citizen. Where would government get that wisdom and integrity? It must come from one of three sources:

a. Divine wisdom: Conventional wisdom at the time of our John I was that the king was God's anointed. If we accepted that, we could also accept that the king has some special, God-given wisdom. We rebelled against that "divinely anointed" king back in 1776.

b. The second possible source of special governmental wisdom is the wisdom of the majority. However, the beliefs of the majority will inevitably be the beliefs of the average person. Majority rule is, after all, essentially an averaging process (or, to be technically correct, a process of finding the median).

c. Maybe some select group is somehow wiser than the average citizen. If so, who chooses those elite rulers, and how do we know that they are really wiser than the rest of us? If we elect them, we are right back to the problems of averaging mentioned in (b) above. If we look for some sort of aristocracy, why are they aristocrats and why should we trust them?

There is no reason to believe that government is any wiser than the average citizen, and integrity is even worse. Government officials are quite as human as the rest of us; some are moral, some are scoundrels. Why would we expect them to have greater integrity than the average citizen? Government integrity suffers from all the problems mentioned above regarding wisdom plus one more: the powerful tend to regard themselves as special, exempt from the rules that apply to everybody else. That applies to the democratically elected as well as to dictatorial rulers. Be it an aristocratic ruling class or officials elected by a majority, all too many believe that what they do is automatically right.

Worse, powerful people develop arrogance and self importance. As Calvin Coolidge said, ""It is difficult for men in high office to avoid the malady of self-delusion. They are always surrounded by worshipers. They are constantly and for the most part sincerely assured of their greatness. They live in an artificial atmosphere of adulation and exaltation which sooner or later impairs their judgment. They are in grave danger of becoming careless and arrogant."[88]

---

88 http://www.nytimes.com/learning/general/onthisday/bday/0704.html

And majority integrity suffers from a mob effect. People as a group will do things they would not think of doing as individuals. People who agree that theft is wrong somehow think it just fine to vote themselves benefits at the expense of others. For example the infamous "bridge to nowhere" in Alaska was to be built with federal tax money, even though there was no real need for that bridge. However a powerful senator wanted it, essentially to buy votes for his re-election.[89]

Majorities have at times supported slavery, invasions of other countries, even genocide. In a democratic system it is those same majorities who elect the rulers. Not only is there no reason to expect government officials to be more moral than the rest of us, they are tempted to increase their own power at our expense. As discussed in Chapter 22, the worst tend to rise to the top.

We may be obligated to obey a law, but we are not obligated to agree with it, nor are we prohibited from opposing it and trying to get it changed. Indeed, if we want to preserve our freedom, we must oppose bad laws. That applies especially to laws designed to give one group special financial or other advantages.

The Prime Suspect

If we want to keep our freedoms, we must be especially vigilant toward those who seek advantage at the expense of others. The prime suspect in that

---

89 The "Bridge to Nowhere" was a bridge to Gravina Island in Alaska backed by that state's Senator Ted Stevens. It would have cost $398 million to serve very few people. Finally, the money was transferred to more urgent projects elsewhere. cf http://www.washingtonpost.com/wp-dyn/content/article/2005/10/22/AR2005102201040.html

regard for each of us? The person we see in the mirror. We must fight our own temptation to obtain unfair help at the expense of others. The government that gives you and me an advantage today may turn around tomorrow and take from us for the benefit of someone else. Even if that does not happen, do we really want to become the beneficiaries of tyrannical redistribution of wealth or power? I would hope that our sense of morality would prevail.

Only that morality, and strict limits on government, can protect our freedoms. Otherwise we will destroy ourselves.

"A democracy cannot exist as a permanent form of government. It can only exist until the voters discover that they can vote themselves largesse from the public treasury." (Attributed to **Alexander Fraser Tytler**) Whether Tytler actually said that is less important than the problem it points out. Voting ourselves largesse from the public treasury will, sooner or later, destroy the country. It will lead to what is called Kershner's First Law: "When a self-governing people confer upon their government the power to take from some and give to others, the process will not stop until the last bone of the last taxpayer is picked bare."

I see only two possible ways to stop that national suicide. One is an electorate wise and moral enough not to give in to that temptation, a protection dependent on an unlikely change in human nature. The other is to put in place and enforce strict limits on the power of government. The writers of the U.S. Constitution gave us the second, strict limits on government power. Only by keeping those limits will we remain free.

Chapter 10 Two Remarkable Documents

In questions of power let no more be heard of confidence in man, but bind him down from mischief by the chains of the constitution. (Thomas Jefferson)

Revolutions. History is strewn with them, including a minor one in Ecuador while I was there as a missionary. That revolution overthrew a military dictatorship, but improved the lot of the citizens hardly at all. That happens all too often, people throw out a tyrant, only to see another take his place. Czarist Russia was replaced by the horror of Stalinist Communism. The French replaced their king with the excesses of the French Revolution. In Cuba, Batista gave way to the tyranny of the Castro regime. Yet every July 4th we celebrate the revolution that created these United States, probably still the freest country in the world.

Why did our revolution succeed while others failed? Because it is easier to destroy a bad government than to create a good one. The revolutionary who ignores the aftermath leaves the door open for new tyrants. Our founders did not make that mistake; they strove mightily to keep their hard-earned freedom. They defined their principles in two remarkable documents: the Declaration of Independence and the U.S. Constitution.

Ours was a revolution not just of government, but of ideas. The Declaration of Independence defined a new philosophy of government. All men are created equal? Really? In 1776 kings were born superior to the common people and ruled by divine right. The Declaration of Independence contradicted that belief, though it took decades, a civil war, and a civil rights movement to free the slaves and destroy official racism.

We are all endowed by our creator with certain unalienable rights, including life, liberty, and the pursuit of happiness? That was another unheard of concept. Unalienable rights are absolute; no government can legitimately deprive us of those rights. That statement automatically limits government power.

Government by Delegation

Next comes a line often ignored but of immense importance. "That to secure these Rights, Governments are instituted among Men, deriving their just Powers from the Consent of the Governed." That stood previous ideas of government on their heads. Government exists, not for kings and other rulers, but for and at the pleasure of the banker, the farmer, the garbage hauler, etc.

That phrase deserves special attention. Government power comes from the consent of the governed. In other words, we the citizens delegate our power to the government. It becomes our agent, to act in our name with such power as we choose to allow. That simple phrase not only means that the people are to rule, but adds another requirement for limited government. We can delegate only the powers and rights we ourselves possess. We have a right to defend ourselves; let's delegate at least part of that right to the police and the military. We have the power to build roads and bridges; let's delegate that power to government. We have a right to demand that a factory not dump mercury into our waters; delegate that to government as well.

There are, however, rights we do not have and therefore cannot delegate to government or to any other entity. We do not have the right to hold other humans as slaves, therefore we cannot delegate to government the right to approve slavery. We have no right to force our neighbor to paint his house the color we prefer; therefore we cannot delegate that right to government. We have no right to force our neighbor to buy the insurance we think he should buy; therefore we cannot delegate such power to government.

This issue of delegation will appear again in Chapter 12 when we discuss bureaucracies.

The Foundations of our Law

The Declaration of Independence is not law; rather it includes a brief description of what law should do. The Constitution, on the other hand, is law and describes how to apply the ideals of that Declaration. It is effectively the power of attorney we give to government to exercise some of our rights for us. It defines how to maintain equal rights and how to keep government subordinate to the people.

Like the Declaration, the Constitution includes ideas that were unheard of when it was written.

The Constitution specifically requires a limited government. Democracies and republics existed before, but the genius of our founders was that they placed limits on what even a democracy can do. Certain laws are prohibited, no matter how many voters want them. At the outset, the constitution prohibited bills of attainder and ex post facto laws. Congress cannot just decide that you are a bad person and declare that you are a criminal; that would make you illegal. A person cannot be illegal, though his actions may be. Nor can Congress decide that an action you committed yesterday was illegal because of a law passed today.

The Bill of Rights provides even more protection. Short of threats, slander or defamation, you are free to say what you want about the president, Congress, or anyone else. We have an unalienable right to our ideas and the free dissemination thereof. And we are supposed to be guaranteed freedom of religion, the right to keep and bear arms, and other protections against overly powerful government officials. Congress may not make laws that restrict those freedoms.

In fact, the constitution deliberately restricts not only the power of government, but the ability of any person or small group of people to exercise what power that government does have. Our president is charged with seeing that "the laws are faithfully executed." He is not supposed to make law; that is the province of Congress. Judges likewise are supposed to judge according to the law and constitution, not make law.

And Congress is designed to protect citizens from a tyranny of the majority. One worry about any democratic government is that heavily populated areas will dominate the rural areas and smaller towns. Or if laws are made by equal vote of the states, the more numerous states with sparse population might dominate the more metropolitan states. The Constitution protects against both of those potential problems. Lest heavily populated states dominate, the senate has equal representation for each state. Lest the more numerous less populated states dominate, the house of representatives gives more representation to populated states. It is a system designed to limit government power and not allow any one group to dominate others.

Other rights have similar constitutional protections. Our government is intended, not to encourage quick action, but to prevent unwise action. The complaints that it does little and moves slowly are justified – and wonderful. Our founders gave us a system that prevents precipitous law-making. The slow process in Congress is a small price to pay for freedom.

Of course the constitution was not perfect, nor is it perfect today. Originally, to keep the country together, it allowed slavery. That is a stain on our history though it was necessary to hold the country together in 1787. Without that compromise, the southern states would have never stayed in the union.[90] Still, we have the best constitution in the world and for that we owe thanks to our founders.

Checks and Balances

The president, the Congress, the courts. What are their legitimate powers? The constitution assigns each a specific function, and it does so for a reason. Congress is to write the laws, the president to see that they are faithfully executed, and the courts to determine guilt or innocence. Beyond that, they can hold each other in check. The president can veto bills, but that power is not absolute. Congress can, with a super-majority, override his veto. The president makes and conducts foreign policy, but only with the advice and consent of the Senate. The courts can overturn unconstitutional laws, but Congress has the power to impeach the president or any judge.

James Madison tells us that the Constitution was written with power widely dispersed to prevent a strong president or legislature from increasing its authority and gradually turning the United States into a tyranny.[91] Sadly, we have forgotten that today, we have a president who unilaterally changes the law.

In *Marbury v Madison,* the Supreme Court established the right of the court to declare laws unconstitutional. That is quite appropriate; if a law violates the

90 Thomas G. West, *Vindicating the Founders, Race, Sex, Class, and Justice in the Origins of America,* Rowman & Littlefield, 1997, pp1-36
91 Clinton Rossiter, ed. *The Federalist Papers,* New American Library, 1961, pp110, 301, 322-323c

constitution it is really not a law at all. The unfortunate side effect is that the court has come to be regarded as the only arbiter of constitutionality. Judges, senators, and representatives, are all "bound by Oath or Affirmation, to support [the] Constitution."[92] In addition, the president must take an oath to "preserve, protect and defend the Constitution of the United States."[93] All have the duty to prevent unconstitutional laws. They are too often derelict in that duty, looking the other way while legislation does violence to constitutional limitations on government power.

Judicial Problems

The judiciary, especially the Supreme Court, deserves special attention for at least two reasons. First, it has the last word on constitutionality. Right or wrong, we are stuck with what the Supreme Court decides. Chief Justice Earl Warren was quoted as saying, "The constitution means what the Supreme Court says it means." Whether he meant only that the court should have the final word on interpretation or that the court could change the meaning, he was right. That court is the nearest thing we have to a dictatorship in the United States.

Second, federal judges are appointed for life; voters have no power over them. Only Congress can remove a federal judge, something seldom done and which has never been done to a justice of the Supreme Court (though Abe Fortas would almost certainly have been impeached had he not resigned). A bad judge can continue to be a bad judge until he dies.

---

92 U.S. Constitution, Article VI, Clause 3
93 Ibid, Article two, section 1, clause 8

Our courts have tremendous power, and we cannot be free unless that power is restrained. There are only three possible sources for that restraint:

First, the self-restraint of the people appointed to our courts. That requires that the president carefully consider such appointments and that the senate carefully evaluate them, not just rubber stamp presidential appointments. Life tenure of judges makes this critical. Below we discuss the requirements for our judges.

Second, Congress must exercise its impeachment power when appropriate. We fire employees in business for failure to do their jobs or for abuse of power; why should judges be any different? They take an oath to defend the Constitution; failure to do so is grounds for removal from office.

Third, we must create a public expectation that judges will exercise restraint and judge according to law and Constitution. Any judge who starts acting like a dictator should be subject to widespread opprobrium. This will help with the first two restraints above. If the public demands appointment of good judges, the president will be more likely to appoint such and the senate will be more likely to reject the unqualified. As citizens we must make it very clear to our hired help that we want judges who will act within the law and defend the constitution. We must contact our president and senators and insist that they require court nominees to meet the requirements listed below.

Qualifications of Judges

We cannot afford judges, especially those on the highest court, who are likely to misuse their power in any way. To prevent misuse of judicial power, we must insist on at least six requirements for every federal judge:

Integrity: We must have integrity in any government official, but especially in judges. Without integrity, other ability becomes a means to abuse the powers of office. An able but corrupt judge will use that ability for his own benefit, not for the good of the country.

Commitment to Constitution and Law: Judges must be committed to our constitutional form of government, and to constitutional law. We have a representative republic with carefully crafted protections against abuse of power. The court must uphold that form of government

Subordination of Personal Belief to Law and Constitution: One mark of a good judge is ability and willingness to set aside personal preference and judge according to the law. To do otherwise would make him a dictator, imposing his own will on the electorate. Justices must recognize that they are "hired hands," employed to serve the people according to the "contract" set forth in the Constitution. They may think that a law is stupid, and in that they may be right. However they must recognize that voters and their representatives have a right to make laws, even stupid laws. If a law, even a stupid law, is constitutional, they must uphold it. If a law, even one they want, is unconstitutional, they must overturn it.

Intellectual Ability: Judges must have the intellectual wherewithal to deal with the issues they will face. Not only are the issues themselves often complex, but there are smart lawyers arguing each side. A justice must be able to consider all aspects of a case, cut through the intellectual fog, and decide on the basis of fact, logic, law and constitution.

Knowledge of Law and Constitution: Judicial nominees must have a sound knowledge of the law and the constitution. They must know and understand the basis on which they are to decide.

The inner strength to stand up for what is right: Judges are under pressure to go along with the majority, with other judges etc. That pressure they must resist. They must decide on the basis of law and constitution.

It is the duty of every citizen to insist that the senate reject any judicial nominee who comes up short in any of those six areas. Laws can be changed, presidents will leave office, but court decisions stand. Unless we demand good judges, those court decisions will destroy our freedom.

An Independent Judiciary

We regularly hear about how important it is to have an independent judiciary. Fine, but we must ask, "Independent of what?" The idea behind judicial independence is that neither Congress nor the president should control the judicial branch of our government. That is great; it is one of the checks and balances our founders built into the constitution. However judges must be very dependent on law and constitution. Anything more or less than that constitutes judicial malpractice. As Chief Justice Marshall wrote:

> Judicial power, as contradistinguished from the power of the laws, has no existence. Courts are the mere instruments of the law, and can do nothing. When they are said to exercise a discretion, it is a mere legal discretion, a discretion to be exercised in discerning the course prescribed by law; and when that is discerned, it is the duty of the court to follow it. Judicial power is never exercised for the purpose of giving effect to the will of the judge, always for the purpose of giving effect to the will of the legislature, or in other words, to the will of the law.[94]

Sadly, we have judges who are quite willing to act independently of law and constitution. For example, Congress passed the Civil Rights Act of 1964 with the explicit promise that quotas would not be required. Yet today we have de facto quotas, mandated by the courts and approved by the Supreme Court. Indeed, most

---

94 Hamburger, op cit, pp 291-292

courts ignore the fourteenth amendment with its requirement that everybody have equal protection under the law. That is dereliction of duty on their part.

Only when we insist on qualified judges, judges who keep their oath of office, will we have courts we can trust.

Protecting the Constitution

If government exists at the pleasure of the governed, the citizens must take responsibility for how that government operates. The wise citizen will no more ignore routine maintenance of his country than would a wise motorist ignore routine maintenance of his car. That means more than voting every couple of years. To really maintain our free country we must make the effort to inform ourselves and to think beyond stage one. We must not just send our elected representatives off to their jobs; we must watch what they do and tell them what we think they should do. They are our hired help, like any employee they need supervision to be certain that they stay on track. When our representatives violate our will or their constitutional duty, we must contact them; give them a bad performance review. Come next election, we can fire them.

We constantly face politicians greedy for power, who would like to increase the power they have. The price of freedom is therefore eternal vigilance, staying on the lookout for both the type of tyrants described in Chapter 22 and for the unwitting tyrant who would protect us from ourselves. We must consider wisely those for whom we vote and the type of government we support. We must resist demagoguery and the attempt of charismatic politicians to unduly empower themselves. Most of all, we must realize that government can be a good servant but a fearful master. We must keep it down as a servant and not allow it to become a master.

Sadly, many politicians tend to think of themselves as elite, better than the ordinary citizens. They isolate themselves from those they claim to represent. They demand privileges in everything from travel to investment. Worst of all, they ignore constitutional restraints on the laws they pass. Those problems should be no surprise; officials who hold citizens in contempt naturally feel no compunction about restricting those citizens. That is a dangerous attitude and those people should not be elected.

One way those elitists gain and keep power is by drawing our attention to only part of an issue. In fact at times they draw our attention to issues of lesser importance while getting us to ignore the most important. Like the magician who makes lots of motion with one hand while the other does the real work, they distract us from what is really happening. They want us to focus on emphatic trifles, or on only one aspect of the whole. That leads to tunnel vision.

Chapter 11 Tunnel Vision

Any durn fool can see what's ahead of him. What gets him in trouble is what he isn't paying attention to.

September 17, 1944, The Netherlands: Parachutes blossomed beneath the C-47s and the Dakotas while gliders skidded to a halt on the ground below. Fighting fiercely, allied paratroopers took control of the north end of the strategic bridge at Arnhem, along with other bridges leading to that critical river crossing. One officer slipped across the border and, in a gesture of obvious symbolism, urinated on German soil. While airborne forces conducted the "Market" part of the Operation Market-Garden, tanks and infantry, the "Garden" part, charged forward on the ground. Field Marshall Montgomery's audacious plan called for the airborne forces to take those critical bridges. Within 48 hours armored forces would relieve the paratroopers and solidify the bridgehead into the Ruhr Valley. The Allies would smash the core of German industry and deny Hitler the materiel he needed to continue fighting. The war would be over by Christmas.

The assault did not go exactly as planned, though that was not for lack of effort. That 48 hours stretched to ten days of hellish fighting; and allied ground forces never did reach Arnhem to relieve the paratroopers. Airborne forces, fighting with inhuman ferocity, were left on their own. One German officer remarked, "In all my years as a soldier I have never seen men fight so hard."[95] It was all for naught.

---

95 Cornelius Ryan, *A Bridge Too Far, the Classic History of the Greatest Battle of World War II.* Simon & Schuster Paperbacks, 1995. p379

Outnumbered and outgunned, the paratroopers faced shortages of food, ammunition, and medical supplies. In a little over a week Nazi troops were back in control, more vicious than ever. They forced all residents of Arnhem from their homes in retaliation.[96] Allied losses exceeded those of the D-Day landings. Of the 10,006 men of the British First Airborne Division who dropped into the Arnhem area, only 2,163 returned. The rest were either killed or captured.[97]

That disaster should never have happened.

What caused the debacle? Let's take an imaginary peek at Montgomery's planning sessions. We see the maps, the planning charts, the great field marshal himself presiding over the proceedings. We see his senior officers, suggesting parts of the battle plan. We see the generals who will command the troops, receiving instructions and asking for the support they will need. So far, so good but what do we not see? Senior Dutch military officers, in exile from their homeland and available to Montgomery. Those officers have conducted training exercises in the area of the proposed attack; they know the terrain and the problems it presents, but they are not at the table. Also missing is an intelligence officer. His crime was finding solid evidence that, contrary to the planners' assumptions, there were many German tanks in the area. When he mentioned that, he was told that he had been working too hard. A doctor was ordered to declare him unfit for duty and send him off for a rest. The planners ignored reams of unpleasant information.

---

96 Ibid, p599
97 Ibid p591

Those planners saw their objective clearly: destroy Hitler's industrial resources and win the war quickly. They ignored clear warning signs, including two major problems:

First, the route to Arnhem was not suitable for armored attack. There was one main road, only two lanes, elevated above surrounding marshy terrain, what the Dutch call polder. Tanks, unable to operate in the polder, were sitting ducks on the road. The Dutch officers, had they been allowed to participate, would have so informed the planners.

Second, the Germans had significant forces hidden around the area. The intelligence officer, excluded from the planning, did all he could to convince the planners of that fact. The reaction was to "shoot the messenger" and ignore his information.

Montgomery and his commanders focused like a laser on the objective. They saw nothing outside their narrow focus.

Tunnel vision was the principal culprit in the failure of Market Garden - and the problem is not limited to military officers.

We Are Not Immune

Tunnel vision can affect all of us. It is the flip side of the stage one thinking described in Chapter 7. Stage one thinking is concerned with the future; we fail to ask "then what?" We thus ignore what can happen going forward. Tunnel vision, on the other hand, ignores information from the past and present. Like Montgomery and his planners, our vision is so narrow that we exclude readily available information. Maybe we just do not like information contrary to our preferences. Maybe we are so intent on the goal that we fail to pay attention. Either way, we pay dearly for our mistakes.

Nowhere is this more costly than in our dealings with government. Politicians paint beautiful pictures of what they will do if only we will elect them, or give them more money, or more power. With tunnel vision we fail to consider all information about candidates and proposed government programs. We lose freedom and suffer economic damage even as we realize that the new rules or programs are not meeting expectations. If we focus only on the promised benefits, the problems and side effects will blindside us.

Bureaucracies naturally have tunnel vision; each concerns itself with only a limited purview, and nobody has general oversight of those rules. The Commerce Department tries to encourage economic development while the anti-trust arm of the Justice Department often discourages such development. I once worked for a company that bought its water from the city. The city fluoridated that water to strengthen teeth. However the EPA allowed zero fluoride in waste water, so it was illegal to allow water straight from the tap to enter the nearby creek – even though that creek already contained natural fluoride.

When different agencies each look after their own concerns, conflicts and silliness are inevitable. Each bureaucracy is a little government unto itself, acting on its own and afflicted with tunnel vision; but with no accountability to voters. Yet each has power over our lives. For example, the Port of Newark is the largest on the east coast. Ships entering that port must pass under the 151 foot high Bayonne Bridge. That is too low for the newer, larger cargo ships so in 2008 the port authority proposed raising that bridge to 215 feet above the water. That was the most cost-effective solution and would cause minimal disruption in the surrounding area. The change required forty-seven permits from nineteen different bureaucracies. Even though the project would not touch any building, rules required an expensive historical survey of every building within two miles of the bridge to be certain no historical buildings were damaged.[98] Work finally started in the summer of 2013.

Nor is tunnel vision limited to bureaucracies. Congress also tends to evaluate programs individually, considering neither the aggregate cost of all laws passed nor how one law may interfere with another.

The upshot of all this is that, we *look at each proposed action in isolation.* Government officials evaluate each rule or expenditure on its own merits – or on the basis of how many votes it will bring in. Furthermore, each agency tends to ignore all the others. If a family acted that way, the wife might call a plumber to repair the kitchen sink while her husband is out buying a new sink for do-it-yourself installation.

Government agencies come by their tunnel vision naturally. Each is expert in only one area and cannot see much beyond that area. One agency may try to preserve a certain species of fish while another works to provide irrigation water to farmers. The irrigation water may change stream flows and adversely affect the fish. What we have is what the British call "quangos," the subject of our next chapter. They spell the death of freedom and of representative government.

Citizen Tunnel Vision

Nor are voters immune to tunnel vision and its ill effects. This affects us in two ways. First, we may fail to see the adverse effects of how we vote. As

---

98 Howard, op cit, pp7-12

discussed in Chapter 7, we may not go beyond stage one in our thinking. Second, we may focus on only one or two issues and ignore others. Neither freedom nor reasonable functioning of the government is possible without attention to everything government does. Freedom of speech and religion, for example, is important. However if we pay attention only to that we may find ourselves blindsided by heavy taxation, onerous and unnecessary restrictions on use of property, or some other government overreach. Our country has a myriad of special interests: abortion, civil rights, child nutrition, the environment etc. etc. etc. Each, if allowed to do so, will claim top priority with voters. Each, if allowed to do so, will distract us from other important issues.

The Voting Tunnel

We must also avoid a related form of tunnel vision, the idea that candidates must agree with us on everything. This leads some to say, "I'm through voting for the lesser of evils. Unless I can vote for a really good candidate I just won't vote." I am sympathetic with that viewpoint; too often I have found no candidate close to my views. But what if we go beyond stage one with that question? If we refuse to vote for the lesser of available evils, what then? Almost certainly, we will be stuck with the greater of those evils.

Almost never will we find a candidate who agrees with us 100%. As the saying goes, whenever two people agree on everything, you can be sure that one of them is doing all the thinking (if any thinking is being done at all). In many cases, reasonable people can disagree. Let us not allow those disagreements to blind us to areas of agreement. This is an imperfect world, populated with imperfect people. Unless we vote for imperfect candidates, we will never vote at all.

If the choice stinks, let's hold our noses and vote as wisely as we can. Then let's see what we can do to get at least one better candidate next election.

Chapter 12 Quangos

The delegation of particular technical tasks to separate bodies, while a regular feature, is yet the first step by which a democracy progressively relinquishes its powers. (F.A. Hayek)

The accumulation of all powers legislative, executive and judiciary in the same hands, whether of one, a few or many, and whether hereditary, self appointed, or elective, may justly be pronounced the very definition of tyranny. (James Madison, Federalist Paper Number 47)

February 2011, Franklin Township, New Jersey. During a storm, a tree falls into a creek and causes flooding. Simple problem of course, just send a tractor to yank the offending log out of the creek. Not so fast, that creek has special protection. Before the township can remove the tree, "The state Department of Environmental Protection requires permits and engineering work totaling $12,000." Flooding continues for twelve days while the town jumps through the hoops required to get that permit.[99] That was a rule made, not by elected officials, but by unelected bureaucrats.

The real government power now rests with the bureaucrats, as you will see should you have a problem with any level of government. Maybe the Internal Revenue Service is treating you unfairly, or Grandma's Social Security payment didn't arrive, or the TSA confiscated your laptop without probable cause. You ask your congressional representative for help and what happens? That representative will almost certainly send your complaint off to where the real power lies: the agency that caused the problem. That agency may listen to someone from

---

99 *Hunterdon County Democrat,* Hunterdon County, NJ, 17 Feb 2012

Congress, or it may not. And if the agency refuses to help? It will take, literally, an act of Congress to do anything about it.

I had two such exchanges, both with unsatisfactory results. My first complaint was that the Forest Service was charging a fee to go above a certain altitude on Mount St. Helens. I was pleasantly surprised that I got as far as I did; I ended up on a conference call with an agent of my congressional representative and the administrator of that National Volcanic Monument. The administrator claimed that they needed the money to build a fancy restroom at the edge of the restricted zone. I pointed out that said latrine was used more by hikers who did not climb the mountain than by the climbers he said should pay for it. Then he claimed that they needed the money to support search and rescue on the mountain. I pointed out that monument personnel do not do search and rescue, that is the responsibility of the local sheriff's departments.

That administrator had no good answer for any point I made, no defense for those fees. Then my representative sent him a letter, with a copy to me, pointing out that climbers were being unfairly charged. The result? Nothing changed.

Later I had a similar exchange with a different representative about such fees being charged on Washington's Mount Adams. He pointed out that the fee was allowed as part of a demonstration program, authorized by a law since expired. The fee is still in place and will probably remain in place, at least unless someone decides to spend the time and money to challenge it in court.

That illustrates the power of what the British call quangos, Quasi-Autonomous Non-Governmental Organizations. We call them bureaucracies. Fortunately, the United States has not officially descended as far as the United Kingdom has. There, quangos are the official source of power. Though not considered part of government, their decisions are binding on the citizens.[100, 101] Our bureaucracies at least pretend to pay attention when a representative calls; sometimes they even help the constituents of that representative. However, I know of no case in which they have actually changed a regulation in response to objections from Congress, save when Congress passed a law forcing them to change.

Not that bureaucracies necessarily pay a lot of attention to the law. For example Congress has refused to pass the so-called "card check" law that would force employees into unions without a secret vote. Some members of the National Labor Relations Board think they have more power than Congress. They are trying to write a rule to effectively make card check the law of the land, even though the constitutionally authorized law-making body refuses to do so.[102] Fortunately they have not yet succeeded.

Bureaucratic Power

There is no greater danger to our freedom than the power of bureaucracies. A strong statement but true, and if this chapter fails to convince you, I urge you to study the subject in greater depth by reading Philip Hamburger's book, *Is Administrative Law Unlawful.* In over 500 pages Mr. Hamburger details the history of administrative law, how our constitution outlawed it, how it has returned, and how oppressive it can be.

---

100   Hamburger, op cit, pp 17-18, 164-179, 246-247, 272-275
101   Hannan, *The New Road to Serfdom,* op cit, pp24-25
102   http://www.usnews.com/opinion/blogs/peter-roff/2011/04/27/unions-try-to-force-card-check-through-nlrb

"Nowadays, however, [bureaucracies] often exercise administrative power with little regard to whether or not Congress delegated it, and with little fear of the deferential judicial review. Administrative power thus has become largely independent of its supposed legal constraints, and is well on its way to becoming the primary mode by which the government controls the people. As a result, the congressional delegation and judicial oversight have come to be fictions – reassuring fables more than real sources of legitimacy."[103] Congress created the various bureaucracies, but has little effective control over them. Like Frankenstein's home-made friend, those agencies thumb their noses at their creator. They write rules having the force of law, but they are not accountable to the people they are supposed to serve. If Congress wants a law about, for example, what kind of baby crib is allowed, that law requires a majority of each house and the signature of the president. However, if a bureaucrat writes a regulation, that rule stands unless both houses of Congress and the president act to overrule it. That turns the law-making process upside down. And while Congress faces elections every two years, the bureaucrats rule indefinitely.

Unelected bureaucrats, far removed from the scene, who neither pay the cost nor live with the results, make decisions for all of us. That is idiocy institutionalized.

The office of Senator Mike Lee provides a graphic demonstration of bureaucratic rule. The senator keeps two stacks of documents. The first is only a few inches high, about 800 pages. The second stands eleven feet high and contains about eighty thousand pages. The first, smaller stack contains all the bills Congress passed in 2013, the second the regulations created by federal

---

103   Ibid, pp501-502

bureaucracies in that same year. *Bureaucracies created one hundred times as much law as did Congress.*[104]

For example, much of the Columbia River Gorge is a national scenic area, created in 1986 and controlled by the Columbia River Gorge Commission. The commissioners are not elected; they are appointed by the governors of Washington and Oregon, and by some county commissions.[105] There is no process to remove them. That commission has power to regulate nearly everything in the gorge.[106] Landowners must beg its permission for any building they want to construct, or any other change in the way they use their land. The commission effectively makes law for the area, law unrestrained by democracy. Landowners get to pay taxes, bureaucrats get to make decisions.

Another example is the Consumer Financial Protection Bureau which "has the authority to administer, enforce, and otherwise implement federal consumer financial laws, which includes the power to make rules, issue orders, and issue guidance."[107] That bureau has not only authority independent of Congress; even its funding is independent. It gets funding directly from the Federal Reserve and is guaranteed 10% of Fed operating expenses in fiscal 201, 11% of Fed operating expenses in fiscal 2012, and 12% thereafter. The Fed is not allowed to deny that amount, nor can Congress reduce its appropriation.[108] And that agency "is empowered to punish "unfair, deceptive and abusive" business practices. While

---

104   Senator Mike Lee, *Our Lost Constitution, the Willful Subversion of America's Found Document,* Sentinel, 2015, p7

105   http://www.gorgecommission.org/

106   http://www.gorgecommission.org/client/PartII_Ch4_20110907.pdf

107   http://www.law.cornell.edu/wex/dodd-frank_title_X

108   http://www.washingtonpost.com/blogs/wonkblog/post/why-the-cfpbs-funding-is-guaranteed/2012/02/15/gIQA1pAQGR_blog.html

unfair and *deceptive* have been defined in other regulatory contexts, the term *abusive* is largely undefined, granting the CFPB officials inordinate discretion to define its own powers."[109]

Other bureaucracies have similar rule-making powers, independent of the legislative and judicial branches of our government. They claim that Congress delegated that power to them, but Congress has no such authority. As described in Chapter 10, the people delegated law-making power to Congress. We did not, however, give Congress any authority to sub-delegate that power. As with any power of attorney, the authorization applies only to the primary delegate unless otherwise specified. Yet bureaucracies are now the primary law-making body in our country.

The Power of Attorney

Suppose you have to be away for a month or so, but you need to deal with some important financial matters. No problem, your friend, Bill, agrees to handle things in your absence. You trust him, so you give him a power of attorney, the right to act as your agent. His actions on your behalf will be just as valid as if you did it yourself.

Everything looks good – until you return and ask your friend how it went. "Sorry, everything broke loose and I just didn't have time. Don't worry though, I sub-delegated it to Don." To Don? Don of all people! If his business sense were ink it wouldn't make a decimal point. Well, you might as well find out how much damage he did.

---

109   http://www.heritage.org/research/factsheets/2011/07/consumer-financial-protection-bureau-unaccountable-and-costly

It is worse than you expected. Don sold your house for 80% of its market value. He bought a speculative stock in your name, a stock that quickly crashed. He accepted 70% payment on a debt owed to you, releasing the debtor from the rest of that debt.

What can you about Don's mistakes? Very little – but that little is more than enough. You simply inform the parties involved that Don was not authorized and the agreements he signed are null and void. Should any of them take you to court, the judge will automatically reject their claims. Standard conditions for a power of attorney do not allow sub-delegation unless specifically authorized.[110] Don's actions have all the force of a pint of dirt trying to dam the Mississippi.

Delegation of Congressional Power

Like the power of attorney you gave Bill, we as citizens give Congress a power of attorney to make laws on our behalf. That power of attorney cannot authorize powers we do not have, nor does it authorize sub-delegation. Unfortunately, Congress and the courts have ignored those standard restrictions. Congress has, without permission from the citizens, sub-delegated the citizens' power of attorney to other agencies. Beyond that, Congress has delegated to those agencies powers that Congress does not have.

---

110   cf John Deacon, *Global Securitisation and CDOs,* Wiley, p581 available at
http://books.google.com/books?id=h56nj72MaJQC&pg=PA581&lpg=PA581&dq=agent+subdelegates+power+of+attorney&source=bl&ots=XpS5BjCRYR&sig=MmSIPIfBQaUYbyfQTjyOErmzP-A&hl=en&sa=X&ei=8vFTVOP_Doa1yQSEtYLQAw&ved=0CE0Q6AEwBw#v=onepage&q=agent%20subdelegates%20power%20of%20attorney&f=false

The writers of the constitution did not intend any sub-delegation of legislative authority. The very first paragraph after the preamble reads, "All legislative Powers herein granted shall be vested in a Congress of the United States, which shall consist of a Senate and House of Representatives." Note the word "all." Nor were the founders ignorant of the need to explicitly allow sub-delegation if they wanted to; some state constitutions in fact did allow sub-delegation of legislative power.[111] The founders clearly understood the concept of sub-delegation; in fact they specifically allowed it in the executive and judicial branches. Article II, section 2 refers to other officers in the executive department while Article I Section 8 says, "The judicial Power of the United States, shall be vested in one supreme Court, and in such inferior Courts as the Congress may from time to time ordain and establish." Yet the Constitution contains not a word that could justify sub-delegation of legislative power.

There is no reason to believe that the founders intended that federal legislative power to reside anywhere but in Congress. There is no authority for Congress to sub-delegate that power.

And the founders knew about extra-legislative power. That question went right back to the battles between kings and Parliament mentioned in Chapter 6, long before our Constitution was written. This is important because supporters of bureaucratic rule-making claim that the Constitution does not allow it only because the founders were ignorant of the concept. There was no such ignorance; the writers of the Constitution not only understood the concept of sub-delegation, they wanted to prohibit it in the law-making process. Congress is the only body

---

111   Hamburger, op cit, pp387-388

constitutionally authorized to make laws.[112] Sadly, those restrictions are today ignored and ineffective.

The Monster Unleashed

How did bureaucratic power escape the bonds of constitutional law? A detailed treatment is beyond our scope here; Philip Hamburger's book, previously referenced, has a good treatment of the subject. Briefly, it goes right back to what we discussed in Chapter 1, the instability of freedom in this world. It is the natural tendency of governments to increase their power unless citizens actively fight that power. The British faced a constant battle between freedom and bureaucratic power. Kings and their supporters wanted "prerogative rule," rule-making power outside of Parliament. Their opponents wanted to restrict law-making to Parliament. That battle crossed the Atlantic to the Americas where our founders deliberately excluded "prerogative rule" when they wrote the Constitution.

That victory did not end the battle. In Germany, bureaucratic rule continued to develop, attracting many U.S. academics and politicians.[113] They decided that the U.S. needed decision-making unrestrained by the constitution. In the 1880s Woodrow Wilson vigorously supported that view. He "emphasized the difference between the province of constitutional law and the province of administrative function.'" His belief was that, "The broad plans of governmental action are not administrative; the detailed execution of such plans is administrative. Constitutions, therefore, properly concern themselves only with those

---

112   Hamburger, op cit, pp1-110. Yes, the book spends that many pages on this subject.
113   Ibid, pp441-478

instrumentalities of government which are to control general law." Wilson was committed to the German idea that constitutional limits did not apply to administrative power.[114]

Apparently it never occurred to Wilson that administrative power is exactly where government meets the people. If constitutional limits do not protect us there, they will protect us nowhere.

Wilson was not the only person with that belief. With such people setting the agenda, bureaucratic power grew until it reached its current condition as the primary law-making force in our country.

The Monster Today

We face an alphabet soup of agencies with power to interpret the law and, in many cases, to make and enforce law. The EPA, SEC, FAA, FCC, NTSB, IRS, NASA, NLRB, and on and on and on. Those agencies are controlled, not by Congress, but by boards of people regarded as experts. Of course we need experts; Congress cannot have detailed expertise in everything from agricultural concerns to zoological problems. Utilized properly, those experts can benefit the country, even the world. The problem is neither their qualifications nor their dedication; most are qualified and many try to do a good job. There are, however, at least six characteristics of bureaucracies that encourage statism and militate against freedom:

> First, they are specialists, subject to the tunnel vision described in the previous chapter. The expert in airline safety must spend so much time keeping up with his specialty that he cannot know much about other areas his rulings may affect.

---

114   Ibid, p464

Second, those bureaucrats are effectively accountable to nobody. If they badly overstep their bounds, a court may slap them down. Otherwise, whatever they decree will stand as effective law, regardless of what the citizens want. And, as discussed below, the bureaucrats have immunity from lawsuits.

Third, checks and balances are missing. Bureaucracies can be lawmaker, judge, jury and executioner. They act without grand jury indictments[115] and defendants have no right to jury trial.[116] In severe cases, the accused may be able to appeal to the judicial branch, but that is expensive, time consuming, and unlikely to succeed. We shall discuss this in more detail below.

Forth, the citizen may have to negotiate a maze of agencies to find anyone who can approve his project or help with a problem. He may need approval from an environmental agency, a transportation board, the planning commission, etc. And those are just the local agencies, heaven help that citizen should he require federal approval.

Fifth, it is difficult in the extreme to fire or even discipline a bureaucrat. They may even be rewarded for poor performance. While I was writing this, the Veterans' Administration was found to be a disaster, with veterans dying for lack of treatment and the problems covered up with outright lies. Yet "78% of VA senior managers qualified for extra pay or other compensation in fiscal year 2013 … [and] all 470 of those senior managers got ratings of 'fully successful' or better."[117] All officers were performing perfectly, but the ship ran aground!

And sixth, most bureaucrats have never worked in the world of the average citizen. They typically spend their entire careers isolated from the people they are to serve. That gives them a tunnel vision, a focus that excludes what most citizens face in their lives and work.

---

115   Ibid, p 241
116   Ibid, pp242-248
117   http://www.cnn.com/2014/06/20/politics/va-scandal-bonuses/

We must deal with those bureaucrats for something as simple as licensing a car. It gets worse if we are trying to run a business. It especially gets worse if we are trying to do something like drill for oil. There is a reason lawyers get rich finding a way to get all the various bureaucracies to approve such projects.

Why are we in this situation? Because we created bureaucracies with more power than accountability. Congress is accountable to the voters every two years, and its power is limited by constitutional processes. Our founders preferred a difficult legislative process to the danger of tyranny, even the tyranny of the majority. They protected our freedom by making it difficult for any one constituency to have too much power.

As mentioned, the current bureaucratic system turns that upside down. Instead of restraints on making laws, we now restrain Congress from protecting our freedoms. A small number of bureaucrats can make a regulation, but it takes both houses of Congress plus the president to overturn that regulation. The bureaucrats are a relatively few people, unelected and in protected jobs, making what amount to laws and with the power to enforce those laws.

Do we have recourse to the courts? For example maybe an IRS agent garnishees your bank account without reason. If he were in private business you could sue him and his company. Not so the bureaucrats. The courts have provided them with more and more protection until today they are essentially immune to lawsuits. Not only are citizens at a disadvantage, but that legal immunity encourages abuse of power. Why worry about following the law or treating people properly if citizens can do nothing about your misbehavior?[118] That armor against

---

118   Hamburger, op cit, pp299-321

accountability is relatively new. "Whereas eighteenth and early-nineteenth-century executive officers had to be fastidious about adhering to the law, twentieth-century officers could afford to be nearly indifferent."[119]

We now have a government of the bureaucrats, by the bureaucrats, and for the bureaucrats.

Bureaucratic Blackberries

The bureaucracy is a blackberry jungle.

Blackberries, the fruit not the smart phone, are delicious – and a problem. Imported to North America in about 1885, the Himalayan blackberry naturalized in the Pacific Northwest by about 1945. They crowd out native plants and prevent the growth of species such as Douglas fir. They "may form impenetrable thickets in wastelands, pastures, forest plantations, roadsides, creek gullies, river flats, riparian areas, fence lines, and right-of-way corridors."[120] They have ripped my clothes during search and rescue operations. In fact they caused at least one search operation when a blind man wandered into a blackberry jungle and could not get out.

Like blackberries, bureaucracies have good and bad sides. We need people to issue drivers' licenses, to oversee management of our public forests, to issue passports and visas, and perform a myriad of other necessary functions. Like a blackberry pie, bureaucracies doing their job can "taste good." On the other hand, bureaucracies can create "impenetrable jungles" of constitutionally questionable regulations restricting our freedom.

---

119   Ibid, p302
120   http://www.invasive.org/gist/moredocs/rubarm01.pdf

We can divide bureaucratic functions into two types. First, they are the executive arm of government, carrying out law made by the legislative branch. In this function their only decision-making authority is to determine what is and is not legal. Is this business paying the taxes the law requires? Did that driver stop at the red light as the law requires? Does this teenager meet the requirements for a driver's license? Rather than making law, they see that the laws are faithfully executed. That is the proper function of bureaucracy[121]

The second bureaucratic function, the unconstitutional function, is the making of regulations and adjudicating alleged violations. Bureaucrats metamorphosed from executing the law to imposing their own will on the citizens.[122] For example, the head of the Environmental Protection Agency is required to make rules by publishing a list of air pollutants that "in his judgment, cause or contribute to air pollution which may reasonably be anticipated to endanger public health or welfare."[123] The opinion of a bureaucrat has the force of law! And that is far from the only situation in which bureaucrats make what amounts to law.

Bureaucratic Legislation

Ostensibly, bureaucracies follow strict procedures for public input before issuing regulations. In practice they often circumvent those procedures. They may engage in "informal rulemaking," also called "notice and comment" rulemaking. This only requires that they publish details and supporting data in the *Federal*

---

121   Hamburger, op cit, pp1-110 discusses this in great and gory detail.
122   Ibid, pp111-128
123   Ibid, p115

Register and allow public comment. Maybe someone will notice, maybe not. How often do you read the *Federal Register?* Maybe someone will comment, maybe not. Maybe the bureaucrats will modify the rule after those comments, maybe not. Then the rules then become binding on the public.[124]

Even worse, agencies may leave the making of regulations to non-government organizations such as trade associations, or even to international bodies such as the World Trade Organization.[125] Groups outside the legislative branch, completely outside our government, even outside our country, effectively make laws binding on the citizens!

This bureaucratic lawmaking affects us all. Every physician, every nurse, every emergency medical technician, is licensed under requirements set by some bureaucracy. The bar association must approve every lawyer before he is allowed to practice. Even barbers in Oregon must meet requirements established, not by the legislature, but by a board of mostly other barbers. Those bureaucracies influence prices we pay, and the competency of barbers, lawyers, and medical people. They do so outside the walls of Congress and state legislatures.

Should we dispense with licenses intended to assure competence? Probably not, though in many cases the standards should be modified. However there is an easy way to put the rules of those bureaucracies on sound constitutional footing. Let the experts in the bureaucracy submit their proposed rules to the legislative branch for approval by majority vote. Thus they could become real law, written as the constitution demands. And the legislature might do something odd – such as not require barbers to have more training than emergency medical technicians.

---

124   Ibid, p112
125   Ibid, p113

Rule of Men, Not Law

Do bureaucratic regulations apply equally to all? Some do, some do not. The executive branch today has power to write the law, to act as police enforcing the law, and to provide the judge who will adjudicate that law. It should be no surprise then that they take the next step and decide that their law applies to some people but not to others. They issue waivers, allowing some people to ignore rules others must obey. No longer are all citizens equal before their law.

Nowhere is this more flagrant than with the "Obamacare" waivers. The president has handed out such waivers, especially to labor unions but also some businesses. Those favored groups do not have to comply with the law.[126] It is probably no coincidence that they are also among the president's strongest political supporters, the people he might like to reward.

Such waivers, then called dispensations, were among the evils our founders prohibited when they wrote our constitution.[127] How did the president get such power today? He claims that Congress delegated it to him, but how could Congress do that? Congress lacks the constitutional authority to exempt some people from the law others must obey. How can Congress delegate a power it does not have?

Constitutionally, laws and rules must be applied equally. We cannot say that a black man must obey while a white man is exempt, or vice versa. We cannot constitutionally say that Joe's business must obey while Jim's is exempt. It is sad that we have such discrimination today, and that the courts allow it. That happens

---

126   http://www.newsmax.com/Newsfront/obamacare-exemptions-unions-republicans/2013/11/20/id/537720/

127   Hamburger, op cit, pp 121-127

when we ignore the Constitution and equal rights, when we let statists exceed the bounds of the Constitution. Bureaucracies unrestrained got out of hand. And that goes beyond rule-making into the judicial arena.

Bureaucratic "Judges" and "Courts"

A horrible possibility: you are accused of violating some rule. An IRS agent claims you underpaid your taxes, or that your health insurance policy does not meet the requirements. Or maybe you are accused of providing more support to a political candidate than the law allows. If found guilty, you may be fined, thousands of dollars in some cases. No problem, you are confident that you are not guilty; and the Constitution assures that you have a right to a jury trial and a presumption of innocence.

Sorry. Those rights do not exist in the bureaucratic "courts."

Charges against you will be much less specific than in a real court of law, and you will likely have no right to confront your accusers.[128] Protections supposedly guaranteed by the sixth amendment are meaningless.

In all probability you will face, not trial in district court, but an administrative law "judge." That "judge" might make the decision, or he might delegate it to staff members.[129] The "judge" might review the staff decision, but he is not really an independent judge. He was hired by the bureaucracy without senate confirmation. He owes allegiance to that bureaucracy.[130]

---

128   Ibid, p242
129   Ibid, p231
130   Ibid, p234

Real judges can act independently without fear of being fired or demoted if they fail to obey some agency boss. At the federal level, "The Judges, both of the supreme and inferior Courts, shall hold their Offices during good Behaviour, and shall, at stated Times, receive for their Services, a Compensation, which shall not be diminished during their Continuance in Office."[131] Administrative "judges," on the other hand, "can be removed or can [be] demoted to a lower pay scale for failing to follow administrative regulations."[132] Even though they are largely protected in tenure and salary, one survey found that 150 out of a thousand of those "judges" complained of threats to their independence and 80 out of a thousand said such threats were a frequent occurrence.[133] That is sort of judge you will face in an administrative "court."

Jury trial? Forget about it. Administrative "courts" use neither grand nor petit juries.[134] That does violence to the Bill of Rights. The Fifth Amendment guarantees, "No person shall be held to answer for a capital, or otherwise infamous crime, unless on a presentment or indictment of a Grand Jury....." Then the sixth amendment adds the right to a jury trial. "In all criminal prosecutions, the accused shall enjoy the right to a speedy and public trial, by an impartial jury of the State and district wherein the crime shall have been committed." And finally the seventh amendment states, "In Suits at common law, where the value in controversy shall exceed twenty dollars, the right of trial by jury shall be preserved." Yet you will have none of those rights in an administrative "court."

How can administrative "courts" get away with such violations of rights? They claim that, because they cannot sentence anyone to prison for more than a year, they

---

131   U.S. Constitution Article III Section 1
132   Hamburger, op cit, p235
133   Ibid
134   Ibid, pp 240, 242-248

are not dealing with "capital, or otherwise infamous" crimes. They thus claim to evade the requirement for grand jury indictment. That in spite of the fact that they often impose huge fines.[135]

The denial of petit jury trial is on even thinner ice. If the proceedings are a suit at common law, they must grant jury trial since more than $20 is always at stake. For any criminal trial they must also allow a jury trial. Their only recourse is to pretend that their proceedings are neither criminal nor suits at common law. Somehow that obvious fiction survives.

With all that against you, do you want to go to trial? Be aware that the government faces a low standard of proof, even lower than a plaintiff in a suit at common law.[136] And you have no right to a public trial; the agency may well close the proceedings so they cannot be publicly visible.[137] The bureaucratic "courts" have judicial power but without the limits placed on regular courts.[138]

But if you lose you can appeal can you not? Well yes, for all the good it will do you. Your first appeal goes right up the management chain of the same bureaucracy that found you guilty.[139]

Appeal to the regular courts? That is allowed, if you want to spend the time and money. The likely result? A rubber stamp on the administrative decision. "Once the agency issues its order, and once enforcement proceedings are commenced in federal district court, 'the sanctioned party is not permitted to litigate the merits of its position in that court.' Moreover, 'should a party choose to ignore an order' issued by the agency, the agency may impose monetary penalties for each day of noncompliance.'"[140] You will almost certainly lose your appeal.

---

135   Ibid, p241
136   Ibid, p250
137   Ibid, p248
138   Ibid, pp 267-268
139   Ibid, pp235-236
140   Ibid, p273

How can such "courts" exist at all? Where does Congress get the power it delegates to the executive to establish courts? Again, Congress cannot delegate a power it does not have, and clearly Congress has no judicial power. The very first sentence of Article Three of the Constitution reads, "The judicial Power of the United States shall be vested in one supreme Court, and in such inferior Courts as the Congress may from time to time ordain and establish." The clear meaning is that such inferior courts are inferior to the Supreme Court, not to the president. Instead we have Congress delegating to the executive the power to create courts, and those courts are responsible to the executive rather than the judicial branch.

Bureaucracies have grown slowly, from administering the law to making law and adjudicating that law. They absorb more and more of the powers constitutionally reserved for the legislative and judicial branches of our government. That trend continues and will be difficult to stop, much less reverse. Yet reverse it we must if we are to regain our freedoms.

Bureaucratic Self-defense

Like any organization, bureaucracies are full of people who will defend their livelihood. Many do want to serve the public, but that desire to serve can become a low priority if their jobs are threatened, or if they get in trouble for taking initiative. Bureaucrats, except those at the very top, are bound by agency rules. The primary objectives of any bureaucracy are first, self preservation and second, following procedures. That clerk at the Department of Motor Vehicles may appear incompetent to you; after all, he did not solve your problem. To his boss he is the ideal employee; all his paperwork is correct and he follows department procedures to the letter. Should he make a reasonable exception for you, he gets a black mark on his record.

Lt. Col. Anthony Shaffer describes some particularly egregious examples of bureaucratic problems in his book, *Operation Dark Heart.* He worked in the Defense Intelligence Agency (DIA) in Afghanistan and received the Bronze Star for his work. However his actions were aimed at successful operations rather than following bureaucratic procedure. The DIA attempted to have that award revoked and eventually drove him out of the army.[141]

Col Shaffer also describes an operation called Operation Able Danger that found evidence, before 9-11, that Islamic fanatics were planning attacks on the U.S. mainland. That information might have prevented the destruction of the World Trade Center and the attack on the Pentagon. Unfortunately bureaucracies were more interested in protecting their own turf than in protecting the country. The bureaucracy with the information refused to share with the bureaucracies that might have acted upon it. Then, after the attacks, Shaffer made that information public in an attempt to encourage correction of the problem. Instead the bureaucrats tried to cover it up, even attempting to destroy the files.[142]

Nor was that the only evidence of bureaucratic compartmentalism facilitating that terrorist act. "In the summer of 2001, an FBI agent was hot on the trail of a suspected terrorist, Kalid al-Mihdhar.... another agent had clues as to Mihdhar's whereabouts. But the FBI has rules against sharing 'intelligence

---

141   Shaffer, Lt Col Anthony, *Operation Dark Heart,* Thomas Dunne Books, 2010, especially p244 though intelligence agency wrangling is described at various points throughout the book.
142   Ibid, pp 17-18, 164-179, 246-247, 272-275

information' with agents in other departments." Then in September, al-Mihdhar piloted the plane that struck the Pentagon and killed 184 people.[143]

Of course we cannot know what would have happened had those agencies shared their information, but we know what happened when they refused to share.

That is the bureaucracy that controls most of our federal government. At present it mostly affects businesses, and state and local governments; but it does not stop there.

Destroying Federalism

Does your local school board control your school system? Don't believe it. That board may make hiring decisions, but it would be very unusual if it decides on policy, discipline, which classes to offer etc. Talk to any teacher and he will tell you that there are federal rules about what he is allowed to do in the classroom. For example, my daughter complained that there were some very disruptive students in one of her classes. I talked to the teacher and found that those were "special" students regarded as having some disability. There were serious federal restrictions on how the teacher could discipline them. The federal bureaucracy is in our children's classrooms, restricting how teachers conduct their classes. That sort of bureaucratic control harms education for all our children.

How about the internet, something nearly all of us use? The FCC wants to control it. They proposed "net neutrality" to control how that service operates. Worse yet, that bureaucracy invited six industry lobbyists to do the drafting.[144] Those lobbyists just might rig the rules to their own advantage.

---

143   Howard, op cit. p42
144   Hamburger, op cit, footnote p 436

Problems with Bureaucrats

Bureaucrats are people, with all the frailties and imperfections of the human race. They can put their own interests above the interests of others. They can have tunnel vision. Nor is there any control over the costs they impose on citizens and businesses. No cost-benefit analysis is required for individual regulations, much less for the aggregate of all the regulations imposed by various agencies. That drives prices up, and it drives companies overseas or out of business.

Bureaucratic Obstructionism

Bureaucracies become hidebound and are one of the greatest obstacles to progress ever invented. Change, except change that increases their power, is anathema. Cooperate with a different bureaucracy? That might reduce their power or cause disruption in their procedures. Change to meet citizen needs? Employees would have to learn a different way to do things, and they might even not need everybody they now employ. Allow a citizen to introduce something new? If it causes problems, the bureaucrat who approved it gets in trouble.

Progress requires change. Change is always risky, and there is hardly anything more risk-adverse than a bureaucracy.

I ran afoul of this in search and rescue. Though most of our missions are close to home, not all are. I took on the task of negotiating a memorandum of understanding (MOU) with the Civil Air Patrol (CAP), something to allow them to quickly fly us to distant missions if necessary. The local CAP leader and I agreed on everything, so we wrote what we thought was a good document. Problem solved? Hardly. Both state and federal lawyers had to approve that MOU. You can guess the result. We are still mostly on our own for transportation.

This bureaucratic inertia is not only expensive; it obstructs both the private and public sectors. Robert Gates tells of the problems bureaucratic inertia and infighting caused in our military efforts in Iraq and Afghanistan. Between people protecting their fiefdoms and their reluctance to change, he was unable to do many things that would have been effective. Even the changes he was able to make were difficult. For example, he believed unmanned aerial vehicles (drones) would be useful. However, the Air Force did not want them; people joined that service to fly planes, not to sit in a bunker manipulating drones by computer. Let the Army fly the drones? Nope, they were fixed-wing aircraft, and the Air Force jealously guarded its fixed-wing monopoly.[145] It took time to break through that barrier, and we do not know how many casualties could have been prevented had those drones joined the battle sooner.

The Result

Bureaucracies give us most of the "benefits" of dictatorship. They provide rule makers not accountable to the voters, "judges" accountable to those rule makers, little recourse for citizens abused, and power beyond what the Constitution allows. The Constitution separates legislative, executive, and judicial powers. Bureaucracy unites all in one organization, the same bureaucracy that makes the rules also provides the "judge." Citizens accused of violating bureaucratic rules will face "judges" employed by that bureaucracy, and subject to discipline if the higher ups disagree with their verdicts. That allows bureaucrats to

---

145   Robert M. Gates, *Duty, Memoirs of a Secretary at War,* Alfred A. Knoff, 2014. Bureaucratic difficulties are mentioned throughout the book but especially described in Chapter 4, "Waging War on the Pentagon," pp 115-148

avoid the checks and balances our founders imposed on the government. And different bureaucracies make their own rules; so many that no human could possibly know what they all are.

"Administrative law therefore should be recognized for what it is: a version of absolute power. Although it is mild compared to other versions, it is more than bad enough."[146] Indeed this bureaucratic power thumbs its nose at the Constitution. "…it returns to the very power that constitutional law developed in order to defeat... It systematically steps outside the Constitution's structures, thereby creating an entire anti-constitutional regime."[147] Sadly, the courts "defer to administrative lawmaking as if it were above the law, thus denying the supremacy of the law of the land."[148]

Why is our judiciary so timid? Why do our judges fail to enforce the Constitution? The precedent was set in 1906. The president threatened drastic action, such as stripping the court of jurisdiction over ICC matters if it did not back off. Such threats were "numerous, systematic, and public.[149] Then, during the New Deal era, Franklin Roosevelt threatened to pack the Supreme Court with extra justices who would do his bidding. The court backed off and acquiesced to his programs.[150] Today the regular court system is reluctant to overturn bureaucratic actions, regardless of constitutionality. Indeed, it seems reluctant to overturn any statist law.

---

146   Hamburger, op cit, p509
147   Ibid, p498
148   Ibid, p499
149   Ibid, p487
150   Lee, op cit, pp145-147

Where Will it Lead?

Not having the gift of prophecy, I cannot tell what bureaucratic tyranny our John IV will or will not face. It is possible that we will tame the bureaucracy, stuff it back into constitutional restrictions. If we do that right, bureaucrats will see that constitutional laws are faithfully executed and leave judgment to the real court system. If we do it wrong, John IV may live under a tyranny of unpredictable power.

We know where such unrestricted executive power has led in the past. The Germans created a powerful bureaucracy to provide order to their lives. Then came Hitler! He inherited that bureaucracy and twisted it to his own ends.[151] Unrestrained bureaucracy is a ready-made tool for any despot who gains power.

Without constitutional restraints, bureaucratic enforcement can threaten citizens, who then have no recourse. We may face repeated audits, delay in processing paperwork, demands for unnecessary information. All those and more are in the arsenal of the politicized bureaucrat. We'll discuss in Chapter 23 some egregious cases in which agencies harassed people who opposed the current administration.

What to do about it? We need legal changes to allow either house of Congress to overturn any bureaucratic regulation. That would restore the restraint on legislation designed into the constitution. If either house of Congress can block a proposed law, surely the same should apply to bureaucratic regulations. Better yet, require congressional approval of bureaucratic rules before they can take effect. As citizens, we must insist that our representatives oppose bureaucratic rule-making and adjudication.

---

151   Ibid, p476

But of course bureaucracy and tunnel vision are not the only obstacles to freedom. Behind many of our problems, indeed the godfathers of bureaucracies and other evils, are citizens demanding government largesse and special privilege at the expense of the entire country. After all, their demands only cost each citizen a miniscule amount.

Chapter 13 Hype and Hide

Anything I want, no matter how expensive, is worth the cost if someone else pays for it.

It has to be one of the oldest scams in the book. Emphasize how great the product is while obscuring what it really costs. Salespeople do it, and politicians do it. The politicians have an advantage because they can force everybody to "buy" if they can just fool enough people to make it into law.

Would you complain about the waste of just under $4 of your money, less than half the minimum hourly wage? That would hardly be worth your time. How about complaining about the waste of almost $1.2 billion? A different amount? Not really. The federal government wastes $1.2 billion per decade on just one duplicate program, people receiving both disability and unemployment.[152] That is less than four bucks for each of us; in 2013 the Census Bureau listed the U.S. population as 316,148,990.[153] Essentially nobody complains about the wasted four bucks, but the people receiving that extra money remember the gift come election time.

Or how about $320 million to build a bridge in Alaska, a bridge to an island with only 50 inhabitants and an airport?[154] That's barely over a dollar per US resident, surely we won't miss that. However, the people in that area, especially

---

152   http://www.washingtontimes.com/news/2014/apr/8/watchdog-finds-more-federal-waste/?page=all
153   http://www.census.gov/popclock/
154   http://www.heritage.org/research/reports/2005/10/the-bridge-to-nowhere-a-national-embarrassment

those who get paid to build that bridge, will be delighted. They will likewise remember that gift next election.

What a sweet deal for the politicians! They send gobs of money to some constituents, thus effectively buying votes. Then they spread the cost so widely that individual taxpayers don't notice. Few even know that we are paying for that bridge to nowhere, or sending millions of dollars to subsidize students in foreign countries. Even fewer complain about it. Then the politicians do it again and again and again, piling program upon program until the aggregate puts us deeply in debt. It is easier to notice the large tax-funded benefit than the thousands of similar wastes you are funding.

We have too many programs with concentrated benefits and diffused costs. This allows politicians to hype the supposed benefits and hide the cost. It is easy to claim that some group would benefit or some problem be solved, if only we were willing to spend the money. It is likewise easy to point out that the money required is only a miniscule portion of our national income. The common mantra is, "Surely a country that can put a man on the moon can..." Or the comparison may be to the cost of a war, or some other great national expenditure. In all such cases, proponents claim that the proposed program is cheap compared to some past expenditure. That is invalid for several reasons.

First, past expenditures are past. They are gone, beyond recovery regardless of how much we may or may not regret that spending. That money is irrelevant to any discussion of current or future spending. Valid comparisons must be with resources available now.

Second, there is no constitutional mandate for federal intervention in local roads, school improvement, foreign students, etc. There is, however, a constitutional mandate for national defense.

Third, the relevant comparison is not to the total budget, but to what is left after meeting previous commitments. This is similar to your household budget. Your disposable income is not what the numbers on your paycheck say; it is what is left over after you pay the mortgage or rent, transportation costs, buy food and clothing, and any other commitments you have. Those previous commitments represent money already disposed of; like past expenditures it is gone, no longer available. Likewise, government disposable income is only what is left after paying all committed expenses, from the pencils needed in offices to the warship for defense. As of this writing, federal disposable income is negative and promises to remain that way for the foreseeable future.

By spreading the cost and concentrating the benefits, politicians buy our votes with our own money, and we seldom even realize how much it costs us.

Getting a Bit Technical

There is another nasty trick that puts us in debt; a way government hides what it owes. This is easy to understand though it does address a technical accounting issue. You may think that anything having to do with accounting has to be as dry as the Sahara Desert, but bear with me please. It won't hurt much, I promise.

There are two common methods of accounting. The simpler is the cash method. Slightly less simple but usually more accurate is the accrual method.

In the cash method you just track money as it comes in and expenses as you pay them. For your household budget you would track income every payday and expenses as you actually pay them. In this method you would not count that big screen TV you bought on credit until you actually pay for it. You may owe a thousand dollars, but if the monthly payment is $20, that is what you count each month.

The accrual method, however, counts not just current income and expense, but also obligations for the future. Under this method you count the cost of that TV as soon as you make the purchase, not when the bill comes due. Of course you can also count income as soon as you earn it, even though payday may be a week away.

We can see the advantages of the accrual method. It allows us to see the entire picture. That big screen TV shows up as money committed. With the cash method we fly blind, we do not see the future obligation to pay for that TV. In fact most large corporations are required to use the accrual method. That gives stockholders a better picture of their real financial status.

Guess which method of accounting our government uses! That's right, the cash method.[155] All those programs Congress created, programs that will require spending for years in the future? They don't count for this year's budget. That is another trick politicians use to hide the debt burden they are handing to us and to future generations.

---

155   http://thehill.com/blogs/congress-blog/economy-a-budget/322139-why-
        we-need-accrual-accounting-in-washington

What it Does to Us

As a result of the above, we have created thousands of ways to give tax-funded benefits to various groups. Each group remembers what it receives while taxpayers forget the cost. In fact, people come to regard those tax-funded goodies as entitlements, something they have a right to whether they earn it or not.

Is a military base obsolete? Congress will likely insist that it stay open. The money it brings in helps re-elect the representative for that district, while the cost is spread so widely taxpayers do not notice.

Does a city want a new convention center? Maybe it can get the federal taxpayers to subsidize the cost. That way, local taxpayers are not out the money, even if results do not justify the price. The real cost is spread over the 300 million people so they don't notice.

Would a road to a tourist attraction bring business to a town? Maybe the federal government will pay most of the cost of that road; it won't cost any individual taxpayer more than a few cents.

Do people want to build in an area subject to flooding? Let's have the taxpayers subsidize the flood insurance; after all the cost to each taxpayer is miniscule.

And on and on and on. We have so many programs of questionable value that we cannot even count them.

The concentrated benefits are visible. The dispersed costs are invisible but expensive. They harm our economy and reduce our freedom. Yet people often think they have a right to them. The next chapter discusses the few rights we do have, rights that do not include entitlement to what others produce.

Chapter 14 You Have a Right to – Nothing

The trouble with socialism is that eventually you run out of other people's money.
(Margaret Thatcher)

The Constitution protects our right to – nothing. That nothing, however, is very important. What can government do to control our speech? Nothing! To control the press? Again nothing! How about to interfere with the free exercise of religion? Nothing again! Nearly all our constitutional rights are what are called "negative" rights. They are rights that protect us from government action, not rights to have government do anything for us. The few constitutional mandates that government take specific actions are really rights to something negative. The mandate for national defense, for example, is really the right to not have foreign powers governing us.

Unfortunately, some today claim that we have what they call "positive rights," the right to have government give us something. The difference between those and the "negative" rights is that the "positive rights" require others to do something for us. Freedom of speech only requires that government not limit our expression. However the "right" to a living wage proposed by some requires employers or taxpayers to pay that "living wage," even if we do not earn it. The right to keep and bear arms requires only that government not act to take our arms. However the "right" to free health care requires that someone else work to provide that care. "Positive rights" say to other citizens, "You work and I will enjoy the fruits of your labor."

This nonsense may have originated with Franklin D. Roosevelt's "four freedoms" speech to Congress, almost a year before the U.S. entered World War II:

> The first is freedom of speech and expression—everywhere in the world.
>
> The second is freedom of every person to worship God in his own way—everywhere in the world.
>
> The third is freedom from want—which, translated into world terms, means economic understandings which will secure to every nation a healthy peacetime life for its inhabitants-everywhere in the world.
>
> The fourth is freedom from fear—which, translated into world terms, means a world-wide reduction of armaments to such a point and in such a thorough fashion that no nation will be in a position to commit an act of physical aggression against any neighbor—anywhere in the world.[156]

Sounds great on the surface, but what if we go beyond stage 1? Roosevelt's speech appealed to emotion, not reason. Look especially at his third freedom. "Freedom from want" imposes a duty on others to provide food, clothing, and housing to those who have not earned it. This creates a "positive right" which imposes servitude on the productive. In fact Roosevelt went even farther, advocating the "right" to a comfortable living and a decent home (though he seems never to have defined what constituted a decent home).[157] Roosevelt's "four freedoms" have made and continue to make mischief in our society. They create unobtainable ideals. We must reject them along with his silver tongue. High-sounding speeches and appeal to "positive rights" are no substitute for the real freedom our Constitution was intended to provide.

---

156   http://www.fdrlibrary.marist.edu/pdfs/fftext.pdf
157   Folsom, op cit, p257

"Positive Rights" Today

"How many legs does a dog have if you call the tail a leg?

" Four. Calling a tail a leg doesn't make it a leg."[158]

Not only politicians, but even educators today push the idea of "positive rights." However calling them rights does not make it so. Nor does calling collectivism "freedom" make it so. Yet there are many who claim that we can redefine freedom however we want. For example, one book, recommended in the national "Common Core" educational standards, claims that "To other Americans freedom includes … the right to education, the right to health care, and the right to meaningful employment...definitions of freedom... are never fixed or final."[159] Let's just define the dog's tail as a leg and it will be a leg. To be fair, that book does a decent job of describing the Constitution, its history and effect. However, on the closing page, the author cannot resist changing the meaning of a word to the statists' advantage.

Entitlements

"Positive rights" are often called entitlements. The statists get away with that verbal sleight of hand because few people think to ask: why is anybody entitled to this so-called entitlement? Nor is anyone likely to ask, "Just where will we get the resources to provide those 'entitlements'?" The use of the word "entitlement" is one of the most pernicious successes of collectivism, often ending the discussion without debate. The wording disguises the fact that, if I am entitled

---

158   Attributed to Abraham Lincoln
159   Linda R. Monk, *The Words We Live By, Your Annotated Guide to the Constitution,* Hyperion, 2003, p263

to something, someone else must give up what he has produced. If my children are entitled to free breakfast and lunch, someone has to work to provide the food they eat. If I am entitled to a cell phone at no charge, someone must design and manufacture that phone and set up the cell sites so it works. Either taxpayers pay for that phone or the people who work in that industry do so for free. Yet all those "entitlements" and many more exist in the United States today.

We have created "entitlements" leading people to believe that they have a right to what others have produced. This diverts resources that might be used to increase our economic well being and at the same time discourages self-reliance. One web site lists over 1600 federal entitlement programs as of 2005. Those range from "1890 Institution Capacity Building Grants" to "Youth Opportunity Grants." The tax money going to those programs totaled nearly two trillion dollars.[160]

Some entitlements are earned. Veterans deserve help in exchange for their service. Social Security recipients have usually paid into the system and deserve to get something back (though maybe not as much as some get). However, it is difficult to make a case that tobacco farmers are entitled to money from the Tobacco Loss Assistance Program, or that we should use tax money for scholarships honoring the late Barry Goldwater, regardless of our opinion of Senator Goldwater. Like the serf masters in the days of John I, some people are getting what others produce.

Most of those programs are relatively inexpensive. Some cost less than a million dollars, some more, and a few cost a lot more. However, when all that money is added up we pay nearly two trillion dollars in "entitlements" to people

---

160   http://funding-programs.idilogic.aidpage.com/

who have not earned what they receive. That money was taken from people who did earn it.

Want to kill some of those programs? Good luck! Their beneficiaries are well organized and will fight for their "entitlements." It seldom occurs to them that they are taking real money from real people. Those "entitlements" come at the expense of the family saving to send the kids to college, at the expense of a widow with what was an adequate income until inflation devalued her husband's savings, at the expense of the entrepreneur struggling to establish a business that would employ people and benefit customers.

Beyond the monetary cost, those programs represent Congress and bureaucrats making decisions for other people. Those decision-makers are far removed from the people who pay the bills, and from the beneficiaries who get the goodies. That is called third-party decision making, and it is a terrible way to make decisions.

Chapter 15 Who Decides? Who Pays? Who Benefits?

Wouldn't it be fun if I could decide how much you should pay for something I will give to somebody you don't even know? At least it would be fun for me.

The Parable of the Pie

Polly's Pie Parlor has an unusual business model. You pick the pie you want, but Polly delivers it to the customer who comes in half an hour later. You get the pie someone ordered half an hour ago; I hope you like his taste. And you won't pay for either of those, instead you pay for the pie somebody ordered two hours ago. No trading of pies is allowed.

That is obviously a silly example – or is it? It is an instance of what is called third-party decision making. One person decides, someone else pays and yet a third person lives with the decision. Yes that happens, maybe not in pie parlors, but it does happen in business, and especially in government.

Government and Third-Party Decisions

Government decisions are inevitably third-party decisions, made by someone far from the scene and who neither pays the cost nor lives with the results. It is worth looking at the problems this causes.

For any decision we must consider: (1) who decides, (2) who pays, (3) who lives with the results, and (4) who has the most knowledge of the situation. The best decisions are made by someone who pays the price, lives with the results, and is knowledgeable about the issues to be decided.

> A person who pays but does not live with the consequences will have an incentive to keep costs down. However, he may not even care about quality or any results that do not affect him.

181

Someone who lives with the results but does not pay has an incentive to get a good solution, but not to control costs. He may go for an expensive solution that is only marginally better than something much cheaper.

A decision-maker who neither pays nor lives with the solution has no incentive to either control costs or find a good solution to the problem. Note that *most government decision makers are in this category.* They neither pay the price nor live with the result.

With government decisions, the decision-makers are usually insulated from both expense and results. However they do have an incentive to appear successful, so they tend to be reluctant to change their decisions. A change would be an admission that they were wrong, not usually career-enhancing. A bad decision is likely to remain in effect, much as the fees on climbers of Mt St Helens and Mt Adams remain in effect.

A person who pays and who lives with the decision, and who gets to make that decision, will have an incentive to balance cost and results. That incentive is likely to lead to the best overall decision, especially if that person is knowledgeable. Third parties are unlikely to have the first-hand knowledge possessed by the people directly involved. Those third parties may be 2,000 miles away from the situation. Furthermore, they may impose a "one size fits all" solution, ignoring differences between places as diverse as a big city like Los Angeles and a rural village where a traffic jam might mean three cars at a stop sign.

Third-party decision makers often think of themselves as smarter and more knowledgeable than the average person. They may even be correct, but the third party tends to have a different type of knowledge than the people at the scene.

That third party is likely to have a theoretical background rather than the knowledge that comes from hands-on experience. Meanwhile, the people directly involved draw on personal experience and on information from others who have such experience. And those who pay and live with the results have an incentive to get more information if they need it.

For example, a rancher in eastern Oregon may have employees who drive 50 miles from town each day, then 50 miles back after work. Employees soon tire of the drive and of the expense of gas and automobile maintenance. The rancher has a hard time keeping good people, so he decides to provide housing right on his ranch. Not so fast! Representatives from urban/suburban areas dominate the state legislature. They do not make that daily commute, they do not lose employees who hate the drive, and many probably don't even know the difference between a bull and a steer. Guess who gets to decide how to run that ranch? That's right, the legislators from urban districts, people who want to prohibit such housing. Land use restrictions require that "Minimum lot sizes in farm and forest zones range from 80 to 240 acres."[161] That restricts the number of houses a rancher may have for himself and his employees.

Ironically, many of the people who support those limits also want to reduce driving, yet their rules force ranch employees to commute from town. That is an example of not only third-party decision making but of stage one thinking. The decision makers do not think beyond the initial objective.

As government acquires more power, we find third-parties making more and more of our decisions. The results are predictable. Our only advantage is that we can blame someone else for the mistakes.

---

161   http://www.landwatch.org/pages/perspectives/accomplishments.htm

Chapter 16 Forget the Facts, Just Sling Mud

About the only exercise some folks get is jumping to conclusions and running people down.

Bumper Sticker Bigotry

"Tea Party sounds so much nicer than Mob of Racists and Homophobes."

That bumper sticker provides one of the most bigoted statements it has ever been my displeasure to encounter. When I see it I'm tempted to ask the car owner how many Tea Party members he or she has actually known. I'm guessing that the answer would be zero. Yet the accusation remains, often accepted without evidence. Tea Party people and other "conservatives" are often accused of bigotry just because they oppose statism.

The essence of bigotry is evidence-free judgment of people as a group rather than looking at individuals and their actions. That is exactly what many statists do to with free men. They automatically label any freedom lover as racist, no evidence required. The news media aids and abets the slander. For example, when some Tea Party activists demonstrated against congressional representatives on their way to vote for "Obamacare," the news claimed that they were using racist language. Yet nobody has been able to find even one recording of such language, in spite of the fact that both media and private individuals recorded every second of the demonstration. Did lack of evidence change how the media represented the Tea Party? Of course not; many in that business hold it as an article of faith that the Tea Party is racist. (See Chapter 27 for more on media bias.)

"Racist" is probably the most common invective thrown at free men, with "homophobe" a close second. Why bother with facts when you can call names? That is bigotry, pure and simple.

Name Calling

In too many cases, name calling replaces rational discourse. People are called extremists, racist, socialist, fascist etc. on evidence as uncertain as a politician's promise. Too often the accusation is regarded as proof, and the deception is often intentional. Statist Saul Alinsky in his book *Rules for Radicals* even devotes seven pages to this tactic. He recommends that his followers pick a target (scapegoat) and personalize it. They should act as if the target is 100% bad and their side 100% good.[162]

Of course this goes both ways. Too often even some free men do things like accuse Barrack Obama of being a Muslim. That is not only unfair but counterproductive. With so much of the media favoring Obama, any false accusation will only work against the accusers – and against anyone the statists and the media can claim is associated with the accusers. They are masters of guilt by association and will use such accusations to tar all free men with the brush of alleged ignorance.

Such accusations often amount to preaching to the choir. People who agree with the accusers take those claims as proof that the accused is next of kin to the devil. However those who disagree are not likely to be convinced by bumper stickers or similar sound bites.

---

162   Alinsky, op cit, pp130-136

There are two dangers, however. First, some people who have not yet made up their minds may accept those accusations and vote accordingly. That puts the misinformed in the voting booth and raises the probability that demagogues will be elected. Second, and much worse, all that name calling leaves little room for rational, evidence-based discussion. An avalanche of innuendo buries the truth deeper than the Mariana Trench.

In fact, the entire name-calling technique smacks of demagoguery. It is a tactic of people who want to hide truth and create false impressions. If those people had evidence for their accusations they would undoubtedly publicize that evidence. The very act of unsubstantiated name calling indicates that the accuser is not being honest, or is blindly accepting the word of someone else who is not being honest. This applies especially to one of the more common forms of name calling.

Godwin's Law

"As an Internet discussion goes on, the probability that someone will be compared to Hitler or the Nazis approaches 100%."

Mike Godwin formulated that law back in 1990.[163] He was correct, but was also guilty of understatement. His law applies to any political discussion, on the Internet or elsewhere. We regularly hear politicians, mainly statists, accuse their opponents of being Nazis. The irony is that the accuser is usually closer to Nazism than is the accused. The Nazis believed in an all-powerful government that would control nearly every aspect of life. That has obvious similarities to today's statists, but it is the opposite of what free men believe.

---

163   http://en.wikipedia.org/wiki/Godwin%27s_law

Whenever we hear an accusation that someone is a Nazi, fascist, or anything similar, we should be skeptical and demand evidence.

Other Sneaky Tricks

One common manifestation of Godwin's law today is what is appropriately called *turnspeak,* that is, accusing your opponents of your own sins. Psychologists call this projection.

Turnspeak goes back at least as far as Hitler's invasion of Czechoslovakia and Poland. Trying to excuse his own imperialism, he claimed that those countries were complicit in a plot to invade Germany, and he even staged a false Polish attack on a German radio station.[164] That is what turnspeak is; turning the facts around 180 degrees as Hitler did when he accused the Czechs and Poles of the imperialism he himself was committing. And it is what all too many in politics do today. Come out against big government and they will likely call you fascist, in spite of the fact that fascism is a form of big government.

One problem the turnspeak victims face is that the accusation many seem so obviously false that it should need no refutation – and it seems trite to refute something so flagrant. Plus refutation risks involvement in a "you are/no I'm not" argument. However, if allowed to go unanswered, the accusation will stick. It is probably best to just do something like point out that the free man is the opposite of a fascist while the statist wants big government just like the fascists did.

However, the real test is when we hear someone else called fascist or something similar. Do we just accept the accusation, or do we examine the

---

164   http://www.warhistoryonline.com/articles/wwiis-first-victim-a-nazi-plot-to-provide-an-excuse-to-invade-poland.html

evidence? Politics creates so much turnspeak that we should be careful about which accusations we accept. If there is solid evidence, we can accept the accusation. Otherwise, we owe it to ourselves and other citizens to publicly oppose the lie.

And there are yet worse forms of political chicanery.

Other Nastiness

False flag operations and *agents provocateurs* are the foulest excrement of politics. The idea is to make opponents look unattractive no matter what it takes, honesty and integrity be damned. The agent provocateur tries to goad his enemy into doing something stupid; for example he may try to get him to appear to agree with a racist remark. The false flag operative pretends to be one of his opponents while doing something stupid or racist. There have been several attempts of these types, especially against the Tea Party. For example, in 2010 a school teacher in Beaverton, Oregon created a web site urging people to crash the Tea Party and to "use misspelled protest signs, make wild claims during interviews or other actions that would damage public opinion of the party."[165] That is an example of a false flag operation – and I know statists who defended that deception. Of course, should that pretender manage to goad his targets into doing something stupid, he will become a successful agent provocateur.

But that was just a rogue teacher, right? I'm afraid not. At least one former high ranking Democrat tried the same trick. Kathy Sullivan, former chairman of

---

165   http://www.oregonlive.com/beaverton/index.ssf/2010/04/school_officials_investigate_beaverton_teacher_who_urged_people_to_crash_the_tea_party.html

the New Hampshire Democratic Party, openly sought Democrats "willing to pose as Tea Partiers and hold up anti-Obama, racist signs at the Tea Parties."[166] It would be difficult to think of a more dishonest dirty trick.

There will always be at least a few liars around, and in politics some will engage in such things as false flag or agent provocateur operations. That should be illegal; perpetrators should go to jail. Such shenanigans attack the very integrity of our political system. Until we have such a law, free men need to identify those deceivers and expose them publicly. And we need to be careful to not fall victim to provocations designed to get us to act stupidly. Of course as fee men, in the Tea Party or not, we must never use such dirty tricks ourselves, and we must try to purge from our ranks anyone who does. If we want the trust of the voters, we must strive to be beyond reproach.

By being aware of the dirty tricks some statists use, we can defend ourselves. That we must do if we are to defend our freedom. Our opponents have those dirty tricks on their side, plus an attractive sounding idea described in the next chapter. Unless we expose them, we will lose our freedom.

The Other Side of the Coin – When the Shoe Fits

I'm confident that nearly everyone would agree: unsubstantiated name calling is bad. It is dishonest and distracts from the real issues. But what if the apple really is rotten? What if a politician is a thief, a scoundrel, even a traitor? Unless the voters know about such things they will not be able to vote wisely. Evidence-based, correct description of politicians is not only good, it is required if

---

166   http://americaswatchtower.com/2010/04/14/new-hampshire-democrats-search-for-tea-party-crashers-to-hold-up-racist-signs/

we are to avoid demagogues and keep our freedom. There is a big difference between unsubstantiated name calling and pointing out verified problems. If a politician has a track record of lies and broken promises, voters should know about it. That is true whether those lies and broken promises were to the public or confined to family and friends.

What should we think of politicians who cheat on their wives, people like Anthony Weiner, Newt Gingrich, Mark Sanford, or John Edwards? Does their private behavior bear on fitness for office? Years ago I saw a quiz intended to measure people's attitudes toward some work issues and help them understand the importance of having the "correct" attitudes. One question asked, "If you found out that your boss was having an extramarital affair, would you think less of him as a boss?" The "right" answer was that no, that should not change how you regard him. His personal life has nothing to do with his work life.

That "right" answer is nonsense.

To believe that a person can have high integrity at work while lacking integrity in personal life is to believe that the person is split into two different characters. It just doesn't happen. If someone cheats on his spouse and not on his employer there is a simple reason: at present he finds it attractive, and of acceptable risk to cheat on his spouse but not on his employer. What will happen when he finds it attractive and of acceptable risk to cheat his employer (or the country)? You don't have to be a rocket scientist to answer that question.[167] Integrity is not situation-dependent. The person who is honest only when honesty

---

[167]   There are a few people who agree to "open marriages" wherein each allows the other as many affairs as he or she wants. However such marriages are, as far as I can tell, officially unheard of among politicians so they need not concern us here.

is convenient, or when dishonesty is dangerous, lacks integrity. When the situation changes, he will cheat. That is true in family life, in business, and in government.

Newt Gingrich, for example, cheated on at least two wives, eventually divorcing both.[168] He then talked of Christian forgiveness, using that to try to convince people that they should support him. As a Christian I believe in repentance and forgiveness, but so what? The issue is trust, not forgiveness. In fact, I am in no position to forgive Gingrich; he did not wrong me. His ex-wives and his children must deal with that. For voters the issue is trust; and trust must be earned. In fact while Christian scripture repeatedly commands us to forgive, I do not know of any scriptural admonition to trust the offender. Jesus even instructed his disciples to be "wise as serpents."[169] Surely such wisdom would include trusting only those who are trustworthy.

In our romantic lives, business, or politics we must require that people be trustworthy. That integrity should be manifest by actions, not just words. The politician who fails to demonstrate integrity by his actions should be rejected – be those actions public or private.

We must seek the truth about our politicians. If they are liars and cheaters, we should know that and not vote for them. If they are falsely accused, we should also know that and not hold the accusations against them. And of course we should refrain from unsubstantiated name calling ourselves.

---

168   http://abcnews.go.com/Politics/story?id=2937633
169   Holy Bible, Matthew 10:16

Chapter 17 Utopian Thinking

I suspect that even most [free men] would prefer to live in the kind of world conjured up in the [statists'] imagination rather than the kind of world we are in fact stuck with. (Thomas Sowell)

Let's admit it, collectivism offers some attractive promises. An easy life, guaranteed food, shelter, medical care, clothing, cradle to grave security. What's not to like? If only reality matched the promise.

Life is full of attractive ideas. Most of us would like a diet high in chocolate, fat, and sugar – and with unlimited calories but no weight gain or health problems. Sadly, nobody has yet invented that diet. There are many such temptations, things that sound wonderful, but are either not available or come with unacceptable costs. Those temptations are the equivalent of, "here fishy fishy, have a nice juicy worm." We swallow the delicious morsel and find the hook. The bad diet is firmly attached to poor health and getting fat. The excitement of fast driving brings an appointment with the judge – or the undertaker. That credit card is so convenient until the bills come due – with interest.

Statist proposals likewise sell us on attractive promises, then we find the hook: loss of freedom, poor economy, and failure to deliver on its promises. When presented with an attractive temptation, we should ask ourselves what it will really cost. Collectivism is no exception; we need to know what it will deliver in the real world.

Collectivism promises that all will have enough, in fact an equal share of this world's goods. In Marx's words, "From each according to his ability, to each according to his need." Nobody will go without and everybody will work happily for the good of the whole. Who could oppose such an arrangement? The problem is not the promise, but reality.

That promise is based on three assumptions, all false:

First, the assumption that people will work as diligently under a collective system as they do when they reap the results of their own labor. The collectivists ignore human nature, especially the fact that incentives encourage effort while a dole encourages sloth.

Second, the assumption that the leaders of such a society will be moral enough to work for the good of others rather than feathering their own nests or amassing power to themselves. Again, the collectivists ignore human nature. They also ignore the empirical evidence of collectivist states where rulers live in luxury while the people struggle for their livelihoods.

Third, the assumption that those leaders have the ability to manage all the gory details of such a society. Again they ignore the empirical evidence that managed economies have uniformly produced shortages and shoddy goods.

Many statists also make yet another assumption, one not strictly necessary to collectivism though it does help them sell their ideas. They assume that economics is a zero-sum game, a fallacy we already discussed in Chapter 3.

Calling economics a zero-sum game can become a self-fulfilling prophecy, or worse. Governments that accept that fallacy engage in "wealth redistribution," taking from the productive for the benefit of the non-productive. Then the people decide that it is no use working hard, the entire economy declines, and zero sum becomes negative sum. There is even less wealth available than before.

Look at the contrast between freedom and collectivism. While free societies often have problems with surplus goods, collectivism is more likely to have chronic shortages. That has been demonstrated repeatedly in the resource-rich countries of the USSR, Cuba, and in the Latin American countries that have tried socialism. Indeed, it is demonstrated in nearly every country that has tried government-mandated collectivism. Utopia works better in theory than in practice.

Do Collectivist Societies Ever Work?

Are there examples of collectivist societies that actually worked? If so, how are they different from the spectacular failures? I can think of four societies that more or less meet that criterion:

> First, the New Testament description of early Christians in Acts 4:32 to 5:11. We have, however, little real information on that system and how effective it was.

> Second, the Kibbutzim of modern Israel.[170]

> Third, my own church's (The Church of Jesus Christ of Latter-day Saints, or Mormon) early experiment called the United Order.[171] And that one only worked for a short time.

> Fourth, the Inca Empire which, though not strictly communal, did have many of the characteristics of collectivism. In that empire people had their own lands but worked those lands in common – and the penalty for working land out of the prescribed order was death. Interestingly, they were required to first work the land of the widows and orphans, then the common people and the land of the ruler last of all.[172]

---

170   http://www.jewishvirtuallibrary.org/jsource/Society_%26_Culture/kibbutz. html
171   http://eom.byu.edu/index.php/United_Orders
172   William H. Prescott, *History of the Conquest of Peru,* Modern Library (No copyright date listed in my copy) p757 This is a dual book, including *History of the Conquest of Mexico* by the same author. Pagination may differ in

Let's examine what those systems had in common. I have not done a full study of the matter, nor do I know of anyone who has. However, I have identified five things that seem to contribute:

First, all had a strong religious motivation. The early Christians, the Jews in the Kibbutzim, the members of my church all had well-known religious attachments. Not so well known was the Inca religion that regarded the ruler (the Inca) as a direct descendent and representative of the sun god.

Second, all were organized around small groups of people. The largest organization would be the Inca Empire, but even in that empire the working of lands of widows and orphans first would have given a feeling of greater intimacy than working large collective farms such as those in the USSR. The early Christians were a small group, and each Israeli Kibbutz is also small enough that people can know each other. Likewise the United Order in my church consisted of local, self-governing areas in which the people could all know each other.

Third, participation was voluntary. Even the New Testament version has Peter telling a cheater that he could have retained his property rather than lying about donating all.[173] The exception was the Inca Empire which was not strictly collectivist and where participation was mandatory.

Fourth, again with the exception of the Inca Empire, all faced enemies that threatened their very existence.

Fifth, they were bound by a major common interest. All were brought together by being of similar ethnicity or religion. I know of no reasonably successful collectivist society without such a common bond.

I believe all or most of those characteristics are required if any sort of collectivist system is to have a chance of success.

---

other printings.
173   Holy Bible, Acts 5:1-4

Religious motivation helps overcome selfishness and encourages people to work for the common good. Many religions teach the necessity of love for fellow man. That love can motivate people to work for the benefit of others, not just for self.

It also helps if the organization is small enough that people know each other. People in such a society are not dealing with some amorphous large government. They know the widow down the street, the orphans, and the handicapped in their community. They see that their efforts directly help those people and that slothfulness will harm them.

A voluntary system allows people to control their own lives rather than being controlled by some other force. That encourages effort and helps morale.

External threats keep people united, helping them see the advantage of working for the common good rather than seeking individual advantage. This reminds us of the quote attributed to Benjamin Franklin at the signing of the Declaration of Independence, "We must all hang together, or assuredly we shall all hang separately."

Large collectivist systems, especially those that reject religion, have no chance of working. That helps explain the colossal failure of communism.

Collectivism Restricts Freedom

The one collectivist promise that has been realized is that collectivism would restrict freedom. The early proponents of socialism openly admitted that it would require a dictatorial government to force people into their system. They expected a deliberate reorganization of society along hierarchical lines. "Freedom of thought they regarded as the root-evil of nineteenth-century society."[174] For example Henri Saint-Simon, an early French socialist, predicted that those who failed to obey the planning boards would be treated like cattle.[175] That bit of honesty lasted until the collectivists realized that people liked freedom. Then they changed their tune and disguised that aspect of their utopia.

With a triumph of obfuscation and public relations, the collectivists promised something they called freedom. Choose your career, or no career at all, and live with the consequences of your choice? Not freedom according to them. They claimed that people weren't really free if they had to work for a living; only the collectivist dictatorship could provide true freedom. Somehow they pulled off that Orwellian Newspeak, long before Orwell wrote his novel, *1984*. They essentially redefined the word. Their "freedom" meant not just the right to choose, but freedom from consequences of that choice. In their mind, government is responsible for housing, feeding, clothing the people, in fact for every human want and need. Where government will get the necessary resources was a triviality not mentioned.

With that semantic sleight of hand, the collectivists convinced themselves and others that freedom was really only available under statist rule. They obscured the fact that such a society would require a government with dictatorial powers, and that that the statist government could not give people their desires without forcing someone to work to provide for those desires. To them, freedom means

---

174   Hayek, op cit p76

175   Henri Saint-Simon, "Letters from an Inhabitant of Geneva to his Contemporaries" in *Henri Saint-Simon (1760-1825) Selected Writings on Science, Industry, and Social Organization* as referenced on page 76 of Hayek's book

dictatorship! And they ignored what we have discussed in Chapter 3 about freedom being necessary to a sound economy.

The result was a triad of collectivist systems, or four such systems if we consider fascism and National Socialism to be different. Though there were other types of collectivism, those were the species to reach wide popularity. Communism and fascism/National Socialism developed on the European continent and sought forceful overthrow of the existing order. Fabian socialism started in the British Isles and expected to gradually transition to socialism through changes in the law. All expected eventual destruction of free choice.

Communism, Socialism, and Nazism

While many nowadays claim that communism and Nazism/fascism are opposites, such was not the case during the early days of those movements. They competed for the same type of mindset and it was not uncommon for a person to start as a communist and become fascist or vice versa. In fact, "Many a university teacher during the 1930s has seen English and American students return from the Continent uncertain whether they were communists or Nazis and certain only that they hated western civilization."[176] Fabian socialism, communism and fascism/national socialism were all based on statist ideas, different manifestations of an underlying statism/collectivism.

The three versions of collectivism promised similar utopias, differing only in how they were administered and how they would be established. In all of them, the economy would be heavily controlled and people would work and share the products of their work. In all those systems, equality was promised, through

---

176   Hayek, op cit p81

redistribution of wealth if necessary. All expected the state to rule and the individual to depend on that state (except in the more wildly utopian version of "mature" communism). Independence and freedom had no part in any of them.

The astute observer will have noticed similarities between Nazism and socialism, in spite of the fact that many think of Nazism as opposite of socialism. That belief is the result of the bad name Nazism acquired during and after World War II. Nazism in fact grew out of the socialist movement and continued to have in common with socialism an antipathy toward capitalism and freedom. With Nazism no longer a significant force in today's world, we shall treat it only briefly.[177] Anyone interested in the subject may read Chapter 12 ("The Socialist Roots of Nazism") of Hayek's book. That chapter describes in some detail how socialism in Germany gave birth to Nazism.

Briefly, if we look at Hitler's original 25 points, what we might call his political platform, we find that several points are demands right out of the socialist/communist handbook:[178]

> 7. We demand that the State shall above all undertake to ensure that every citizen shall have the possibility of living decently and earning a livelihood. If it should not be possible to feed the whole population, then aliens (non-citizens) must be expelled from the Reich.

---

[177] There is an unfortunate though small movement in parts of Germany and the United States to force National Socialism on the world. That movement is composed largely of bigots who hate people different from themselves. Unfortunately, the statists have managed to lump those bigots with free men, even though the neo-Nazi has little in common with the citizen working for lower taxes and less intrusive regulation. In fact freedom and Nazism/fascism are opposites.

[178] http://www.historyplace.com/worldwar2/riseofhitler/25points.htm

11. That all unearned income, and all income that does not arise from work, be abolished.

13. We demand the nationalization of all trusts.

14. We demand profit-sharing in large industries

16. We demand the creation and maintenance of a sound middle-class, the immediate communalization of large stores which will be rented cheaply to small tradespeople, and the strongest consideration must be given to ensure that small traders shall deliver the supplies needed by the State, the provinces and municipalities.

17. We demand an agrarian reform in accordance with our national requirements, and the enactment of a law to expropriate the owners without compensation of any land needed for the common purpose. The abolition of ground rents, and the prohibition of all speculation in land.

18. We demand that ruthless war be waged against those who work to the injury of the common welfare. Traitors, usurers, profiteers, etc., are to be punished with death, regardless of creed or race.

21. The State has the duty to help raise the standard of national health by providing maternity welfare centers...

25. In order to carry out this program we demand: the creation of a strong central authority in the State, the unconditional authority by the political central parliament of the whole State and all its organizations.

Karl Marx would have been right at home with those demands, but no free man could tolerate them, especially number 25. Hitler, however, saw clearly that number 25 was crucial to his aims. Without that central and unconditional authority, no collectivist can implement his programs.

Internecine Warfare

Statists claim that, because Fabian socialism, fascism, and communism often fight each other, they are all different. Are they really? Or are they simply competitors, seeking similar goals? The latter is clearly the case. While there are variations, all want statist, central control of the economy and life. The fascists would like more of a corporate statism while Fabian socialists and communists would prefer more overt government control, but the result is much the same for the people: government controls everything. And, theory aside, the results fail to live up to the promises.

Nazism/fascism, communism, and Fabian socialism are not different species of animal. They are different sub-species, fighting to see who gets the support of the unwary. They are all statist.

Words Are Not Enough

Collectivists of all stripes present attractive, mostly self-consistent theories. They claim that their theories are science, but theory without empirical confirmation is speculation. It is not science, regardless of the ardor of its supporters. Unfortunately, the statists have convinced people that their theory is sound in spite of evidence to the contrary. That is another triumph of public relations; too many people fail to compare collectivist promises to the reality of results. If they did, they would notice things like the old USSR under communism. That was a country blessed with tremendous natural resources, yet the people in general lived in poverty. Some of the workers were fond of saying that they had a good system on the job, "They pretend to pay us and we pretend to work."

In spite of the lofty claims, no collectivist country has ever come close to the per capita production of the United States. As we shall see in the next chapter, a planned society does not work, at least not for the common people.

Chapter 18 Planning: the Individual and the Collective

The socialists believe in two things which are absolutely different and perhaps even contradictory: freedom and organization. (Elie Halevy)

In a country where the sole employer is the State, opposition means death by slow starvation. The old principle: who does not work shall not eat, has been replaced by a new one: who does not obey shall not eat. (Leon Trotsky)

Organizations. Most likely you are a member of at least one, probably more. You may belong to a church, a club, a service organization, almost certainly a family, and it is probable that you have some place of employment. In all those organizations you work with other people toward a common goal. That is great; we can accomplish more working together than we could if we each went our separate ways. Statists, however, take this too far when they make organization mandatory, with individual choice not allowed. In a free country you are not forced to join any group, and you can resign from a church, volunteer group, your job, or any other group to which you belong. Not so the captives of government collectives.

The resident of a completely statist country cannot easily leave, and may even risk being shot on the way out. He may not even be allowed to choose his employment. Does he have an opinion? Better keep it to himself unless he wants to see the inside of a prison. He is subject to that rule 24 hours a day. He is a stranger to individual choice. Milder forms of statism, though not as stringent, still restrict choice – and too often they "progress" to the more stringent forms.

Our concern here is not voluntary association with an employer, church or club, but the forcible transfer of decision-making power from individuals and businesses to the government. It matters little if that government be communist, socialist, dictatorship or some other form of collectivism. All such governments limit the power of the individual to determine the course of his own life.

As discussed previously, most of today's so-called liberals are really statists. It is time to discuss statism, the idea of strong government control.

Statists object that freedom allows inequalities. Those who have more ability and work harder will have more, as will their descendants (until they become wasteful or lazy and lose it). In fact some will have more simply due to luck. They also point out that the poor may lack good medical care and similar benefits. While those accusations are true, we must be careful about the proposed solution. It is easy to find problems, and nearly as easy to propose solutions. It is a bit more difficult to make those solutions effective without causing other problems, often more serious problems. The statists too often ignore the problems their solutions create. They confuse proposals with actual solution of problems.

In the U.S., much of this confusion comes from misinterpretation of the Great Depression and of the economic effect of World War II. Milton and Rose Friedman tell us, "The depression convinced the public that capitalism was defective; the war, that centralized government was efficient. Both conclusions were false. The depression was produced by a failure of government, not of private enterprise. As to the war, it is one thing for government to exercise great control temporarily for a single overriding purpose shared by almost all citizens and for which almost all citizens are willing to make heavy sacrifices; it is a very different thing for government to control the economy permanently to promote a vaguely defined 'public interest' shaped by the enormously varied and diverse objectives of its citizens."[179]

As we shall discuss later, government intervention did not solve the Great Depression, it prolonged it. Yet many today use that Depression to justify automatic government intervention in response to any problem – and to increase statist power. In the words of Rahm Emanuel, "You don't ever want a crisis to go to waste; it's an opportunity to do important things that you would otherwise avoid."[180]

Indeed one of history's most colossal failures was the result of well-intentioned attempts to solve the problems mentioned above. Communism, an extreme form of statism, was supposed to fix inequality, poverty, lack of medical care and the other problems of free society. The results were the exact opposite of the intentions. Poverty was rampant, the government class was "more equal than others," medical care, housing, and food were abysmal for most of the people. Why? Why was statism such a failure? The answer is to be found in the difference between statist planning and that done in a free society, the difference between central planning and individual choice.

179   Friedman, Milton & Rose, op cit p85-86
180   http://www.nationalreview.com/liberal-fascism/203838/never-let-good-crisis-go-waste

Faith in Statism?

There is an increasing tendency among modern men to imagine themselves ethical because they have delegated their vices to larger and larger groups. (Reinhold Niebuhr)

Implicit in statism is a belief that government is somehow wiser and more moral than the average citizen. Without that wisdom and integrity, there is no reason to trust government. John I, our medieval serf, lived in a society in which the king, the duke, even the lord of the manor, were regarded as wiser and more moral than the peons. Had that been true, there would have been no reason to do away with serfdom.

Communism demonstrated that government has no special wisdom, nor is it less likely to abuse power than is the average person. Good intentions may be comforting, but they make a poor supper. What I saw in the divided city of Berlin provided an example. On one side of the wall business thrived, people smiled and went about their business in modern buildings, then went home to enjoy their time off. On the other side, war damage was unrepaired twenty five years after the war, business was slow, and people had the look of hunted animals. Nobody who values freedom would want to live the East Berlin of the communist era.

Even milder forms of statism turn social theory and personal preference into law. Be it the old official state church or modern political correctness, that creates silliness at best and institutionalized idiocy at worst. For example, Portland, Oregon outlawed "snout houses," houses on which the garage projects out in front.[181] What business does the city have, forcing architectural preferences of a few politicians on everybody? If people want to avoid those houses they can buy a different style. They can even live in neighborhoods where voluntary covenants prohibit such houses. It is, however, a serious infringement on freedom when government decides what kind of house everybody should live in.

Individualism and Planning

But does "planning" necessarily mean a statist society? A society in which planners in a central, authoritarian government control the lives of the people? That need not, indeed should not, be the case. We can remain free and still employ foresight and clear thinking regarding our common affairs – if we wisely distribute the decision-making and avoid coercion to the greatest extent feasible. To quote Hayek, "The question is whether …. it is better that the holder of coercive power should confine himself in general to creating conditions under which the knowledge and initiative of individuals are given the best scope so that *they* can plan most successfully; or whether a rational utilization of our resources requires *central* direction and organization of all our activities according to some consciously constructed 'blueprint'."[182] (Emphases in the original)

Government can provide an environment that encourages freedom and individual choice, or its planners can decide nearly everything for the citizens.

Consider apartment rents, for example. The statist would have central planners determine how much rent a landlord is allowed to charge, as is done for

---

181   http://www.nytimes.com/2000/04/20/garden/in-portland-houses-are-friendly-or-else.html

182   Hayek, op cit. P85

many apartments in New York City. The law there limits increases in rental rates, especially for apartments likely to be occupied by lower income renters. On the other hand, cities like Portland, Oregon have no rent control at all; apartments are only required to conform to the building code and land use planning laws. The resulting competition among apartment owners gives renters more choice and assures that there are adequate numbers of apartments available. In New York, the incentive is to build only apartments that will not be rent controlled, even at times to abandon controlled buildings. That causes a shortage of low-cost rental units and encourages cutting corners on maintenance. It also breeds corruption, as exemplified by Congressman Charlie Rangel who hardly suffers from low income but kept multiple, rent-stabilized apartments.[183]

Notice that there is planning in both cities. In New York, the planning is done by government officials who dictate prices. In Portland, the landlords do the planning; they build to meet demand. In other cities, even the land use laws may be relaxed or non-existent, allowing yet more individual initiative and competition. The question is not if there shall be planning, but who shall plan and decide: the state or the citizens?

Communism: Promise vs. Results

The communist state represents the ultimate in central planning. Planners gave quotas to farms and factories, telling them what to produce. It even assigned people jobs. The result was one of the most spectacular failures in human history. The five year plans failed. The factories and farms did not meet their quotas, and what they did produce was often shoddy. The people were held captive in a

183   http://www.nytimes.com/2008/07/11/nyregion/11rangel.html?pagewanted =all&_r=0

system that produced shortages of nearly everything except misery. Even their showplace factories were found to be safety and environmental nightmares.[184]

That statist system was hardly either wise or moral.

Clearly there are problems with freedom. However, those problems are not nearly as serious as what happens when we allow a statist government to rule our lives, whether we label that government "progressive," "positive," "modern" or anything else. Freedom leads to more production and more goods for everyone – and it produces the goods people are willing to buy. Statism leads to less for everyone except the ruling class.

The goal should be not elimination of inequality, but enhancing life for everyone. In places like the United States where the "poor" often have cars, large screen TVs, air conditioning and other niceties, it would be difficult to claim that freedom has harmed the poor. They may have less than do the rich, but they still have more than the average resident of a collectivist country.

Collectivism does not help the poor, nor is it inevitable.

---

184   http://countrystudies.us/russia/25.htm

Chapter 19 The Inevitability of Collectivism

We were the first to assert that the more complicated the forms assumed by civilization, the more restricted freedom of the individual must become. (Benito Mussolini)

San Diego, California, 19 December 1980. With less than three minutes left, the SMU Mustangs enjoyed a 45-25 lead over the BYU Cougars. Cougar fans headed for the exits while Mustang fans started celebrating. Make up a 20 point deficit in three minutes? No way! The third annual Holiday Bowl football game was effectively over, and BYU no longer had a chance.

Somebody forgot to tell the BYU players.

A touchdown pass reduced the deficit to 45-32.

An onside kick and a quick march down the field cut the lead to six points.

SMU got the ball, but the Cougar defense rose to the occasion and BYU took over – with only 13 seconds left to play. Two incomplete passes left time for one more play.

BYU quarterback Jim McMahon launched a "Hail Mary" pass. His tight end, Clay Brown, surrounded by four SMU defenders, somehow came down with the ball in the end zone. Final score: BYU 46, SMU 45.[185]

In life and politics, as in sports, we should never give up on a good cause, even when everyone thinks we are beaten. Such is the case with freedom vs. statism today. Statists appear to be winning. They claim that collectivism is inevitable. Resistance is futile and we might as well just all go along. The statists

---

185   If anybody is interested, BYU fans know this as the Miracle Bowl. SMU fans undoubtedly feel differently. Interestingly, though BYU is a "Mormon" school, that final pass went from a Catholic to a Catholic.

are "on the right side of history," their opponents of course "on the wrong side of history." Since collectivism is coming anyway, we might as well do what we can to make it work.

Nonsense! If free men give up, the statists will win by default. Like my favorite team, we are down but not out. If we continue to defend our freedoms we can win – and coming generations are depending on us. Like the players in the 1980 Holiday Bowl, we *must not give up.*

Technology and Monopoly

Statists claim that collectivism inevitable, but why would that be? The statists agree with Mussolini's claim that modern technology favors the huge company. In their mind, size gives those companies an insurmountable advantage; unless constrained, they will dominate the market. Since nobody can compete with them, we should just have government-controlled monopolies or even government-owned businesses.

Really?

Here's an experiment. Go to your local electronics store and see if you can find an IBM computer. If you are lucky, nobody will laugh at you. Yet for years IBM had a near monopoly on the computer business. Or you might look for a Nokia cell phone; that company dominated the market at the turn of the century. Competitors had no chance, right?

Somebody forgot to tell a few entrepreneurs how hopeless it was. IBM no longer makes personal computers and Nokia is out of the cell phone business. Some upstarts got busy elsewhere, even in a few garages. Apple, Microsoft, Compaq, and others ignored the "fact" that they could not compete with the monolith. Though IBM remains in business, it has nowhere near monopoly power. Technology was going to make that company unstoppable. Instead, that same technology allowed competitors to prosper.

Maintain a monopoly without government help? Probably impossible. Not only IBM and Nokia, but other near monopolies have fallen to upstarts. Even Standard Oil, the archetype of a powerful monopoly, could not have maintained that position forever. Before being legally broken up, the company was losing market share to changing technology. Automobiles and the electric light displaced kerosene, Standard's primary product. New competitors entered the market and Standard's near monopoly vanished.[186] The lasting monopolies are those legally protected from competition: utilities, taxi companies, and bus companies, etc.

Technology, far from harming small companies, provides opportunity. As we progressed from vacuum tubes to individual transistors to the modern integrated circuit (sometimes called a semiconductor chip), it became easier for the upstarts to do business. It does take a huge investment to manufacture the actual chips, but those chips need software and other components before they can work in the computer, the cell phone, or the digital clock. Anyone with the requisite skills and a computer can write software or create a web site. Today's "apps," used in cell phones, tablets, and other electronic devices often come out of somebody's garage, living room or bedroom.

---

186   While conventional wisdom holds that Standard Oil grew by predatory practices, there is some dispute on that point. The company started its growth by finding creative ways to increase efficiency and cut costs. A reasonably complete treatment is far beyond the scope of this book. Those interested can find more information at
http://www.theobjectivestandard.com/issues/2008-summer/standard-oil-company.asp

Even computers present no great obstacle to the entrepreneur. If you want to compete with Dell computers, you only need facilities, a few people, and components; a small investment will get you started. Some people even assemble personal computers at home, either for themselves or for sale. Knowledge and skill are more important than a big bank account.

Technology is not a barrier to new competitors. Instead it creates opportunity.

Another claim is that economies of scale favor the monopoly. Only partly true. There are economies of scale, but there are also dis-economies of scale. While a large company can buy raw material or components more cheaply than a smaller competitor, it also has a large, bureaucratic organization. Major decisions require several layers of approval and at any one of those levels someone can block a promising idea. The smaller competitor is more nimble; it can run with an idea before that idea even reaches the decision point in a bigger company.

The Small, the Nimble, and the Washing of Hands

What does a $3,000 investment in 1964 have to do with washing your hands? A great deal if you are a typical American. In that year, Robert Taylor used $3,000 of his savings to start a company he called Minnetonka. His company progressed from dealing in niche markets to soaps, fragrances, etc. Then in 1977 he introduced something initially called the Incredible Soap Machine. You may have heard of it by its current name: Softsoap. It was innovative and beneficial to customers who no longer had the mess a bar of soap would create.

How did Minnetonka fight off the bigger competitors, companies like Procter & Gamble, Armour-Dial, or Colgate-Palmolive? Initially it didn't have to;

those hide-bound companies did not want to risk the investment necessary to introduce their own versions of liquid soap, nor did they want to compete with their existing brands. They preferred to let Taylor take the risk. Only after Softsoap became popular did they show interest. Then Taylor pulled another innovative trick: he locked up the entire supply of the pumps used to dispense his product. That gave him another 18 to 24 months to build market share before bigger competitors could sell their liquid soaps.

In 1987, ten years after the introduction of Softsoap, Taylor sold the brand to Colgate-Palmolive for $61 million. He got rich. You and I got a more convenient way to wash our hands.[187]

Economies of Scale?

A large organization also costs money. Joe may be the only manager of his ten-person plumbing company, and he may have only one secretary/receptionist. However a large company such as General Motors requires layers upon layers of management and support personnel. Secretaries, mail clerks, purchasing agents, human resources people, etc. All expect paychecks and benefits. The big company requires more management and support personnel for each "worker bee" than does a small operation.

And there is more waste in a bigger company. Joe will notice if his plumbers spend two hours talking about a football game before they go to their assignments. Those employees will mend their ways or Joe will replace them. If employees at General Motors waste two hours a day, it is likely nobody will

---

187   Adam M. Brandenburger and Barry J. Nalebuff, *Co-opetition*, Currency Doubleday, originally published 1996, pp149-151

notice. Likewise, in a larger company, employee theft may go undetected while it will be more obvious in smaller companies.

There is undoubtedly an ideal size for companies in each industry. That size strikes a balance between economies and dis-economies of scale. For Joe's plumbing, remaining small has advantages. For automobiles, the capital equipment is expensive, tipping the balance toward a larger corporation. However even building cars has a limit on what the economies of scale gain the company. And we note that government, being inevitably the largest organization in any country, will suffer most from dis-economies of scale.

So, no, economies of scale do not force us into monopolies, either the corporate or the government kind.

Complexity and Collectivism

Some statists have followed Mussolini in claiming that, as society becomes more complex, we need more central control. Another nice theory murdered by a gang of cold-blooded facts. Observation and thought will show that the opposite is true. The more complex the society, the more difficult it is to manage and the more impossible central planning and collectivism become. If you doubt that, you are invited to consider how you would manage a tiny part of a national economy, say the production of shoes.

You need to know how many are needed and in what sizes. You would look at the number of male and female citizens in the populace and their ages. That is a good start but you are far from done. People need different kinds of shoes, for the office, for construction work, for farming etc. Children need shoes suitable for play, and everybody should have some suitable for exercise.

What about preferences? Are you going to allow different styles? Will you provide for hikers, skiers, boaters and other special needs? How will you determine how many of each should be produced? Will the country's rulers get better shoes than the janitor who cleans their offices? There are probably hundreds of shoe types possible, each needed in twenty or more different sizes. Produce too many of a size or type and some go to waste, too few and someone goes without.

Once you finish the gargantuan task of determining how many shoes of each type and size to produce, you can move on to other tasks. Where will you get the raw materials, the equipment, the facilities, and the workers to make those shoes? You need leather for the uppers so you need to be certain that enough cattle are slaughtered to provide that leather. In the process you may upset co-workers who are trying to provide enough milk for the country, or those who manage meat production and are already plagued with an excess. You need machinery for your factories, but for that you compete with another co-worker who is trying to equip coat factories.

The problems multiply for every component of your shoes. Shoe manufacturing draws on nearly every part of the economy: mining, machinery, agriculture, transportation, etc. Furthermore, each component you need raises similar questions. The farmer cannot produce cattle to make your leather without feed and land for those cows. The land that provides his hay can also be used to produce carrots, potatoes, cabbage etc.

Competing supply chains tie our entire economy together. A change in any demand can cause shortages or excesses in seemingly unrelated commodities. An extra demand for ice cream can cause farmers to keep marginal dairy cows instead of sending them for slaughter. That can cause a shortage of leather which in turn causes a shortage of baseball gloves. Children with no baseball gloves may turn to other pursuits and cause shortages of other toys. Manufactures of baseball bats suddenly find themselves plagued by a surplus.

That spreads throughout the economy. Every item in the grocery store requires a myriad of inputs before you put it on your table, and every one of those inputs competes for resources with other commodities.

In theory, all our economic matters are governed by mathematical rules called differential equations. We just solve those equations and everything will be great, right? Easier said than done – by a long shot. Even the simplest differential equations require calculus and can be difficult to solve. The equations that govern the economy are not simple; they can involve hundreds of terms, most not precisely known. Worse, because of the interdependence of the economy, all those equations are coupled together. You cannot solve just one; you have to solve nearly all of them at the same time. The math required would be horrendous, even if we knew enough to write the equations.

Do you think you could successfully manage shoe production for a country, or even a village? If not, think of the difficulty of managing an entire economy, all those complicated equations with terms not precisely known, all of them coupled together. No wonder managed economies don't work. It doesn't even work to manage just part of an economy. Because the whole is interconnected, you cannot change one part without causing changes throughout. Many of those changes will be unanticipated, and often your best intentions will create problems. We might try to do it without the mathematical tool of differential equations, but we still need to know the details and how they affect each other.[188]

An effective managed economy remains unavailable – and there is reason to believe that man, with his lack of omniscience, will never create such an economy.

Unfortunately, that impossibility really does not prevent some from trying; and to try they must impose their ideas on the citizens – with or without the consent of those citizens. There are people with enough intellectual arrogance that they think they can do it. I believe that arrogance comes from two sources. First, they lack of understanding of the problem and its difficulties. Second, they have what Thomas Sowell calls the unconstrained vision, or the vision of the anointed.[189] Such people simply do not recognize their own limitations and thus feel free to overstep their abilities at the expense of others.

Complexity and Free Enterprise

So how does a free society handle the problem of a complex economy? We know it works; it has been working for centuries. There are occasional problems of surplus or shortage, but in general free enterprise meets our needs quite well. In the United States, we can almost always find what we want to buy at about the price we expect to pay. That is true whether we are looking for a candy bar, a

---

188   Economist Casey Mulligan gives a good description of how one law, the "Affordable Care Act" affects the economy in the November 2014 issue of *Imprimis* published by Hillsdale College. A .pdf version is available in their archives at http://imprimis.hillsdale.edu/archives

189   See Sowell's books, *A Conflict of Visons* and *The Vision of the Anointed,* described in the bibliography.

computer, or a car. Contrast that with the long lines, shortages, and shoddy goods that faced shoppers in a managed economy like the USSR.

Our system of uncontrolled economy works, and works quite well. How does that happen? We've already mentioned Leonard Read's essay, "I Pencil." That essay describes both the complexity of making a pencil and how it actually happens. The essence is that each company involved produces what it can sell. None of the people involved need know anything beyond their immediate business. The clay mining company knows how much clay it can sell at what price. It cares not if its clay is going into pencils or ceramics. Likewise the copper mine, the graphite supplier and the rest of the people producing things that will eventually wind up as parts of pencils. As demand increases, they increase production or raise prices. As demand drops, they either find other markets for their products or cut back on production.

Why does this system work so well? It is because each worker, each manager, each business owner, can make decisions on the information available to him. That information comes, not from central planners or differential equations, but in the form of orders or sales.

Beyond that, each company is responsible for its product. If output is shoddy, the company will lose customers and probably go out of business. If the company produces a good product at a fair price, it may prosper. Nobody is telling the company that it must produce 2 million pairs of shoes or 10,000 cars lest the manager go to jail. Nobody is guaranteeing that company a market, even if its quality stinks. Management must decide how much to produce and is free to reduce production if necessary to maintain quality, or to increase production if demand increases.

In a complex society, free enterprise is a big advantage. It is the only system shown to meet our needs and wants. Both private monopolies and public collectivism fail. Complexity does not make collectivism necessary, it makes freedom necessary.

However there is yet one more force that often pushes for collectivism while making it unworkable: divergent desires.

Special Interests and Collectivism

Here's a fun thought. What if you were suddenly able to make a change or two in the law, any change you want and nobody can stop you or change it back. What would you do? Outlaw abortion? Reduce speed limits? Eliminate those limits on freeways? Limit what can be shown on TV to what is suitable for children? Impose socialized medicine?

Such a question gets to the heart of why some people want statism. In their minds, their ideals are so important that everybody should accept them. Some want socialized medicine, others insist on severely restricting private automobiles. Some want education to emphasize self esteem; others want emphasis on the arts or science. Those people naturally tend to support unlimited government in order to impose their ideas on everybody.

However, many of those special interests are opposed to each other. They agree that we need a more powerful government, but once we have it, they would agree on little else. The anti-abortionists would lock horns with those who want population control. In education the self-esteem proponents, those who want emphasis on the arts, and those who want to emphasize science would fight each other. Some would demand disarmament, others a more powerful military. Even

220

should those special interests succeed in imposing collectivism, their battle would be hardly begun. They would fight each other until one side won, or until some tyrant took over and imposed his will on the lot of them.

Collectivism will not give the special interests what they want. There are too many special interests seeking different things.

"Special" Special Interests

Of all the special interest groups in the country, two deserve particular attention. Not only are they supremely powerful, but we often don't even think of them as special interests. They are first, government and second, the education establishment. Yes, both fit the definition of "special interest," a group of people seeking their own advantage even at the expense of the general welfare. In fact, managers in both are quite as likely as managers in business to engage in "empire building." If they can get more people working for them, they will justify getting paid more.

Government: Back when the Post Office was officially part of the federal government, a friend worked as a postman. He found that he and others could deliver all the mail on their routes in about half a normal work day. He dropped an idea in the suggestion box. Every time a postman retired or left for other work, instead of hiring a replacement they could combine routes and continue doing that until the work load matched the number of postmen. Bad mistake! The big boss downtown called him in for a royal reprimand. "Do you know how I get paid?" he demanded! "I get paid by the number of employees under me. If I do what you suggest, I will lose money."

That postal supervisor was protecting his own empire, and we can be certain that he is not the only such person in government. Even today, while the Postal Service is semi-independent of government, Congress will not allow such simple changes as reducing delivery days. I suspect most people would be quite satisfied if the mail were delivered only three days a week (that would mean three days with no bills arriving for one thing). However a minority demands service six days a week. Postal workers are part of that minority; reducing deliveries would eliminate jobs.

Of course the "empire building" temptation is common, both in government and in private business. However government special interests have a monopoly, plus a temptation beyond that in most businesses. They are tempted to expand not only their spending but also their power. As discussed in Chapter 22, power is addictive, and greed for power is at least as dangerous as greed for money. Government officials form a special interest seeking to increase both power and income.

Education: The education establishment is part of government, but is so big that it deserves separate treatment. Plus, in education there is another factor important to people like professors. Universities and professors are greedy for prestige, and that prestige comes from big budgets, fancy buildings, and publication in academic journals.

A salesman of electronic instruments once told me what happened when he sold an oscilloscope to a university professor. Next day a professor down the hall called with only one question: What do you have that is more expensive than what the other guy bought? He bought the most expensive oscilloscope the company offered. Of course such things happen in government and industry as well, but not as often as in education where prestige is paramount.

Nor are educators immune to "empire building." You can check this for yourself by looking at the number of administrative employees in your school district. Unless that district is unusual, non-teachers will outnumber the teachers. At the university level, increasing administrative costs are becoming a national scandal.[190]

We need good education; our way of life depends on it. However we do not need the bloated administrations and other costly features that the empire building educational special interest has imposed on us. Even the conventional wisdom that we need to reduce class size is at least questionable.[191]

Monopolistic, empire-building government agencies try to increase their size and power. That is a natural human tendency.

No, it is not inevitable

With all those forces favoring collectivism, we might be tempted to give up. That we must not do. The game is not over. Collectivism is not inevitable. As I write this, it appears that the statists have the upper hand. In fact at times it

---

190   A internet search on something like "increase in university administrators" will find lots of information on this subject, including http://online.wsj.com/news/articles/SB10001424127887323316804578161490716042814.

191   An internet search on something like "class size doesn't matter" will find studies supporting both sides. For example https://www.aaeteachers.org/index.php/blog/647-new-study-class-size-doesnt-matter and the opposing view at http://www.washingtonpost.com/blogs/answer-sheet/wp/2014/02/24/class-size-matters-a-lot-research-shows/

appears that freedom is 20 points behind with only three minutes to go. However, the game is not over and we must continue to play – hard. Our freedom and happiness, and that of our children and grandchildren, depend on us. We must defeat the statists, both the well-intentioned and the tyrannical (who are sometimes the same people).

Chapter 20 Statism and Democracy

The statesman who would attempt to direct private people in what manner they ought to employ their capitals, would not only load himself with a most unnecessary attention, but assume an authority which could safely be trusted to no council and senate whatever; and which would nowhere be so dangerous as in the hands of a man who had folly and presumption enough to fancy himself fit to exercise it. (Adam Smith)

Diversity. Does it include the right to dissent from the official, government belief system? Can a church expect employees to not publically oppose its doctrine? Not according to the statists. They want everybody to think alike. Today, homosexuality and same-sex marriage are a quasi-religion that the statists try to force on the world; and they oppose the right to disagree with their belief. For example, the *San Francisco Chronicle* editorialized against Roman Catholic schools expecting their employees to refrain from public support of homosexual marriage.[192] Those schools are private, supported by tuition and the Church. They do not force anyone to attend either their schools or their church, yet the statists want to force them into the same box as public schools. Statists want to force people to support their secular quasi-religion. Such things as baking cakes and taking photographs for same-sex weddings are mandatory, even if that is contrary to deeply held religious belief.

Statists thus deny the right to free exercise of religion, then they go farther and try to establish a state quasi-religion from which nobody may dissent.

---

192   www.crisismagazine.com/2015/archbishop-attacked-over-catholic-schools. That source links the original editorial which, unfortunately, requires a subscription to access.

The statists insist that everybody think like them. Free men believe in freedom of belief, speech, and association.

Should diversity be allowed? That question separates the statist from the person who believes in liberty. It is a question of control vs. freedom. The statist wants to control everything, to dictate even aesthetics. He wants us to like what we are told to like. The believer in democracy wants to regulate only when there is a pressing need for regulation. Otherwise, we can determine our own preferences and act on those preferences.

It is a matter of who makes decisions in our lives, government officials or the individuals living those lives.

For example, let's look again at John III and his attempt to start his own taxi company. The city rejected his application on the grounds that there was no public need for another taxi company. Why should that be an issue? Do authorities have some superior wisdom that allows them to decide, both for the entrepreneur and for his potential customers, if a new taxi company should offer its services? Freedom would allow an entrepreneur to start his business and let the customers decide.

Unity of Purpose

One statist complaint is that, in free societies, ideas, efforts, and aspirations are guided by the different whims of individuals. Everybody runs off in different directions and there is no overall authority to decide how people should live. The collectivist wants to replace that with a common, unifying goal. If collectivism is enthroned and individualism suppressed, everyone will work for the same ends. Be it communist dictatorship, Fabian socialism, or simply the control of industry, the collectivists want "everybody on the same page." To them, the idea that people would work for their own ends is anathema, even when those different ends result in advantages for everyone. The irony is that many of those statists support, even demand, diversity of skin color and gender, yet they demand conformity of opinion and aesthetics.

That is a stark contrast between statists and free men. The free man welcomes diversity – real diversity, not just skin color and gender. He happily allows the sale of Windows based computers, Macs, and Linux systems. If one person wants a Ford while someone else prefers a Chevy, that is no problem for the free man. The statist, on the other hand, opposes individuality; everybody must fit in with the "right" ideas. This difference in mindset explains why the statist, while supportive of democracy in the abstract, often opposes and tries to overturn democratic decisions. Two examples will suffice.

Democracy in the Abstract but not in Reality

In the region of Portland, Oregon and Vancouver, Washington, there is a push to increase the amount of light rail. That includes a new bridge across the Columbia River that would, at great expense, include light rail. There is no question that something should be done, the existing bridge is old and inadequate. The issue is not the automobile and truck lanes, but the cost of including light rail, something Vancouver voters soundly rejected. Citizens in the Portland area, though not allowed to vote on this particular project, have opposed most extensions of light rail elsewhere. Any official who really believed in democracy would accept that and move on. Not the Portland authorities, nor the governor of Oregon. They have extended light rail into some areas over the objections of the residents. And, as I write this, the governor is continuing to push to include light rail on any new bridge, even if Oregon residents have to pay the entire cost. That is an anti-democratic response, not respectful of the will of people.

Another example is the very existence of the European Union. Initially, the plan was to have it ratified by a vote of the people in the various countries. That lasted until the first two countries (France and the Netherlands) to vote rejected it soundly. That ended the attempt to get democratic approval for the new European Union – but not the creation of that union. A team of lawyers made the proposed constitution unreadable by the average person. Then the governments imposed it on their countries without further consultation with the people. Those statists favored democracy – but only if the voters agreed with them.[193]

Such an attitude is, unfortunately, common among the politically powerful, especially the statist/collectivist types. Their respect for the citizens does not extend to citizens who disagree with them.

Democratic Statism?

Can a statist/collectivist government be democratic? Can we just vote for statist policies or powerful leaders, then impose them on everyone? In small, religious organizations, maybe. We saw some indication of that in Chapter 17. However, those organizations were not only small, they were voluntary and dissenters were free to leave. What happens if we scale that up to an entire country and make it mandatory?

First, collectivism is well, collective. It regards with suspicion anyone different from the norm, at least in political terms. The statists may accept people

---

193   Hannan, *The New Road to Serfdom,* op cit, pp42-43

who wear weird clothing, but they get upset when someone openly criticizes their government. The individualist, the odd duck who rejects the "wisdom" of the collective is not welcome.

Second, who will rise to the top in any collectivist government? As we shall discuss in Chapter 22, those people tend to be tyrannical, wanting to bend others to their own will and beliefs. Such people do not tolerate differences gladly. A "benign dictatorship" it may be, but a dictatorship it will remain, with "liberty" only for those who agree with the rulers. Goodbye freedom.

If We Have Perfect People

But what if we have voters and elected officials willing and able to put aside their own desires for the benefit of their fellow man (if we could find them)? Their desire would be to create the best possible system for everyone. Wouldn't that overcome the difficulty? Sadly, no. Even such a moral society would still make shipwreck on the shoals of reality. Human ability is as limited as is human morality, and righteous desires do not overcome those limitations. This would take us right back to the question of who has the ability to manage such things as shoe production in a perfectly moral country. The desire might be there but, as indicated in the Adam Smith quote at the beginning of this chapter, no human or group of humans would be able to manage all the details necessary to make a collectivist country function smoothly.

Values to Impose on the Country

And what if we could overcome the problems of morality and ability? Would we then have our utopia? No, there remains yet one more obstacle. In a statist society, everyone would want to impose the best values possible on the collective – but what are those best values? In a world of limited resources, how will they allocate those resources? Some will want heavy emphasis on medical research and treatment, others may think that efficient production of food and clothing takes priority. Then there will be those who put quality of life as the first objective and therefore want more music, art, and literature. Others will emphasize the preservation of natural areas, while yet others may want more scientific research.

For such a society to work, voters and officials would have to be not only perfectly moral and capable, but also in near perfect agreement on the issues. Such unanimity is as elusive as snow in Florida.

Seeking Agreement

How can we deal with the fact that normal people disagree with one another? There is a way, though that way is not compatible with collectivism. The solution is to apply the law in areas of general agreement and leave other decisions up to individuals. Government should pass laws against murder, child abuse, theft etc. and should do things like provide roads that are generally useful. As long as the law limits itself to areas of near total agreement, there is no problem. In Hayek's words, "When individuals combine in a joint effort to realize ends they have in common, the organizations, like the state, that they form for this purpose are given their own system of ends and their own means.... The limits of this sphere are determined by the extent to which the individuals agree on particular ends; and the probability that they will agree on a particular course of action necessarily decreases as the scope of such actions extends."[194]

In other words, the more things government meddles in, the less chance that citizens will agree. We can agree that we need national defense, law enforcement, and things of that nature. However once government starts deciding issues like what kind of retirement programs everybody must have, agreement will come only by force.

Democratic peoples can reach general agreement in only a few spheres. Outside those areas, wide disagreement is certain. Limiting government power to areas of agreement will encourage respect for and compliance with the law, and make for a happy citizenry. Forcing people to violate their personal values will create strife and provide excuses for contempt of the law, even for violation of that law. Laws outside those areas of agreement should be passed only rarely, for the most urgent of reasons, and only if they fit the requirements for external costs and benefits described in Chapter 6. We should avoid, insofar as is feasible, any forcing of the values of one person or group on anyone else.

Democratic governments work best if their laws are limited to areas of widespread agreement.

The Results of Seeking a Common Goal

At the start of this chapter we noted that the collectivist wants to replace freedom of choice with a common, unifying goal. In the statist mind, we should all be working toward the same end. But what happens when it comes time to agree on exactly what that common end should be? Unfortunately that is a

---

194   Hayek, op cit p103

question often postponed until we devise means of reaching that yet-to-be-determined common goal. We give decision-making power to a plurality, to elected officials, or even to bureaucratic "experts" removed from politics. That not only creates the means of seeking common goals, but allows those entities to determine what those goals shall be. Hayek compares this to a group of people agreeing to travel together without first agreeing where they intend to go. Most, if not all, end up at a destination not of their own choosing.

We see that in the socialistic countries of the world; and we see it in the United States of America. Many complain about how slowly Congress moves, but they fail to notice what created that problem. Government is asked to rule on everything from health care to the kind of light bulbs allowed, issues so varied that consistent majorities are impossible. As government reaches into more and more issues, it becomes less and less likely that people will agree. In fact, even on a single issue there are likely to be so many options that a majority becomes impossible without compromise, vote trading etc. Should we be surprised then that Congress delegates much of that law-making to the "experts" in the bureaucracy? Or that those "experts" impose rules most of us don't like, even some rules we think are silly? We have too many laws with no commonly accepted goals.

Nor can a common goal be reached by dividing that goal into smaller objectives. Plans are of necessity complete, the parts interrelated and dependent on one another. Splitting off the parts creates confusion and destroys effectiveness. The transportation planners, the food planners, the medical care planners may each provide a plan, but how will those plans fit together without an overall plan? And the differences of opinion among the people naturally militate against an overall plan.

To split up economic planning would be as foolish as it would be for a general to split up battle plans. If he gives each subordinate the ability to plan his part of the battle as he sees fit, the result will be uncoordinated actions and certain defeat. Instead, the general will create a single plan for each battle and order everyone to follow that plan. However the general has two great advantages: First, he has one and only one objective and can dedicate his entire planning and resources toward that one objective. Second, he has command authority; he can order everyone to follow his plan. Thus he can plan effectively and marshal his resources toward that one plan and its single objective.

The economic planner, on the other hand, must deal with many objectives, and different people will value those objectives differently. The people in the potato department will do as they see fit, regardless of what that does to the soap department. Neither can exercise any authority outside his limited bailiwick.

To correct that problem we have "taken the politics out of" many decisions, turning those decisions over to "experts" not accountable to the voters. That solves the authority problem. However there is no reason to expect the experts to have the same values as do the citizens. Inevitably they will impose their own value system on the community. As discussed in Chapter 12, we have given power to bureaucrats but have not sufficiently controlled how they use that power. In fact, we cannot control how they use their power without eviscerating their ability to "overcome politics." We have compounded that problem by giving power to separate agencies while providing no overall authority. That splits the plan into smaller, uncoordinated plans that may even work against one another.

Coordinating the Plans

There are two possible solutions to that problem. The first is to create some unelected overall authority, not accountable to the people. That way lies serfdom; such an authority will have dictatorial powers. That was what brought Hitler to power. Many Germans detested him personally, but thought him the only person strong enough to solve their problems.[195]

The other possible solution is to limit government power to areas of wide agreement, to allow it power over only the necessary external benefits and costs. That is the road to freedom, what the writers of the United States Constitution bequeathed to us if we can regain it. Only by limiting the scope of government can we protect ourselves from serfdom. Only in that manner can we give our John III and John IV the freedom John II enjoyed.

To quote Hayek again:

> It is the price of democracy that the possibilities of conscious control are restricted to the fields where true agreement exists and that in some fields things must be left to chance. But in a society which for its functioning depends on central planning this control cannot be made dependent on a majority being able to agree; it will often be necessary that the will of a small minority be imposed upon the people because this minority will be the largest group able to agree among themselves on the question at issue.... It is now often said that democracy will not tolerate 'capitalism.' If 'capitalism' means here a competitive system based on free disposal over private property, it is far more important to realize that only within this system is democracy possible. When it becomes dominated by a collectivist creed, democracy will inevitably destroy itself.[196]

---

195   Ibid, pp108-109
196   Hayek, Ibid, pp109-110

A Means or an End?

It has been said that democracy is the worst form of government except for all the others that have been tried. (Winston Churchill)

If capitalism is necessary to democracy, what about the reverse? Is democracy necessary to capitalism? Or more importantly, is democracy necessary to freedom? And does democracy guarantee freedom? Would that it were that simple; nice theories again collide with cold-blooded facts.

Does democracy guarantee freedom? Before the U.S. Civil War, any slave in the southern United States could have answered that question. Indeed any black person in the U.S. South could have answered it during the Jim Crow era.

Is democracy necessary to capitalism? Again the facts say otherwise. From the trading empires of Arabia to modern military dictatorships, undemocratic regimes have often allowed free enterprise. Why not? They like the tax money that is most readily obtained from wealthy subjects, and those subjects are most likely to obtain their wealth through trade, manufacture, or other businesses.[197] Dictatorships may put some restrictions on free enterprise, even control who is allowed to engage in capitalistic business. However, they often allow a great deal of economic freedom. This has worked better in the past than at present. Today, economic freedom is likely accompanied by information about personal freedom. Once the people see what a free society is really like, it becomes difficult to deny

---

197   Personal note: In graduate school I had a friend whose family used the government's desire for tax money and hard currency to escape mainland China. They established an export business and soon "discovered" that they needed a representative in Hong Kong to manage that end of the business. The government gave permission. Then the business grew and they needed more people in Hong Kong so more of the family moved there. That continued until they got the entire family to Hong Kong, whereupon they closed the business.

personal freedom. The Chinese learned that at Tiananmen Square, and they may learn it again if they continue their present course.

So democracy does not guarantee freedom, nor does lack of democracy always prevent economic freedom. What does that tell us? Simply that democracy should not be an end in itself. It should be a means to an end, and that end is personal and economic freedom. Indeed it tells us that even a democratically elected government must be restrained. Otherwise it becomes, as Benjamin Franklin said, "Two wolves and a lamb voting on what to have for lunch."[198]

Democratic government has proven the greatest system on earth for personal and economic freedom, and for economic growth. However, unless restrained, it risks regression to tyranny. That tyranny may consist of the majority oppressing a minority as in Sri Lanka (see Chapter 22), or the democracy may give way to overt dictatorship.

As Churchill implies, democracy is beneficial, but by itself is not enough; it must be accompanied by restraints on government power. It should be regarded, not as an end in itself, but as a means to the end of protecting freedom. And it must include the rule of law.

---

198   http://www.americanhistorycentral.com/entry.php?rec=469&view=quotes

Chapter 21 The Rule of Law

Rules which make it possible to foresee with fair certainty how the authority will use its coercive powers in given circumstances and to plan one's individual affairs on the basis of that knowledge. (F.A. Hayek)

A policeman approaches, gun drawn. "Put your hands on the top of the car and spread your feet. You are under arrest."

"What is going on? I haven't done anything wrong."

"Want to bet? Last month you cut down that tree in your yard, the one shading your garden. It is a felony to cut any tree in this city without a permit."

"But that law was passed only last week. What I did was quite legal."

"It is not legal now, and you are a felon."

"What about the mayor? Just yesterday I saw a landscaper cut down a tree at one of his rental houses. A friend in the permit department assures me that the mayor didn't even try to get a permit."

"Do you really think the mayor has to obey the same laws you do? And by the way, the mayor doesn't like those daisies in front of your house. As soon as you get out of jail you better replace them. The mayor prefers chrysanthemums."

You feel your hands yanked behind your back, then the cold steel of handcuffs around your wrists.

The Meaning of Rule of Law

The above, admittedly overblown, illustrates three important aspects of the rule of law:

First, the law should not be changed retroactively. For that reason the U.S. Constitution prohibits ex post facto laws.

Second, the law is supposed to apply equally to everyone, from the president to the panhandler on the corner. In countries with official aristocracies that may not be the case, but that is how it is supposed to work in the United States. It matters not who your parents were, what office you hold or held, who your friends are. Everyone is subject to the same laws and the same punishments. We may follow that standard imperfectly, but a standard it is, something we must strive for.

Third, the law was determined by one man, the mayor who demanded that people plant his preferred flowers.

Rule of law prohibits those kinds of arbitrary actions, plus one more.

Remember Robin Hood? In legend he was declared an outlaw. Not what he was accused of doing, the man himself was declared to be illegal. That is called a bill of attainder and is also unconstitutional. In countries that allow bills of attainder it is not necessary to convict a person of any specific crime; authorities just outlaw him. That may be convenient; sometimes we are confident that someone has committed crimes, but we just cannot get the evidence for a conviction. It is tempting to just say that the person is an outlaw and lock him up.

There are two problems with bills of attainder. First of course, we may be wrong. It is easy to convince ourselves that someone is a really nasty character and has committed some horrible crime when in fact he may be innocent. Or he may have done some nasty things that didn't violate the law, so we go beyond the rule of law and punish him anyway. Second, and even worse, authorities may use this to outlaw their political enemies. That happens in tyrannical regimes even today. If you lived in one of those countries and said something against the government, you might be declared an "enemy of the state" or "enemy of the people" and locked up. Tyrants love such rulings; they have less worry about people who express inconvenient opinions

The Law Does Not Say

What if you decide to do something unusual, something most people would not think of doing? It could be anything from doing a handstand on your roof to publishing really strange poetry. The law says nothing one way or another about your endeavor, so you go ahead. In the United States that is perfectly fine, what is not specifically prohibited is legal. Not in continental Europe! "To the Eurocrat, 'unregulated' is more or less synonymous with 'illegal.'"[199] In Europe, if you want to do something strange you better get government approval first.

That is another difference between freedom and statism. The statist expects people to get government approval before anyone can take action. The free man says, "Go ahead unless there is a law against it, and we won't make such a law unless there is good reason for it." The statist wants to regulate everything. Daniel Hannan, member of the European Parliament, often asks in that parliament why they need a new EU directive. The typical answer is, because there isn't one.[200] Somebody might do something without first asking, "Mother may I."

In a free society, everything is legal unless specifically made illegal. In a statist system, everything is often illegal unless specifically allowed. One has rule of law, the other has the rule of men.

---

199 Daniel Hannan, *Inventing Freedom*, op cit p80
200 Ibid

How Do We Get the Rule of Law?

It was the most boring high school assembly in memory, at least the first part. Our congressman spoke and blew enough hot air to bake Alaska. I don't remember what he said, but I do remember thinking it was about as useful as a snowmobile in the Amazon jungle. It was so bad that the principal had our government teacher speak after the congressman finished. He was much better; he compared the rule of law with the rule of men. He explained that we have fixed laws, established by duly constituted legislative bodies. We can depend on those laws, both to protect us and to allow us freedom to engage in legal activities. No arbitrary authority changes the law on a whim. Violations of law are prosecuted on the basis of evidence.

I found our teacher's comments very impressive; that is the way the law should work. Only later did I see the problem: any government is ultimately a rule of men. It is men and women who make laws. More importantly, it is men and women who enforce them, who decide if the accused is guilty or goes free, who decide if the law shall be enforced on everybody or only on some of the people. In short, it is men and women who decide if the law shall be only so many words, or if we will really abide by the rule of law. And those men and women are subject to temptation. They may apply their own desires and prejudices rather than what the law actually says. Unless restrained, powerful politicians and bureaucrats will create a rule of men. We will have rule of law only if we insist that our officials follow the law and constitution.

As I write this, we have a president who has decided that he can pick and choose which laws he will enforce and which he will ignore. He has unilaterally changed immigration law, the requirements for being on welfare for a limited time, and even parts of his own signature health care reform law. The health care law is especially interesting. That law makes it illegal to sell health insurance policies that do not meet certain requirements. After many complaints, the president decided, unilaterally, that he would allow the sale of policies that do not meet requirements. Then, when some in Congress suggested officially changing the law to allow what the president was doing, he threatened a veto. That is rule of man, not rule of law.

Did the president help the people with his unilateral decision on which insurance policies can be sold? Maybe, maybe not. It is certain that he created the confusion normally attendant to rule of men rather than of law. Citizens do not know if the president is going to change the law again tomorrow. He could decide that the law applies after all and invalidate all those insurance policies.

Sadly, we have people in positions of power who ignore Constitution and constitutional law, and instead use their power to change the law to their own taste. Those people also often change their rules to fit the situation; citizens cannot know what the rules say at any given time.

Changing Law- The Bucking Bronco of Life

Most anybody can sit on a horse that is standing still, or even walking. Once that horse starts to trot, canter, or even gallop it becomes more difficult to stay aboard, but still not too bad. However if the horse jumps, bucks, twists, and turns in all sorts of crazy directions almost nobody can stay aboard. The place a rider must sit changes so rapidly that such horses cannot be used for ordinary purposes.

The few people who can remain on bucking broncos for a few seconds win lots of money in rodeos.

A constantly changing legal code becomes the bucking bronco of daily life. Of necessity, the rule of law limits the frequency of changes in that law, a limitation we effectively have with congressional law. Though there is no constitutional restriction on how often a law can change, our legislative process assures that few changes will happen quickly, and that is a good thing.

Why must we limit the changes in the law? This is best answered with a consideration of the opposite. What would happen if the law were to change daily? If what was legal yesterday is illegal today but may change again tomorrow? You plan carefully to get your tax return done on time. Then comes the announcement: the filing date has been changed and returns must now be submitted a month earlier. Or one day you are allowed to turn right on a red light, next day that is prohibited but then the next week it is allowed again.

James Madison warned about this during the debate over ratification of the Constitution. "It will be little avail to the people that the laws are made by men of their own choice, if the laws be so voluminous that they cannot be read, or so incoherent that they cannot be understood; if they be repealed or revised before they are promulgated, or undergo such incessant changes that no man who knows what the law is to-day can guess what it will be to-morrow. Law is defined to be a rule of action; but how can that be a rule, which is little known and less fixed?"[201]

A constantly changing law has all the bad effects of arbitrary rule by men. Yet a collectivist society, with its myriad of rule-making bureaucrats, can change the rules as often as the bureaucrats like. Indeed, a collectivist society requires

---

201   James Madison, "Federalist Paper Number 62"

"flexibility" to meet the changing demands on a system expected to control everything. That will negate the rule of law.

Rule of Law and Collectivism

Collectivism requires state control of decisions. How much wheat shall we plant? What price shall we charge for that wheat, and for everything else bought and sold? How do we handle the unexpected storm that reduces the harvest? How many winter coats shall we make and what do we do if this winter is warmer or colder than normal? How could any legislative body appropriately deal with such details? If they tried, situational changes would quickly make their decisions obsolete.

The collectivist solution is to appoint bureaucrats to manage such things. Aside from the difficulties those bureaucrats face (see Chapter 19), that is the rule of men, not of law.

Collectivism must control so many details, in the face of so many changing conditions, that rule of law becomes impossible. Bureaucrats, quangos, people not constrained by law, must decide. They must have power to act quickly, a power subject to abuse. They may or may not be people of high morals and wisdom, but they will face a task beyond human ability. How will they decide between workers who want higher wages and the unemployed who might get jobs if wages were lower? Between farmers who want better prices and consumers who want less expensive food? Between environmentalists who want less energy consumption and citizens who want warm homes in the winter?

As planning expands, more and more such dilemmas raise their ugly heads. Bureaucrats acquire more power while citizens acquire more uncertainty. It is rule of men, not of law.

The problems of such ad hoc rulings are at least two-fold:

First, any such ruling will reflect the judgment of the bureaucrats who make the ruling. That judgment may or may not reflect the values of most citizens.

Second, such a ruling can seldom be anticipated; they often become effectively ex post facto laws. Furthermore, some other bureaucrat may treat the same situation differently and make different rules.

Once the law becomes too far reaching, it will inevitably become the tool of bureaucrats rather than a fixed and known legal code. True rule of law requires that the law be limited in scope, and it must be clear and understandable.

Legal Clarity?

Imagine that the police are after you again. A city ordinance makes it illegal to allow an excessive number of weeds to grow in any yard, and the police accuse you of violating that ordinance. Why are they ticketing you and not your neighbor? His yard has at least as many weeds as yours. Could it have anything to do with your letter to the editor opposing some police actions while your neighbor wrote in support of those actions?

If you go to court, how will you defend yourself? Mention your neighbor's yard and the judge will point out that his neglect, if such it be, does not justify your weed patch. Comparison with your neighbor's yard won't work, but something else might. You can point out that conviction requires proof beyond reasonable doubt that you violated the law. That would require proof that your weeds were excessive, but what does "excessive" mean? The word has no clear, specific meaning. If the term is not well understood, how can there be proof that your yard had an excessive number of weeds? A good judge would say that the law is unconstitutionally vague and dismiss the case.

It doesn't always happen that way. Harvey Silvergate has documented several cases in which federal law was unclear and the Justice Department took advantage of that to punish companies and their officers for supposed infractions. "Troublingly, the doctrines of misleading the citizen and 'void for vagueness,' which federal courts have applied in numerous cases with regard to state statutes... have not been applied consistently or with equal rigor in federal cases...."[202]

This even extends to putting citizens in situations where they cannot avoid breaking the law. In 2006 Christ Church in Greenwich, Connecticut discovered that the organist had loaded child pornography on his church-issued computer. The organist was fired and the computer turned over to attorney Philip Russell. That made Russell a criminal since possession of child pornography is illegal. Nor could he ethically turn the evidence over to police, that would betray a client. He destroyed the illegal material and for his trouble was charged with obstruction of justice and destruction of evidence. The law made it a crime to "knowingly alter, destroy, [or] mutilate any...any document or tangible object with the intent to impede, obstruct, or influence the investigation or proper administration of any matter."

202   Harvey A. Silvergate *Three Felonies a Day, How the Feds Target the Innocent,* Encounter Books, 2009. p xxxv

The law governing such situations was vague and difficult for even a lawyer to follow. The court ignored those trivialities and eventually Russell plea-bargained to a lesser charge.[203] Had he kept the evidence he would probably have been charged with possession of child pornography. By destroying it he got himself charged with destruction of evidence. Federal authorities ignored the fact that Russell could have had no intent to interfere with any investigation; he did not even know such an investigation was in progress.

This gets worse. Do you think that a court ruling that a law is unconstitutionally vague settles the issue? Think again! Walter L. Lachman and Maurice H. Subilia, Jr. were charged with selling materials that would help India develop nuclear weapons. The case hinged on the definition of materials "specially designed" for such weapons. The jury convicted, but then lawyers discovered that Commerce Department officials had given seminars where they taught that such materials did not meet the "specially designed" criterion. They also discovered an appellate case that decreed that the materials were not specially designed for nuclear uses. Judge Douglas P. Woodlock declared a not guilty verdict. Did that settle the issue? Nope. The government appealed and that same appellate court this time ruled that the materials were so designed. That court also ruled that, in spite of the same court giving diametrically opposed rulings on the wording, that wording was not unconstitutionally vague. The defendants were again convicted![204]

Mr. Silvergate provides more such examples of vague laws being used to get convictions or plea bargains. In many cases, prosecutors "climb the ladder,"

203   Ibid, pp159-165
204   Ibid, pp224-232

forcing employees or friends of their target to testify, sometimes perjuring themselves, to avoid risk of prison. The feds find it easy to do this; they claim that they can indict a ham sandwich. With threats of indictment, they frighten people into giving testimony that may or may not be true. That allows prosecution of people higher up in the targeted companies, often on the basis of questionable testimony.

That is not rule of law, nor is it compatible with freedom. It is rule of men – often the worst kind of men.

Rule of law can only exist under a limited government. The laws must be few and clear. The people's representatives must be able to manage them, and the people must be able to understand them. Such a limited government not only enhances freedom, it restricts opportunity for demagogues and other obnoxious people.

Chapter 22, The Rise of the Sour Cream

People took the favorable developments [created by freedom] for granted. They forgot the danger to freedom from a strong government. Instead they were attracted by the good that a stronger government could achieve – if only government power were in the "right" hands. (Milton & Rose Friedman)

That's all we need, leaders wise enough to manage all the complicated details involved in big government, and moral enough to work for the benefit of the people rather than for their own selfish interests. Do you know of such people? If so, please tell the rest of us where to find them and how to put them in positions of power and keep them there. Meanwhile, government officials will come from the people actually available in this imperfect world. Some are well-intentioned and wise. Some are well intentioned but foolish. Some are tyrants. Perfection eludes them all.

In fact our leaders come from a self-selected group: from people who seek positions of power and who have the ability to obtain that power. Some honestly seek the welfare of the country; some seek their own selfish ends. Do they have greater wisdom and integrity than the rest of us? History regards that question as a bad joke. Rulers, especially statist rulers, are seldom paragons of wisdom and integrity. This is most obvious among the dictators of the world, but even free countries are often plagued by the perverse.

Types of Statists

Statist rulers vary in cussedness. There are the "soft dictator" or "overprotective parent" types who genuinely want what is best for the people. They impose their own ideas on the country, from controlling what is in school lunches to forcing citizens to save for retirement and to buy health insurance, even telling them what that insurance must cover and that they must put retirement savings in a government run system. To "help and protect" the people, the soft dictator will set up a nanny state, including systems that provide oversight of the population – you cannot protect the people from themselves without some means of controlling them. That fosters dependence and prepares a people to acquiesce to whatever the authorities decree.

At the other extreme is the slave master such as the Kim family in North Korea or the Duvaliers in Haiti. They treat their people as property, forcing them to support extravagant life styles for the elite. And should a slave master take over a soft dictatorship, he will inherit the existing nanny state mechanisms and turn them into tools of tyranny. Overprotected citizens, like overprotected children, are easily misled.

So what kind of people rise to the top in a collectivist country? Stalin, Hitler, Mao, Castro, Pol Pot, and others. Misery makers all, they ruled with iron fists and treated their people, not as citizens to be served, but as pawns to use as they saw fit. Why are so many collectivist rulers despots? Is that accidental, or do the tyrannical have some advantage in the quest for power? We shall see why the latter is true.

Sour Cream

"The cream rises until it sours." The delightful book, *The Peter Principle,* uses that term to describe employees who get promoted into jobs they cannot do. There they stay, ineligible for further promotion. That is an interesting and useful concept, but not our concern here. We are concerned with the "cream" that is sour before it rises, the cream that rises *because* it is sour. Control freaks, tyrants, people who would force their ideas on others. Those people are the "sour cream," who obtain power because they want to control the rest of us.

Honey attracts flies.

Money attracts the greedy.

Government attracts the power-hungry.

That is just the way things are. And the more powerful the government, the more it will attract those of tyrannical mindset.

There are two reasons despots rise to the top in statist systems. First, they want that power – badly. Second, they are willing to do what it takes to reach the top, ethics be damned. Their favorite tool is demagoguery, which we shall discuss shortly. However we should first correct a common misconception, an erroneous belief about the dangerously powerful.

Concentration of Power

"We're for the people, they're for the powerful." During the 2000 presidential election, that was Al Gore's campaign slogan. It was a lie. Gore wanted to increase the already stifling power of the most powerful organization in the country. He and other demagogues would have us ignore the real power, the danger that threatens our freedom. They distract us with attacks on lesser threats while they increase the most dangerous power of all.

Statists claim, without evidence, that corporations and the wealthy are dangerously powerful. They never mention the most powerful entity of all: the federal government. If we really want freedom we must limit that government power. Statists want to go the opposite direction. They propose a transfer of power from individuals and businesses to a monopolistic government. That is a change not just in location, but in the very nature of power. No corporation can force people to obey its edicts, but the humblest government bureau can do just that. And the bureaucracy has no competition.

You don't like General Motors cars? Fine, buy a Ford, a Dodge or a Toyota. In fact, you need not buy a car at all. But what if you don't like the type of baby crib that the Consumer Product Safety Commission approves? Tough, nothing else is available. Or you don't like your local school system? At least you are allowed to send your children to private school – but in most cases you must still pay the government school, just as though you were sending your children there.

The power of government is inherently different from what any corporation or other private entity can have. It is a concentrated power, with no competition. Even if that government is not run by demagogues, it will have power over our lives that corporations can only dream of. The exception is the crony capitalists, those corporations in alliance with government and which get their power from government. For example, many insurance companies expect to gain more customers as Obamacare forces people to buy insurance. Such abuses will increase as government power increases. The potential damage is unlimited.

Our Defense Against the Nefarious

What can we do about it? There are two defenses. First, we must jealously defend constitutional, limited government. Limiting government power will limit the damage any demagogue can do. Second, we must carefully examine political candidates and reject the demagogues and the power hungry.

That last may be difficult, often we face an unhappy choice between two statists. As mentioned before, sometimes we have to hold our noses and vote for the lesser of evils.

And we must stay in contact with our representatives. They want to get re-elected; they will pay attention if the voters demand it. One state senator gave some friends of mine a lesson on that fact. They had been in the state capital testifying against a bill. After hours of that, the senator finally took pity on them. She took them aside and said in effect, "You need to understand that we don't care about your charts and statistics. What we care about is getting re-elected."

If we make it clear to politicians that their re-election depends on defending freedom, they will respond. As described in Chapter 10, we must maintain our Constitution by constant vigilance, and by keeping our representatives on a short leash.

The first line of defense is keeping demagogues out of office. The second is constant oversight of our hired help.

So let's look at how demagogues work and how we can keep them out of power.

Demagogues

Passions. Prejudices. Loaded words. Meaningless words. Imprecise words. Implying that aberrations are the norm. Behind a smokescreen constructed of such deception lurks the demagogue. With appeal to emotion he obscures reason. With loaded, meaningless, or imprecise words he persuades the unthinking. With passion and prejudice he sets us against each other. Making isolated aberrations appear the norm, he divides and conquers. Power is his goal and he cares not for the trouble he causes. Adolf Hitler plunged the world into the most destructive war in history. Jim Jones led his followers into mass suicide. Pol Pot created a hell on earth for his people. Other demagogues have caused similar problems.

Nor is the U.S exempt. Campaign ads and slogans typically appeal to emotions but say little or nothing. "Hope and change?" Hope for what? Socialism? Freedom? Tax-funded gifts to everyone? That was left to the voters' imaginations. Change? That could mean anything from absolute dictatorship to anarchy. The slogan was meaningless.

Are Republicans exempt? Hardly. I remember a full-page ad with the republican candidate's name in large print, along with the office he was seeking. It showed him beside a tractor with a farm in the background. A nice, pretty picture – and nothing else. Not a word about his qualifications or what he expected to do if elected. What did that tell the voters? Nothing! All image, no substance.

Pick a politician at random; look at his campaign slogan and advertising. Chances are it will have no real meaning. If you want to know his qualifications and intent you have to look elsewhere – and really work to get the information.

Nor is this limited to politicians. We have race baiters and others who encourage us to jump to conclusions before the facts are in. By so doing, they distract us from the more important issues while gaining power or money for themselves.

In Chapter 5 we discussed the false rape accusations involving Tawana Brawley, the rape charges against the Duke Lacrosse Team, and the shooting of Trayvon Martin. Those cases became national scandals, to the detriment of the falsely accused and even of at least one witness who refused to toe the party line. The race-baiting demagogues picked those isolated cases and used them to present an overblown perception of racism – while lining their own pockets and enhancing their own celebrity.

Meanwhile, the greatest danger to Blacks is not white men or police, but other black men. Of every thousand Blacks murdered, some 930 are killed by other Blacks.[205] That fact holds the key to prevention of many murders, yet it is hardly ever publicized. That is not to say that prejudice does not exist, it does. It is only to say that the major cause of Blacks being murdered is not white on black prejudice, but the behavior of some Blacks. Failure to address that problem sentences many young Blacks to death.

Unless we ignore the demagoguery and demand real information, we will fall victim to misinformation and bigotry. It may or may not become as bad as what happened in Ceylon, but it will harm us.

Demagoguery, an Example

Ceylon, 4 February 1948. One hundred elephants, decked out with white pantaloons and ruby necklaces. Golden-robed chieftains. Maidens and bare-chested youths dancing with bells on their ankles. All are celebrating freedom from British rule. Even Britain's Royal Duke & Duchess of Gloucester join the celebration. Prime Minister D.S. Senanayake raises the Lion Flag. Ceylon, later known as Sri Lanka, is no longer a British colony.[206] The celebration goes on for a week. Optimism reigns, and why not? The economy is good, the people educated, and the two ethnic/religious groups get along well.

---

205   http://www.bjs.gov/content/pub/pdf/bvvc.pdf
206   http://www.sundayobserver.lk/2008/02/03/plus01.asp

Ceylon (now Sri Lanka), 1984. Civil war rages, the culmination of decades of turmoil and discrimination. Peace and optimism? Only distant memories. The misery of war goes on. Why?

Before we look at the cause, we need to know a little about that new country. The population consisted largely of minority Tamils and the majority Sinhalese, differing in religion and language as well as ethnicity. The better-educated Tamils held a majority of government positions. The Sinhalese, whose native territory was more fertile than that of the Tamils, gravitated to agriculture. During the colonial period that worked well, there was essentially no animosity between the two groups.

Enter the demagogues, prime culprit one Solomon Bandaranaike. Sinhalese by birth, raised as a Christian and educated at Oxford, he did not even speak Sinhalese until he decided on a "divide and conquer" strategy to gain power. He converted to Buddhism, learned Sinhalese, and became an extremist for the Sinhalese language, culture, and religion. He used the classic technique of the demagogue: create a victim class, then stir up that class against its supposed oppressors. If done "right" the "victims" do not even think about why they lack the advantages of their "oppressors," they simply follow the demagogue.

Bandaranaike did it "right." He had little in common with the low-paid people he claimed to represent, but he promised to help them against the Tamil "oppressors." It worked. He became prime minister, then set out to increase his power by more demagoguery, more blaming of the Tamils for all the country's ills.

With the populace polarized, peace fled. The Sinhalese took complete control of the government and only Sinhalese was allowed as a government language. Other demagogues piled on, treating the Tamils as outcasts and restricting them from education and employment. Government power increased and freedom was restricted – steps toward serfdom. The rulers confiscated and attempted to manage businesses, predictably worsening the economy. All the fault of the Tamils, of course.

The Tamils complained and trouble brewed. Bandaranaike finally realized that he had gone too far, but fanaticism unleashed is a wildfire in dry brush. Attempts at compromise came too late.

Eventually poetic justice prevailed. Bandaranaike died at the hand of his own creation, assassinated by a Buddhist fanatic who believed he had not gone far enough. His death did not end the trouble. Ethnic strife fed on itself and unleashed a civil war that lasted until 2009.[207] At least that was its official end; racial strife torments those poor people to this day.

Bandaranaike is only one example. Milosevic caused similar problems in the former Yugoslavia. Hugo Chavez used class division to gain and maintain power in Venezuela. Others created similar tyrannies. Compiling a reasonably complete list would take more time than I want to spend, nor would you want to read such an account. This chapter is depressing enough already.

Any politician who bases his campaign on emotions, class division and similar distractions should get a big boot in the backside. We must think carefully about the type of people we are electing. Demagogues tend to rise to the top in any statist system, or even in free governments if we allow them to do so. Power attracts them, and they are willing to do what it takes to obtain that power. If we

---

207   Thomas Sowell, *Affirmative Action Around the World, An Empirical Study,* Yale University Press, 2004, pp78-79, 85-89

understand their motives and methods, we will be better able to counteract them. What gives demagogues the ability to advance at our expense?

Aid to Tyranny

In the latter part of the 1980s Nancy Foner studied nursing homes by volunteering in a non-profit home regarded as above average. She noted two nursing aides, Gloria and Ana. Gloria was mean and abusive to the residents. She would yell at them, order them to eat, and even went so far as to leave an immobile resident in an awkward and precarious position, supposedly as a joke. Another aide intervened and prevented a possible fall. Ana, on the other hand, was kind. She called one resident "Mama" and gently coaxed her to eat. She applied makeup to a resident who was unable to move her arms, and showed other kindnesses to those elderly residents.

It is obvious which care-giver most of us would prefer, but what did the nursing home administration do? Gloria was highly regarded and even put her in charge when the supervising nurses were away. Ana? She was constantly in trouble, reprimanded for taking the time to be kind to the residents. Ana failed to meet bureaucratic regulations while Gloria complied to the letter.[208]

That, on a small scale, demonstrates how bureaucratic rules give advantage to the heartless and punishes people for kindness and personal integrity. Government unrestrained lives by those bureaucratic rules and provides a similar advantage to heartless power-seekers. They are the people willing and able to manipulate the system for their own advantage.

---

208   Howard, op cit, pp78-79

Personality Problems

What kind of person is attracted to politics or other positions of power, and has what it takes to obtain that power? Be it a candidate for high school class secretary, president of the United States, or prime minister of some socialist country, what is that person like? Most likely he is an extrovert. He thrives on attention, and people are attracted to him. The contemplative, less extroverted type is easy to overlook – and much less likely to seek public office. That biases elections toward the extroverts, the back-slappers, the charismatic. They get people excited – but then what? Are such people the best leaders? Allow me to tell you about one of them.

I stood at ease with the other soldiers, enthralled as the commandant of the jump school spoke. One of the most effective teachers I ever had the pleasure to meet, he not only helped us learn the techniques of parachute jumping, he motivated us to jump out of perfectly good airplanes, a thousand feet above the ground. His charisma was amazingly effective, both as a teacher and as a motivator. Because of that charisma he never got another promotion.

In a previous assignment he commanded a brigade of paratroopers. The wind was blowing, hard enough that regulations prohibited airborne operations. You can guess where this is going. Yes, he got his troops fired up. They were tough paratroopers; a little wind wouldn't bother them. Let the wimps follow that silly rule. Out of the C-130s they went – two of them to their deaths. His charisma, unrestrained by wisdom, was dangerous as long as he was commanding officer.

Charisma can be a problem. Timothy Judge of the University of Florida business school says that being an extrovert is correlated with being chosen as a leader, but not with being a good leader. "We go for these effervescent leaders when what's really needed is a dull, focused, plodding [type] building effective groups and organizations."[209] Leadership requires two distinct but unrelated abilities. First and most important, the leader must make wise decisions. Second, he must motivate people to act on those decisions. Motivation without wisdom only leads people to Hell faster. It is the demagogue, the potential tyrant, who is most likely to motivate without wisdom.

Charisma attracts votes. It also causes people to act without thinking. Extroverts are the people likely to win elections, but not the most likely to make good decisions. The only possible solution is for voters to pay more attention to substance and less to image.

Beyond Personality

There are two opposite reasons for [supporting democracy]. You may think that all men are so good that they deserve a share in the government of the commonwealth, and so wise that the commonwealth needs their advice... On the other hand you may believe fallen men to be so wicked that not one of them can be trusted with any irresponsible power over his fellows. (C.S. Lewis)

Charisma alone does not a successful politician or tyrant make. The life of the party, the guy who entertains co-workers, the neighbor who enthralls us with his stories, all spice up our lives without seeking office. Political power requires something more. Not every charismatic wants political office, and even many who

---

209   U.S. News and World Report, November 2009, p26

have such desires lack the requisite drive. The people who obtain that kind of power pay a price to get it.

Be it a democracy or a dictatorship, advancement requires determined effort, including acquisition and organization of supporters. In a democracy, those supporters are voters and the campaign workers who convince those voters. In a dictatorship supporters must be those already in power, or people with the ability, often military ability, to overthrow those in power. In either system, competitors must be removed or rendered powerless. Only the most able and determined reach the top. That ability and determination can be used either to advance freedom or to enslave the people.

Who has the motivation, the drive, to make that effort? Only those most committed to their goals. Some of course want to help others. Some want power. Some are worse than others but all have a tendency to run roughshod over competition to reach their goals. Before we go farther, let's discuss the worst of the worst.

The Poison Cream

"It's all about me, and nothing is my fault." That could be the motto of any narcissist, but especially of the psychopath. Not all psychopaths are violent. Some are white-collar criminals. Some stay within the law, though seldom within normal ethical boundaries – and they fool people with ease. The white-collar psychopath is a talented deceiver. He uses his personality, his mind, and his silver tongue to separate people from their money, to acquire high-paying jobs, or to reach positions of power. He is the ultimate narcissist; and as far as can be determined he has, literally, no conscience. He is, however, charming, persuasive, often charismatic – and a world-class liar. He could run a red light, hit your car, and convince you that it was your fault. He is "cream" that is not only sour, it is poisonous – and he uses that characteristic to climb the ladder of power.

Psychopaths are almost certainly over-represented in political office. They like power, and their charm and lack of conscience help them obtain it.[210] They use that charm to distract citizens from the real issues, and to gloss over illogical thinking. They appear so wonderful that we seldom notice their logical fallacies, dishonesty, and other problems. Should we notice those defects, they are good at diverting our attention, making us ignore obvious problems.

The political psychopath is essentially a white collar criminal, expert at manipulating others. He is outgoing and makes friends easily, though the friendships are often short-lived. He creates an image of himself as a wonderful and inspiring leader – and inspiring he is! He collects dedicated followers who fail to think critically. He will typically have a group of pawns and patrons who pave his way to advancement. Those pawns and patrons refuse to believe any evidence against him.[211] He gets things done, but seldom to the betterment of the country. His motivation is his own selfish ends, and he will do what it takes to reach those ends. Our liberty depends on keeping him out of office.

How can we, citizens untrained in psychology, recognize the psychopath? Sorry, we can't. Even those qualified to diagnose the condition cannot do so at a

---

210   http://www.theatlantic.com/health/archive/2012/07/the-startling-accuracy-of-referring-to-politicians-as-psychopaths/260517/ Although this is a popular treatment, it does draw on some research. However as far as I can determine, research in this area is still in its infancy.

211   Paul Babiak, PhD and Robert D. Hare, PhD, *Snakes in Suits, When Psychopaths go to Work,* Harper 2006. Those characteristics are described throughout the book.

distance. That is the bad news. The good news is that we do not need a solid diagnosis. We need only know that a candidate has signs consistent with the condition. Any candidate having most of the characteristics of psychopathy is qualified only for rejection, be he a true psychopath or not.

Psychopaths are described as "without conscience, incapable of empathy, guilt, or loyalty to anyone but themselves."[212] They will have most of the following traits:

Superficial

Grandiose

Deceitful

Lack of remorse

Lack of empathy

Refusal to accept responsibility

Impulsive

Lack of goals

Irresponsible

Poor behavioral control

Adolescent antisocial behavior

Adult antisocial behavior[213]

Those traits are red flags, the growl before the dog bites. They warn us to avoid the candidate, though the personality of the psychopath distracts from that warning. Note, however, that lack of goals will not show up in the political

---

212   Ibid, p19
213   Ibid, p17

psychopath. That psychopath does not lack goals, he has very ambitious goals – all relating to himself.

Psychopaths may even fool the experts. For example, a former policewoman with psychological training worked on a crisis line two nights a week. She prided herself on her "ability to detect aberrance in other humans – both because [she] had that innate skill and through experience and training." She was greatly impressed with a wonderful young man who worked with her. Even when evidence of heinous crimes emerged, she had difficulty accepting his guilt.

The former policewoman was crime writer Ann Rule. Her young coworker was Ted Bundy, one of the most prolific and cruel serial killers in U.S. history.[214]

Like Ted Bundy, non-violent psychopaths and similar people are world-class deceivers; they will snare us unless our caution matches their deception, unless we look beyond the facades. Difficult though it may be, we must keep psychopaths and similar people far away from positions of power.

At present psychopathy is poorly understood, even the terminology is a bit uncertain. Psychopathy, sociopathy, personality disorder, and perhaps others names can apply. We know neither its cause it nor how to treat it. Indeed we know of no good way to recognize it. That lack of knowledge is a disadvantage, but with care we can keep such people out of office. Research is ongoing; maybe by the time you read this we will know more.

---

214   Ann Rule, *The Stranger Beside Me,* Pocket Books 1989, pxxxvi. Note that this book has been re-published several times with added information and commentary each time. Previous editions may lack this particular quote.

Powerful Problems

Not only psychopaths but other power-seekers often reach high office. Why are the powerful so perverse? What keeps the nice guy, the person of integrity, from reaching the top in a statist system? In one word: conscience. Statism is founded on the idea of a powerful state, superior in every way to the individual. One question and one only determines if an action is good or bad: does it advance the state? Lie to the people? Fine, if it helps the cause. Murder opponents? Do it, they cannot be allowed to spread their nefarious ideas. Lock up citizens in the gulag and treat them like slaves? Certainly, if that helps the collective. Have children spy on their parents? Of course, the state must know if those parents are considering anything rebellious.

The Power of the Unethical

This leads directly to the reasons why the unethical rule in statist societies. Suppose that, in a free country, your boss orders you to do something highly unethical. Your conscience objects and you can refuse; but what if you live in a collectivist country? There, your individual integrity is worse than useless; it only gets in the way of doing what the state demands. If you want to advance, or even keep your current job, you must ignore that integrity; bury it so deeply that nobody will even suspect it exists. You must never oppose the state, no matter what it demands of you. The state and only the state will decide what is good and what is bad; and the only question will be if it helps advance the state. If it does, anything goes, and you may not question your orders. Everything from small lies to murder of opponents is fair game. Indeed one prominent "manual of tactics" for collectivists explicitly states that action for the masses must supersede conscience; ethical standards must stretch with the times.[215]

This is a conflict of interest – big time. Monopolistic government decides what is right and what is wrong, and that same government benefits from what it decides. Historically in this country, churches and philosophers have taught right from wrong, then government made laws on that basis. When government declares that it has a monopoly on deciding right and wrong, the potential damage is again unlimited. Government, unrestrained by independent thinkers, will decree a "morality" to its own benefit.

Up the Statist Ladder

Who can move up in such a system? Not the man who insists on mercy, kindness, and treating everybody with respect. No, promotions go to the ruthlessly obedient, to the person who obeys without question. If he has a conscience at all, he has learned to ignore it. This is tailor made for the psychopath. Murder, deception, anything to carry out the wishes of the state, it won't bother him at all. Non-psychopaths can advance only if they have, as the Bible says, "their conscience seared with a hot iron."[216] The psychopath has no conscience to sear.

It is no accident that the Stalins, the Castros, the Hugo Chavez types rule the statist countries of this world. They and only they are willing to do what is necessary to advance in such systems. Their only ethic is power and serving

---

215   Alinsky, op cit. P25, 30-31. The entire second chapter of that book tries to show that normal ethics can be ignored to reach the goals of the collectivist organizers

216   *Holy Bible,* 1 Tim 4:2

themselves. Our collectivist friends are fooling themselves when they think that tyrants rule only by accident in statist countries.

An Attack of Conscience?

And what if someone in the ruling circle of a statist country should have an attack of conscience? Will he dare voice his doubts? Not if he is wise. Even if the others in that ruling circle agree with him, they will not dare say so out loud. Instead they will ostracize him, probably purge him and send him to the gulag.

Leon Trotsky learned that lesson the hard way. Though still a committed communist, he opposed Stalin's version of communism. Stalin first removed him from office, then exiled him, and finally murdered him and his family. Nor did that sort of enforced groupthink end with Stalin's death; statists continue to murder dissidents abroad. For example, in 2006 Alexander Litvinenko died a painful death in London, poisoned by polonium-210 after he had the temerity to defect from Russia and to speak out against his former bosses.[217]

Groupthink is mandatory in a statist country. Nobody dares express any thought contrary to the accepted doctrine. The entire group may want change, but nobody will dare mention it aloud. The status quo stays stuck on quo, no real progress allowed. And that status quo includes repression of the people.

Collectivist Rulers

Put all the above together and what have we got? Statist or collectivist rulers self-selected from the dregs of humanity. They obtain power by unethical actions, and they punish their fellow-man for any desire for freedom. Even should

---

217   http://www.bbc.com/news/uk-19647226

they have a change of heart, they find themselves trapped, forced to continue those unethical actions. The survivors, the people who reach the top, are the people willing to lie, steal, spy, deceive, and otherwise cheat to acquire and retain their power. Some are psychopaths; some have just learned to ignore their conscience. All place their own desires above the good of the country.

Castro in Cuba, Allende in Chile, Stalin in the USSR, the Kim family in North Korea, Chavez in Venezuela, all those and more got their power by actions that would violate the conscience of most free people. It is no surprise that their selfish desires continue to govern their lives. As it must in any collectivist country, the sour cream rises to the top, and there it stays.

Sour Cream in a Free Country

Are free countries immune to sour cream? Would that it were so! Even there the narcissist, the psychopath, the control freak, sees possibilities for power in government; he sees voters as fodder for manipulation. Even the honest politician can become addicted to power. All those try to increase their power at the expense of freedom. The power-hungry exist in free countries as well as in dictatorships.

As described in Chapter 1, freedom is an unstable state. Like a man working on a steep roof, we must fight to keep our balance in a precarious place. Unless we work at it, our home-grown control freaks will lead us to statism. Only constant alertness and effort will restrain their nefarious ambition. And we have reason to remain alert.

Power Seekers in the United States

Much as I wish it were otherwise, deception and demagoguery are alive and well in the U.S. I must mention the characteristics of some U.S. leaders, including a deception that affected me personally.

In 1969, along with millions of other young men, I received an "invitation from the president," a draft notice. The Vietnam War raged and the army needed cannon fodder. Though I went to Germany instead of that "tropical paradise," it took two years of my life. The U.S. got heavily involved in that war because of an event that never happened. Allegedly, North Vietnam twice attacked a U.S. destroyer in the Gulf of Tonkin. The first attack was real, but the second was not and commanders knew it. However some officers twisted the facts and Secretary of Defense McNamara lied to Congress to get the Gulf of Tonkin Resolution, authorizing the president to do whatever he deemed appropriate.[218]

Would the United States have been as heavily involved in Vietnam without that deception? There is no way of knowing. However it is certain that our leaders mislead us at the time. And that is not the only lie our leaders told us.

Sadly, at this writing (2014), we have a president who seems not to hesitate to lie, and some congressional leaders and media people who support him in that. The president knowingly misled the citizens with a claim that, under his proposed health insurance reform, they would be able to keep their insurance and doctor if they wanted. In another case, when an Islamic fanatic murdered our troops in Fort Hood he blamed "workplace violence," refusing to acknowledge that the murderer was an Islamic fanatic who had openly expressed his desire to aid our enemies. In yet another case, his administration flagrantly and knowingly blamed

---

218   http://www.usni.org/magazines/navalhistory/2008-02/truth-about-tonkin

the murder of our diplomats in Libya on a video that the murderers had probably never seen. Authorities refused to mention the fact that our own intelligence had determined that the killers were Islamic terrorists and that the video in question had nothing to do with the attack. Other examples abound. Our president seems to regard truth as optional at best.

By the time you read this, will we have an honest president, or another liar? That depends on citizens, citizens who either vote wisely or swallow the line of demagogues.

We have not yet descended to the state of Nazi Germany or Stalinist Russia, but it is ominous when our leaders lie so facilely. Their ethics seem to approach those of the statist/collectivist system. The honesty required in a free country is nowhere in sight. How long can we maintain any semblance of freedom if we do not replace such people with leaders whose values are more compatible with a free people?

Innocent until Proven Guilty?

I cannot accept your canon that we are to judge Pope and King unlike other men, with a favourable presumption that they did no wrong. If there is any presumption it is the other way, against the holders of power, increasing as the power increases. Historic responsibility has to make up for the want of legal responsibility. Power tends to corrupt, and absolute power corrupts absolutely. Great men are almost always bad men, even when they exercise influence and not authority, still more when you superadd the tendency or the certainty of corruption by authority. There is no worse heresy than that the office sanctifies the holder of it. (Lord Acton)

I close this chapter debunking another misconception. Politicians accused of misbehavior often claim that they are innocent until proven guilty. For example, some in Congress so defended President Clinton during the latter's impeachment.[219] Utter nonsense! A person is either guilty or not guilty, and no verdict will change that fact. The accused is not innocent until after the trail, he only has a right to be *considered* innocent in the court of law. An incorrect verdict means a miscarriage of justice, but changes underlying guilt or innocence not at all.

In the second place, the right to be considered innocent until proven guilty applies specifically in courts of law and to those accused of a crime. It does not apply to politics. We must hold our politicians to a higher standard. They come to us seeking our votes, essentially asking for a job. Like any job applicant, it is up to them to show us why we should hire or retain them, and it is up to us to investigate their qualifications. If they are accused of bad behavior, we have no obligation to look at the evidence – and the burden is usually on them to show why the accusations are false. There is one caveat however. Politicians have been known to make false accusations against their opponents. We must be careful about accepting such accusations.

In a democratic system we get the leader we deserve, a George Washington or a Joseph Stalin. Only by actively seeking and supporting candidates of integrity and wisdom, candidates committed to freedom, will we overcome our current problems. We must thoroughly investigate those candidates, their backgrounds and integrity. And we must cut through the fog of mis-communication they so often use to hide their intent. Our freedom depends on it.

---

219   http://www.washingtonpost.com/wp-
    srv/politics/special/clinton/stories/delegation091298.htm

Chapter 23 Communicating Confusion

The naive radicals think that under Socialism the "people" will run everything. Actually, it will be a clique of Insiders in total control, consolidating and controlling all wealth. (Leon Trotsky)

It is significant that the nationalization of opinion has proceeded everywhere [together] with the nationalization of industry (E.H. Carr)

The collectivist has a problem, two problems in fact. Both are rooted in the need to create at least the perception of unanimous support. Significant opposition would encourage everything from black markets to open rebellion. "To make a totalitarian system function efficiently, it is not enough that everybody should be forced to work for the same ends. Although the beliefs must be chosen for the people and imposed upon them, they must become their beliefs, a generally accepted creed which makes the individuals as far as possible act spontaneously in the way the planner wants."[220]

Two problems obstruct that unanimity:

First, there are always some who prefer to remain free, who will continue to oppose statism. Left alone, those people will propagate their ideas and create dissatisfaction. That dissatisfaction poses a danger to the rulers.

Second, even those who enthusiastically seek collectivism support a theoretical version, an ideal statist society. They are less supportive of the versions of collectivism actually available in this imperfect world. The rulers must lead them to believe either that things are wonderful in spite of small problems, or that the problems are temporary and will soon disappear.

---

220   Hayek, op cit p171

Those sources of dissatisfaction must be hidden lest they contaminate the rest of the people. Deception becomes a necessity.

The deceivers use two primary techniques. The first and most difficult, they hide the facts, twist them beyond recognition, or replace them with faulty assumptions. The second technique is faulty reasoning from those alleged facts. The warning for citizens is obvious. We must examine both the supposed facts and the reasoning leading from those facts to the conclusion. If either is faulty, we must reject the conclusion.

Nor need the deceivers even realize that they are deceiving. They may just be slipshod in reasoning or fact-finding. It is human nature to seek evidence for what we prefer to believe. We easily ignore or misconstrue facts and make prodigious leaps of ill-logic to support our biases.

Skewed Statistics

For example, supporters of gun control claim that 70% to 90% of guns in the hands of Mexican criminal cartels come from the United States. "Mexican drug cartels get most of their guns from the United States."[221] That is the only part of the statistics they emphasize. However their source goes on to qualify the claim, saying that 70% of the guns *recovered and submitted for tracing* come from the U.S. That source, however, does not specify what percentage of those recovered guns was submitted for tracing. A much better discussion, but one the politicians seldom mention, clarifies. According to the GAO report:

---

221   http://www.wola.org/commentary/four_facts_about_gun_legislation_and_
     cartel_violence_in_mexico

Some 30,000 firearms were seized from criminals by Mexican authorities in 2008.
Information pertaining to 7,200 of that 30,000 (24 percent) was submitted to the U.S. Bureau of Alcohol, Tobacco, Firearms and Explosives (ATF) for tracing.

Of those 7,200 weapons, the ATF could trace only about 4,000.

Of that 4,000, some 3,480 (87 percent) were shown to have come from the United States.

Almost 90 percent of the guns seized in Mexico in 2008 were *not* traced back to the United States.[222] Guns obviously from other sources, guns with no serial numbers, were not traced and not likely to have originated in the U.S. The sample was badly skewed. When we look at the whole picture, it is very different from what we see if we fixate only on one slice of available information.

We need to examine carefully all supposed evidence, be it for the side we support, the side we oppose, or our own carefully constructed arguments. Only thus can we hope to cut through the fog of contradictory and unsupported claims such as the following about Obamacare.

Spin, Spin, Spin

"The non-partisan Congressional Budget Office report says that Obamacare will cost the United States the equivalent of 2 million to 2.5 million full time jobs."

"The Congressional Budget Office report clearly states that Obamacare will not produce an increase in unemployment."

---

222   http://www.stratfor.com/weekly/20110209-mexicos-gun-supply-and-90-percent-myth#axzz3ENVMNE9w

Both statements refer to the same report, and partisans have distributed both quite widely. What does the report really say?

"The reduction in CBO's projections of hours worked represents a decline in the number of full-time-equivalent workers of about 2.0 million in 2017, rising to about 2.5 million in 2024."[223]

However it adds:

"The estimated reduction stems almost entirely from a net decline in the amount of labor that workers choose to supply, rather than from a net drop in businesses' demand for labor."[224]

So the reduction in employment is a combination, mostly people voluntarily not working (subsidized by taxpayers) and some job loss. The claim that it is "almost" all voluntary is of course rather hazy; what does "almost" mean? Clearly, some jobs will disappear, and some people will voluntarily leave the workforce. However involuntary unemployment will be neither as great as one side claims nor as negligible as the other side would have us believe.

Both sides engage in selective quotation of the source. One side ignores the fact that many people are expected to voluntarily depend on taxpayer subsidies instead of their own earnings. The other ignores the fact that there are some real job losses, and glosses over the fact that taxpayers are subsidizing voluntary unemployment. Both sides are misrepresenting the facts.

Interestingly, the statist side upped the ante with creative semantics. They invented the term "job-locked" to describe people who work for a living. They

---

223   http://www.cbo.gov/sites/default/files/cbofiles/attachments/45010-breakout-AppendixC.pdf, p117

224   Ibid

seem to think that working for a living is a bad thing. Then House Minority Leader Nancy Pelosi said, "What we see is that people are leaving their jobs because they are no longer job-locked."[225]

As that example shows, neither side is guiltless in the battle of information; both twist facts and engage in questionable reasoning. However there is one weapon in this battle that belongs totally to the statists.

The Ultimate Information Weapon

Here it is: the information weapon that comes naturally to the statists, but which free men cannot use. Should they use it, they cast aside the mantle of freedom and enter the statist camp.

That weapon is control of speech and of the press, control of the information and reasoning to which citizens are exposed. Collectivism requires suppression of contrary views, either officially or by such measures as peer pressure, ridicule etc. No statist society can coexist with freedom of information, nor can a free society exist without it.

In the "advanced" collectivist regimes such as Hitler's Germany or North Korea today, this can be rigidly enforced. Dissent is a ticket to the gulag or the concentration camp. However it need not start that strictly. We have, even in the "free" countries, growing restrictions on free speech.

Many college campuses in the U.S. have what amount to speech codes, prohibiting advocacy of certain viewpoints. For example, the University of Kansas placed a professor on administrative leave after he sent an anti-NRA

---

225   http://hotair.com/archives/2014/02/05/pelosi-fighting-job-lock-lets-americans-follow-their-passion-like-leaving-the-workforce/

tweet.[226] From the other side, Modesto Junior College prohibited students from distributing copies of the U.S. Constitution in observance of Constitution Day. Their policy was that such speech is free as long as it is approved five days in advance and limited to a small "free speech area." Happily that policy has been changed as a result of a lawsuit supported by FIRE, the Foundation for Individual Rights in Education.[227]

In an even more onerous example, the University of Minnesota had planned to require "cultural competence" of all education students. That was intended to include reeducation, weeding out, or refusal of admission to those deemed not to meet the narrow definition of culturally competent. "The proposal, initiated by the college's Race, Culture, Class, and Gender Task Group, sought to require each future teacher to accept theories of 'white privilege, hegemonic masculinity, heteronormativity, and internalized oppression.'"[228] That would have put our precious young people at the mercy of teachers with a narrow viewpoint. Fortunately, wiser heads defeated that proposal.

Send people to prison for speaking against the accepted belief? Not yet, but some suggest it. Assistant Professor Lawrence Torcello of the Rochester Institute of Technology says, "We have good reason to consider the funding of climate denial to be criminally and morally negligent. The charge of criminal and moral negligence ought to extend to all activities of the climate deniers who receive funding as part of a sustained campaign to undermine the public's understanding

226   http://www.thefire.org/cases/university-of-kansas-anti-nra-tweet-results-in-professors-suspension/
227   http://www.thefire.org/cases/modesto-junior-college-students-barred-from-distributing-constitutions-on-constitution-day/
228   http://www.thefire.org/victory-for-freedom-of-conscience-as-university-of-minnesota-backs-away-from-ideological-screening-for-ed-students-2/

of scientific consensus."[229] He wants to make it a criminal offense to oppose accepted dogma.

The global warming/climate change issue is certainly controversial, as it should be. Both sides get paid, some by industry and some by taxpayers. However, censorship of scientific discussion is not only unconstitutional, it is the surest way to stop scientific progress. Galileo was forced to recant his claim that the earth revolved around the sun. Will we return to similar scientific censorship today?

Nor are such restrictions limited to campuses. There is a trend to oppose even the mention of certain viewpoints, especially those contrary to the wishes of "protected" classes such as homosexuals, minorities, or certain religions such as Islam. There is a growing belief that people have a right not to be offended. That is a very slippery slope; the definition of what is offensive is often left to the "offended." They can claim offense at all sorts of things and the "offender" has no way of knowing beforehand what is offensive today and what will be offensive tomorrow.

Let us be clear, there is such a thing as offensive speech, and those who use it should be ashamed of themselves. However, freedom requires the right to freely disseminate ideas; and that freedom has led to progress in many areas. We must allow speech we disagree with as well as speech we favor. If we restrict what people may say, we replace freedom with statist control. That opens the door to the thought police.

---

229   https://theconversation.com/is-misinformation-about-the-climate-criminally-negligent-23111

Official Federal Speech Restrictions

Attempts to inhibit free speech have even spread to the federal government as the Internal Revenue Service selectively audits some organizations. An official Treasury Department examination of that organization reports, "The IRS used inappropriate criteria that identified for review Tea Party and other organizations applying for tax-exempt status based upon their names or policy positions instead of indications of potential political campaign intervention."[230] The IRS not only went after Tea Party groups, it extended this special treatment to "political action type organizations involved in limiting/expanding Government, educating on the Constitution and Bill of Rights, social economic reform/movement." And that was *after* two revisions of IRS criteria intended to solve the problem.[231]

Who decided that educating on the Constitution and Bill of Rights was worthy of extra IRS attention? As of this writing, we do not know. What we do know is that those audits were aimed at particular political positions. The effect, and probably the intent, was to discourage those viewpoints.

Statist efforts to mislead go beyond limiting information, serious though that is. The flip side is creation of biased, even untruthful, propaganda. Once the authorities have control of available information, it is easy to propagate falsehoods. Hitler's blame of the Jews for his country's economic problems, Stalin's accusations of treason against anyone he suspected, and many other evils happened when there was no alternate source of information. Truth ceased to exist; there was only "information" that aided the statist program. Statist controls create an "ethical" objection to even listening to contrary viewpoints. Then they

---

230   http://www.treasury.gov/tigta/auditreports/2013reports/201310053fr.pdf p2
231   Ibid, p38 on paper, p44 in the .pdf

use their propaganda machine to generate "information" that militates against freedom and supports collectivism.

Lies, Deliberate and Flagrant

The Soviets were masters of deceit, and their falsehoods continue to cause problems today. For example, as though animosity between Jews and Arabs were not already bad enough, they spread the forgery *Protocols of the Elders of Zion* throughout the Arab world.[232] That stirred up existing animosities and contributed to the continuing violence in that part of the world.

Lt General Ion Mihai Pacepa is the highest ranking eastern bloc intelligence officer ever to defect. He knows how the USSR worked, how it got its satellite countries to do much of the dirty work. His book *Disinformation* describes their methods. While lying and skullduggery are nothing new in international relations, the USSR raised that to a whole new level. Mao claimed that a lie repeated a hundred times becomes the truth, and the Soviet bloc used that to its advantage. The standard technique was to start with a kernel of truth, build lies around that, then continue repeating the lie. Eventually people forget the truth, or those who know the truth die off. The lie becomes "truth."

---

232   *The Protocols of the Elders of Zion,* aka *The Protocols of the Learned Elders of Zion,* is a pre-Soviet Russian forgery claiming to be a Jewish plan to rule the world. It has created havoc throughout its history, including being instrumental in Hitler's crusade against the Jews. cf. http://www.history.ucsb.edu/faculty/marcuse/classes/33d/projects/protzion/DelaCruzProtocols Main.htm See also Pacepa, Lt General Ion Mihai and Professor Rychalk, Ronald J., *Disinformation, Former Spy Chief Reveals Secret Strategies for Undermining Freedom, Attacking Religion, and Promoting Terrorism,* 2013, WND Books, pp 96-97, 99. Soviet Bloc distribution of that forgery is documented in Pacepa's book, pp 262-263

Modern science has shown just how Mao's claim works. Psychological research has found that people tend to accept the familiar. Repeat something many times and it becomes familiar, thus accepted as true. That is not 100% effective, if something is obviously false it won't work. However, it is very effective for claims not obviously false.[233] As citizens, we must be on the lookout for such "proof by repetition" from politicians and from others.

Disinformation, as opposed to misinformation, uses other entities to distribute the falsehoods. For example, Mother Jones is a well-known statist publication that would like to be accepted as independent. It may in fact be independent today, but Pacepa shows that it was initially linked to the KGB through connections of its founders. Also, the KGB effectively managed the World Council of Churches and other such organizations. This technique allows the creators of the disinformation to stay at arm's length and create the impression that the lies are coming from neutral sources.

Pacepa's main example (covering nearly 140 of the 355 pages) is the character assassination of Pope Pius XII, intended to discredit religion in general and Christianity in particular. Pius XII was regarded as a hero for his work in saving so many Jews during World War II. Then the Soviet bloc went to work. They put out repeated disinformation, waited until the people who really remembered events died off, and even created a misleading dramatic production (*The Deputy*, also called by other names). Soviet intelligence thus painted him as Hitler's pope and got a lot of people to believe that he did nothing to protect the Jews and even assented to the Holocaust. That is an example of what they called

---

233   Daniel Kahneman, *Thinking Fast and Slow,* Farrar, Straus and Giroux, 2011, pp61-64

"framing." They changed a person's reputation, painted him as just the opposite of what he really was. Framing in fact goes both ways. They slander a good person, or make an evil man appear good. The latter is often used for such things as painting former KGB leaders as kind reformers.

A major disinformation success, already mentioned, was the wedge driven between the Islamic world and the west, and especially between Islam and Judaism. Though there was already animosity there, Soviet bloc actions made it much worse. Along with the *Protocols of the Elders of Zion*, they distributed "documentation" that the US was a Zionist country whose aim was to transform the Islamic world into a Jewish fiefdom. Pacepa's organization alone distributed thousands of copies of that intellectual poison every month. Sadly, they were quite successful.[234]

With control of information, statists are in position to change ethical expectations.

Statist Ethics

Ethics may vary, but every group has some rules that it expects people to honor; even organized crime has certain expectations of its members. Statist societies are no exception, indeed such a code of conduct is more important in collectivism than in a free society. Free men can be different, weird, even loose cannons as long as they do not interfere with others. Not so the collectivists. They must not step out of line lest the collective mind lose focus, or independent thinking lead to unacceptable ideas. Such societies strive for tight surveillance of

---

234   Pacepa, Op Cit pp 262-263

their people, but they cannot watch everybody all the time. Only by creation of a new set of ethics can the collectivists fully control the people.

To accomplish that, they must impose a system of ethics founded on their prime good: advancement of the collectivist society. And they must prevent people from learning the advantages of any other system. They invert the biblical injunction, "For he that is not against us is on our part." (Mark 9:40). Their motto is effectively, "what does not advance our cause is evil."

For the fully statist society nothing is neutral, even amusements, art or science. Anyone who disagrees with the official line is an enemy of the people. That applies especially to anyone with the temerity to publicize information or belief contrary to what the authorities decree shall be truth. It is "unethical" to contradict those authorities. While there are exceptions, such twisting of ethics is common among those who want to control their people.

The Infallibility of Statist "Ethics"

Biological science under Stalin was an especially appalling example. Trofim Lysenko gained control of Soviet agricultural science with his "socialist genetics." His methods, mandated on collective farms throughout the country, eviscerated production and played a key role in repeated famines and the death of millions. Evidence mattered not at all, his ideology was what was important. Scientists who disagreed risked the gulag.[235] Lysenko set back Russian biological science decades.

On the other hand many statists, including both the Soviets and post-Soviet Russians, excel in the fields likely to impress the rest of the world. The Russian

---

235   http://www.britannica.com/biography/Trofim-Denisovich-Lysenko

space program was and remains first-rate. Russian chess players dominate the game. They spend lavishly on their athletes in order to show that their system is the best in the world. They also produce the best theoretical mathematicians in the world, useful for cracking the codes of the free world. Out of sight of the world, they present a different picture. The USSR's famous factories were environmental nightmares. Their medical system provided good care for the elite, but the common people made do with what amounted to third-world care. Their collective farm system, on some of the richest agricultural land in the world, frequently left people hungry.

What system of ethics created those public successes and hidden failures? It was a system designed to control people. The people had to be led to support the diversion of resources to the newest rocket or sports success, but never complain when they went hungry and lived in bad housing. They had to have pride in the world-class ballet troupe, but be satisfied with poor clothing for themselves. The rulers created an ethic that ignored individual needs while glorifying the public accomplishments of the state. It helped that authorities controlled the press; they could exaggerate accomplishments and hide problems. They could even make trivialities seem like great accomplishments; a world chess champion is nice, but hardly a replacement for adequate housing. Yet by emphasizing the chess champion and blacking out news of the housing, they moved people toward the national groupthink they sought.

And those who disagree? The Soviets and other statists deal with them easily. Their opinions are illegal attempts to undermine the state. They are enemies of the people. Their sedition gives aid and comfort to the enemy. A few years in the gulag should show them the error of their ways.

It is important that this national ethic apply to all aspects of life. Much like military service, collectivism requires uniformity. And, much like military service, you cannot have uniformity if people are allowed to have their own ideas, even about minor things like their clothing. The person who acquires a better suit or dress may begin to think for himself about other things. This ethical system must penetrate every aspect of life – and it must do so with the force of law. If it is wrong it should be illegal, no matter how trivial.

Because nobody can think of all possibilities ahead of time, much control must be ad hoc. The authorities will decide, even ex post facto, that something should not be permitted. That has a big advantage: they can ignore violations by the favored and apply such ad hoc rules to people deemed undesirable. No need for trivialities such as proof that the offender violated any law.

"Totalitarianism... condemns any human activity done for its own sake... Science for science's sake, art for art's sake are equally abhorrent to the Nazis, our socialist intellectuals, and the communists... it might produce results which cannot be foreseen and for which the plan does not provide."[236]

As mentioned, not all statist systems indulge in all these measures. However all do restrict freedom and some use all possible techniques to control their people and what those people are allowed to believe.

Multiplicity of Rules and Regulations

In addition to ad hoc rules and flexible laws, collectivist governments can take advantage of the sheer number of regulations. They multiply rules to the point that it is nigh impossible to avoid slipping up and breaking some law. Then

---

236   Hayek, op cit, p177

they arrest, or sometimes blackmail, anyone suspected of lack of loyalty. So what if they did not know about that law they inadvertently broke? Ignorance is no excuse.

I fear that we are creating such a monster in this the U.S. today. Not only have Congress and state legislatures passed a tremendous number of laws, but they have created bureaucracies, the quangos of Chapter 12. Those bureaucracies have the power to effectively make law, but are essentially accountable to no-one. Do you think you can go a week without violating some law or regulation? Maybe one you don't even know about? Probably not, especially if you run a business. And even if you somehow manage to comply with all the laws and regulations, those bureaucracies have the power to "investigate" you for possible violations. That requires your time, money, and maybe your employees' time to defend against an agency with unlimited resources. They can continue to harass you as long as they chose. Guilty or not, you can suffer sullied reputation and the cost of defending yourself against those investigations.

One example is Catherine Engelbrecht who founded the organization True the Vote, an effort to oppose voting fraud. She and her husband were targeted by the IRS, OSHA, the FBI, and the BATF.[237] While it is impossible to prove beyond doubt that those actions were ordered by the president or others high in his administration, that organization is only one of many anti-statist groups that federal bureaucracies have investigated. Why is it that so many administration opponents "just happen" to be chosen for investigation while statist groups and administration supporters were much less likely to face such scrutiny?

---

237   http://www.nationalreview.com/article/348756/true-scandal-jillian-kay-melchior, see also http://canadafreepress.com/index.php/article/61052.

As of this writing, there are some congressional investigations in progress, looking at the evidence of partisan retaliation by the IRS and other agencies. Results are not yet known, but we do know that the real duty to prosecute malfeasance in office rests with the Department of Justice. The very administration accused of malfeasance controls the department charged with prosecuting any violations. Can we expect them to properly investigate themselves?

It is really up to the voters to hold officials accountable for misuse of their power.

What about issues not overtly political? Does the U.S. have rules on them today? Not officially, but in many cases "political correctness" supersedes evidence. One of the most widespread such cases is the question of differences between men and women. Many statists today have an unquestionable belief that, beyond biological plumbing, there is no difference. That is founded on political correctness, not evidence; science points in quite the opposite direction. Yet anyone with the temerity to suggest that the differences in hormones and brain structure might lead to differences in preferences is likely to be ostracized. Lawrence Summers was forced to resign as president of Harvard University, largely because he suggested looking at science to see if biological differences might cause the imbalance of women and men working in the sciences.[238] [239]

Other "untouchable" questions are the value of affirmative action and the cause of homosexuality. The "politically correct" belief is that affirmative action

---

238   http://www.thecrimson.com/article/2005/1/14/summers-comments-on-women-and-science/

239   http://www.washingtonpost.com/wp-dyn/content/article/2006/02/21/AR2006022101842.html

helps minorities, and that homosexuality is genetic. There is still plenty of dissent on those questions, but the self-appointed elitists excoriate those dissenters. Science matters not a whit; anyone disagreeing with them is automatically considered bigoted. Such dogma, unsupported by empirical evidence, threatens our freedom and our ability to advance. Progress requires rational discussion of different ideas.

Statism on the Attack

Collectivism is not idle; it continues to attack "mere" empirical fact. In the mind of the extreme statist, "The word 'truth' itself ceases to have its old meaning. It describes no longer something to be found, with the individual conscience as the sole arbiter of whether... the evidence warrants a belief; it becomes something to be laid down by authority, something which has to be believed in the interest of the organized effort and which may have to be altered as the exigencies of this organized effort require it."[240] Free men must combat that mindset. (Though truth be told, a few defenders of freedom try to use the same tactic. In that they harm their own cause.)

Attacks on citizens who support the "wrong" side in political issues threaten our freedom. We are not (at least not yet) hauling people off to gulags or concentration camps, but the effect is similar – an ethical system that stifles opposing viewpoints. This is not yet general, but on many campuses student newspapers and others openly oppose even the mention of contrary views. For example, one Harvard editorial advocated firing anyone doing research that might

---

240   Hayek, op cit, p178

produce evidence contrary to political correctness,[241] while at Swarthmore a student claims, "What really bothered me is, the whole idea is that at a liberal arts college, we need to be hearing a diversity of opinion,"[242]

When universities excoriate anyone who would use science to examine facts, and when they try to limit information to a narrow range, we are well on our way to politically mandated "truth" ruling our lives while real truth remains an outcast.

Without dissent, our freedom is dead and buried.

Independent Thinking – Is it Widespread Enough?

What fraction of the people really engage in independent thought? How many think critically about important issues? I know of no solid information on the subject but, based on people I've talked with and met on line, would guess that it is a rather small percentage. That is a sad situation, but it is the probable reality. That has to tempt the collectivists; they will try to tell people what to think. If the ideals and tastes of the majority are directed by fashion, advertising and fads, why not just provide some "intelligent" direction for those people? If they are to follow somebody's lead, why not that of the "right-thinking" elites? Why not use the power of the state, or of herd instinct, to direct everybody's thinking into the "intelligent" path?

A powerful government may have the ability to do that. Indeed, just convincing people that certain viewpoints are in style may accomplish the same

---

241   http://www.thecrimson.com/column/the-red-line/article/2014/2/18/academic-freedom-justice/

242   http://www.nationalreview.com/article/371625/attacking-diversity-thought-jonah-goldberg

thing. However the ultimate cost is incalculable. In the first place, only the arrogant would think that their ideas should be the only ones allowed. In the second place, interaction of differing beliefs is the way new ideas are discovered and erroneous beliefs discredited.

Only people of independent mind can create progress, and they do their best work when they interact with other independent thinkers. Channeling all thought into the same rut destroys thinking. That is the bad news. The good news is that even a minority of critical thinkers can counteract that problem – if they are allowed to disburse their thinking widely.

"The tragedy of collectivist thought is that, while it starts out to make reason supreme, it ends by destroying reason because it misconceives the process on which the growth of reason depends."[243]

Our job, as citizens, as free men and women, is three-fold:

First, we must do all we can to assure freedom of thought and expression. We must fight the statists and others who would, by legal means or peer pressure, interfere with freedom of information.

Second, we must think carefully and critically ourselves; then do our part to distribute the results of sound thinking to other citizens.

Third, we must encourage everyone to think critically about politics and similar issues. We must ban groupthink.

If even a significant minority of free men and women will do that, we can counteract the statist/collectivist propaganda.

---

243   Hayek, op cit p180

Chapter 24 Private Property

No man but feels more of a man in the world if he have a bit of ground that he can call his own. However small it is on the surface, it is four thousand miles deep; and that is a very handsome property. (Charles Dudley Warner)

Let's revisit our John I. How would his life change if some generous aristocrat were to give him a lot of money? Less than we might imagine. Yes, he could afford better clothing; maybe even build a new, nicer home. However, he still belongs to the land. Without his lord's permission he cannot leave. The lord of the manor could still require him to work the demesne land and to pay his share of the produce. Even should that lord allow him his freedom, it will be difficult or impossible for him to purchase a place of his own. Land is under the control of the king and aristocracy; private property as we know it today does not exist.

Contrast that with John II whose ability to leave his old boss and seek employment elsewhere is unlimited. He can buy his own land as soon as he has enough money to pay for it, or he might even borrow part of the price of that land. Even John III can freely change employment, though government rules limit his ability to establish his own business. In terms of freedom, he again stands between John I the serf and John II the free man.

Where will John IV fall on the scale of freedom? That again depends on us. Will we move toward freedom? Or toward the government ownership that is part of serfdom, socialism, and communism? The answer affects both freedom and the economy.

Means of Production and Other Capital

The farm, the factory, the foundry. Who should own and control those and other means of production? How about ownership of retail establishments? Homes and apartments?

Those questions get to the heart of the difference between collectivism and freedom. The collectivist, with all good intent, wants common ownership of means of production, and often of means of distribution and even living quarters as well. He believes such common ownership will solve our problems. If only that worked in practice as well as it does in theory!

The free man, on the other hand, wants to allow private ownership of all those resources. He believes that, in spite of the inevitable inequalities in such a system, private property is the best way to provide the goods and services we need, and certainly the best way to support freedom.

Which idea is correct? We need only look at the various countries that have tried each method. We discussed elsewhere the fact that, in the United States, even those regarded as poor inevitably have big-screen televisions, air conditioning, plenty to eat, even cars. In communist countries, workers wait in line for bread. The collectivists provide equality in misery; the free market provides plenty but with inequality.

Why the difference? Is there something fundamental about private property that enhances production and freedom? There is. As former communist Max Eastman pointed out, "...the institution of private property is one of the main things that have given man a limited amount of free-and-equalness that Marx hoped to render infinite by abolishing this institution. Strangely enough Marx was the first to see this. He is the one who informed us, looking backwards, that the evolution of private capitalism with its free market had been a precondition for the evolution of all our democratic freedoms. It never occurred to him, looking forward, that if this was so, these other freedoms might disappear with the abolition of the free market."[244]

Advantages of Private Property

Private property extends beyond ownership of land and buildings, important though that is. It extends to ownership of companies, patents, copyrights, and to other assets involved in the production of goods and services. Freedom and economic advancement require citizen control of those assets. Otherwise it is government, not citizens, controlling production and thus controlling our lives.

One advantage of private ownership is that it encourages the owner to care for his property lest it deteriorate. That applies not only to physical property but to intellectual property as well. That is why companies are so protective of trademarks, patents, and copyrights. Not only do they want to protect their temporary monopolies, they do not want low quality counterfeits besmirching their reputations. That requires that they not only protect intellectual property against misuse, but also keep their quality up so customers trust them and know what to expect from that company. And while things like patents may not deteriorate from lack of use, neither do they return the investment unless the owner actually cares for them by producing what customers want.

We see some problems of public ownership in the thousands of public housing projects in the U.S. Those buildings, so nice and shiny when new, quickly become run-down and damaged. Residents, with no real ownership, see no reason

---

244   Hayek, op cit. p136

to provide the care that a homeowner normally exercises. On a larger scale, farms, factories, etc. in the old Soviet Union were much less productive than similar facilities in the free world. Ownership provides incentive to care for the property.

The Non-property Owner

What of those not fortunate enough or diligent enough to acquire property of their own? Would they be better off under collectivism? Not really.

Suppose you live a country where the government owns all property, or at least all means of production. You are unhappy with your current employment so you decide to seek a different job. Sorry, the employer is the same, no matter where you go. Any new job you find will still be working for the collective, under pretty much the same conditions as your old job. You might get lucky and find a kinder boss, or it could go the other way and put you under a worse supervisor. And when you apply for that new job they just might tell your current boss that you are seeking another job, and he might punish you for disloyalty. You are probably better off to just put up with the conditions where you are.

On the other hand, what if you are unhappy with your job in a free country? There you can seek employment elsewhere and probably find a job with a company not connected with your current employer. That encourages employers to treat good employees well; they do not want to have to train replacements. Of course, not all companies are enlightened enough to treat employees well. However the free market offers choice to employees, choice not available in collectivist systems.

The same applies if you are unhappy with living quarters. A collectivist government builds and owns all the housing and has little incentive to build anything better. In contrast, in a free country different builders compete for customers, offering different floor plans and amenities. One family may want a large recreation room while their friends prefer a fancy kitchen for gourmet cooking, and yet another family may prefer a less expensive home so they have more money for recreation. Each family can pick out a home according to their taste and ability to pay.

Even if you own no more than the clothes on your back, you have many advantages, including career advantages, in a country where property is privately owned.

Career Advancement

What if you want to advance in your career, either in your current occupation or something different? In a free society you can learn new skills or improve the skills you have. You might take night classes, get a more skilled co-worker to mentor you, or otherwise improve your abilities. By so doing you not only advance your career; you become more productive, and contribute a bit more to the general economy. You may move up the ladder where you have been working, or you may move to a different company. It is true that there are some incompetent or uncaring bosses who will not recognize your improved skills, and that there are companies in which company politics plays a major role. However you can always seek a position where your new skills will be useful and rewarded.

But what happens if you want to advance in a collective society? That depends on your supervisor. He may recognize and appreciate your diligence and promote you. On the other hand he may not recognize that improvement, or even feel threatened by your qualifications. Since you have limited or no chance of changing the company you work for, your only hope is to impress your current boss. Workers in that situation tend to spend their efforts "polishing the apple" instead of improving skills. Organizations become more competent in apple polishing than in getting the work done. No wonder collectivist countries tend to produce less than do free countries, and to produce shoddy merchandise.

Private Property and the Economy

I've been kicking around this old world long enough to remember when everybody was afraid of the USSR. That country had military might comparable to that of the United States. Both countries were heavily armed with nuclear-tipped intercontinental ballistic missiles, enough of them that people believed that last ones fired would only bounce the rubble from the first strikes. We lived with the appropriate acronym MAD, for Mutually Assured Destruction. The theory was that neither country would dare attack the other since retaliation was certain and would wipe out both countries. It wasn't very comforting, but at least we didn't start shooting at each other.

Then, during the Reagan years, the Soviets folded. Why? Any military depends on support from the home economy and the Soviets just couldn't keep up. The U.S. economy, over and above maintaining a high standard of living for citizens, produced enough military materiel to overwhelm the Soviets in the arms race. Russian military adventures are still a problem, but at least the risk of nuclear war is now somewhat lower.

Why did the U.S. economy do so well? Our private enterprise, capitalist system encourages hard, smart work. It rewards those who produce what their customers want and punishes the wasteful and inept. Both individuals and corporations can own such businesses. The proceeds pay owners, stockholders, and employees. Then the prosperity spreads as those people spend money with other businesses. Tax money from those profits enables government to buy everything from paper clips to aircraft carriers. Private property, including ownership of corporate stock, has allowed that economic miracle.

And corporations are part of that economic miracle.

The Corporation in Free Society

Statists commonly denigrate the corporation. They like neither the legal protection such businesses have nor the fact that large corporations control so much production. Truth be told, corporate structures do cause some problems, but are those problems worse than what we would have without that legal protection? Let's look at that question, including advantages and disadvantages of corporations.

Suppose a friend offers you a chance to invest in a business he is starting. It looks like a good idea, but he needs two million dollars to buy equipment, acquire office space, and pay employees until he can start turning a profit. If he can raise a quarter of that amount, a bank will loan him the rest. You happen to have $50,000 available, you could invest that and own a tenth of the company. Would you do it? Consider two possibilities:

First, maybe the company does very well, repays the loan and in a few years your share of the profits amounts to $20,000 per year. You can either collect that as dividends or sell your share of the company for upwards of a million dollars.

The second possibility is grim. The company might fail, or at least not do well enough to repay the loan. A competitor may push prices down, or an employee error might expose the company to a lawsuit. Now, as owner of a tenth of the company, you are liable for a tenth of the debt, maybe $150,000! You lose not only your $50,000 investment but another $100,000 besides!

Do you invest in that business?

That illustrates a major obstacle to any unprotected investment. Few investors want to expose the rest of their resources to such things as lawsuits or having to pay off business loans. Indeed, there is hardly any limit to lawsuits, and nobody wants to own any part of that liability. Under those conditions, investment would be negligible and the economy terrible. Fortunately, there is a way out.

The legal protection for investors comes from the idea of legally limited liability. Both limited liability companies (LLCs) and corporations can protect investors. Once such businesses are established, only the actual assets of the business are at risk. A legal judgment against a company may be millions of dollars, but no stockholder will lose more than the value of his stock. Your friend can establish an LLC or a corporation and, even if the company loses everything, you will lose no more than what you invested.

The disadvantage is that lenders and others may be left holding the bag, but that is the price we pay for a robust economy. And it encourages lenders to be careful with the money they loan.

There is yet another benefit of the corporate structure. Assume you make the investment and it pays off, big time. Your tenth of the business is now worth a million dollars, maybe more! However, your children are graduating from high school and you want to sell part of your stake in the company to pay their college expenses. If the business lacks any corporate protection, or even if it is an LLC, you may have a hard time finding a buyer. Not a problem if the company has "gone public," it will be traded on a stock exchange and you can sell your share, or part of your share, easily. You would probably consider that when you make your initial investment. Do you really want to make a large investment without a convenient way to sell when you need the money?

Without the advantages of publicly traded stock, it would be more difficult to attract initial investors.

For all their disadvantages, corporations have boosted our economy greatly. They are an important part of our economic freedom and prosperity.

Private Property, our Economic Engine

Private property is what drives our economy. It produces food, clothing, housing, transportation and other commodities. It provides the tax money to support government programs, from education to national defense. No collectivist system comes close to what the free market can do for us.

That free market provides what we need to live, and gives us opportunity to create everything from a good road system to a strong military.

Chapter 25 Freedom and Security

He who sacrifices freedom for security deserves neither. (Benjamin Franklin)

Franklin was guilty of understatement. Security in this world is a mirage, even should we trade in our freedom. Such a trade will only buy the supposed security of the slave – security dependent on the whim of the slave master. Life is risky; the most we can do is trade one risk for another.

Appointment in Samarra

Baghdad, about 200 BC: "Master, what shall I do? I went to the market as you instructed, but there Death met me! He pointed his finger right at me."

"Abdul, you are not only a faithful servant but a good friend and I would not lose you. Take my best horse and flee to Samarra. You can be there by nightfall."

The master then went to the market to confront Death. "Why did you threaten my servant? You are supposed to take people gently, not frighten them."

"Truly I am sorry; I did not intent to frighten anyone. I was reacting to the shock of seeing Abdul here in Baghdad. You see, I have an appointment with him tonight, in Samarra."[245]

When we flee one risk, we should be careful that we are not running to a different danger, perhaps worse, danger.

---

245   "Appointment in Samarra" is based on an old story, repeated in many places. One source is Joel Ben Izzy, *The Beggar King and the Secret of Happiness*, Algonquin Books of Chapel Hill, 2003, p107-108

Our world is full of risks. There are drunk drivers, earthquakes, lightning, tornadoes, disease, and other natural killers. We cannot eliminate all risk, and if we try to trade freedom for security we will expose ourselves to new risks. The authorities we would depend on for security may fail to provide the promised protection, or even use us for their own ends.

Dealing with Risk

There is a field called risk management which is, I believe, misnamed. In most cases we do not and cannot manage risk; what we manage is ourselves. We can drive carefully and stay off the road at especially dangerous times. We can buy insurance and prepare a safe place should the tornado strike. We can reduce the probability of heart problems through diet, exercise, and avoiding tobacco. How we manage ourselves is up to each of us; government can neither eliminate all risk nor protect us from our own bad choices. When authorities promise safety, the more likely outcome is more restrictions, little risk reduction, and an increased probability of government-induced (iatrogenic) problems.

What government will provide is a one-size-fits-all rule that precludes freedom and inhibits progress. Consider medical treatment for example. The Federal Drug Administration requires new medications to be proven safe and effective before they can be sold. That sounds good, but what does it do to people who might benefit from those medications? As I write this, that rule is under question for at least one disease. Much of Africa is suffering an epidemic of Ebola, one of the nastier illnesses known to man. Victims suffer vomiting, diarrhea, fever, possible impairment of liver and kidneys, and both internal and external bleeding. The average fatality rate is about 50%. There is no currently accepted treatment beyond supportive therapy.[246] However there are new medications, including one called ZMapp that shows great promise. If you had Ebola, would you want to try that medication? The choice would be to take the risk of unexpected side effects or suffer the effects of Ebola.

In this case an exception was made. The drug was used on at least two human patients, both of whom have apparently recovered.[247]

To give or not to give ZMapp to an Ebola patient? If the law is understood strictly, the drug should not be used. There is a "compassionate use" exception for unapproved drugs in exceptional cases. However getting approval is usually time-consuming. Ebola patients do not have that much time, so in this case an "exception to the exception" was made and the drug was quickly allowed.[248] Strict enforcement of the normal rule would have imposed a high risk of death on those two people. They would have been safe from any ZMapp side effects, but that would be small consolation at their funerals.

The Alpha and the Beta, the A and the B

The above is an example of what is formally known as alpha versus beta risk, also sometimes called type one versus type two risk. It is a concept that affects government action regularly. Alpha risk, after the first letter of the Greek alphabet (α), is the risk we usually think of; we do something and it causes harm. For example we give a patient experimental treatment for Ebola and it makes him sicker or even kills him. Beta risk, after the second letter of the Greek alphabet

---

246   http://www.who.int/mediacentre/factsheets/fs103/en/
247   http://www.cnn.com/2014/08/04/health/experimental-ebola-serum/
248   Ibid

(β), is the risk of not doing something beneficial. We fail to administer the experimental medication and the patient we would have saved dies. We forgo the good we might have done. The problem is that alpha risk is visible while beta risk is not. We will probably learn if the treatment harms the patient. The doctor and pharmaceutical company may get sued. Beta risk, on the other hand, is usually invisible. Nobody knows about the patients we could have saved. Government therefore restricts alpha risk but usually ignores beta risk.

This goes beyond medical issues. A new building material or technique might make housing more accessible, but it is difficult to change building codes. Nobody will realize how much more affordable housing could have been had the code been changed. Automotive advances might help reduce energy use, but if they are delayed we'll never know how much energy we might have saved.

Alpha, Beta, Gamma, (A, B, G)

Since we're throwing around Greek letters, let's put in one more: gamma for government. Gamma (γ) is the third letter of that alphabet, it does sort of sound like our G. How does this mathematical mess of alpha and beta risk affect government?

Government is a bit different than most entities. It doesn't just take risks; it imposes those risks on its citizens. It is one thing for a citizen to suffer after he willingly took a risk; it is quite something else if he suffers because someone else imposed that risk on him. If an Ebola patient refuses treatment with ZMapp, his death is on his own hands. However, if he dies because government refused to allow a treatment, that government is guilty.

Like other uncertainties, there are risks from both government action and inaction. However there is yet another difference between government and private risk. Because government action often consists in restricting private action, the alpha and beta roles can be reversed. When government prohibits an action, it causes the beta risk of foregoing the potential benefits from that prohibited action. When it allows or even mandates an action, it creates the alpha risk of the damage that action might cause.

In most cases, taking action creates alpha risk, taking no action allows beta risk. However government action often creates beta risk by prohibiting potential positive outcomes.

To return to our ZMapp Ebola treatment, the doctor prescribing ZMapp runs an alpha risk that his action will have side effects. If he refuses to prescribe it, he runs the beta risk that the patient will not receive an effective treatment. When government steps in and prohibits the use of that medication, it is in the same position as the doctor who refuses to prescribe it; it causes a beta risk of not helping the patient. That is one reason government should be careful about restricting private decisions. Of course we need some rules about medical practice, but those rules should allow a trade-off between possible harm and possible benefit, between alpha and beta risk.

Improving Security

We can improve security in some areas but, contrary to statist belief, that improvement need not come from government. In fact prior to the Great Depression we had no federal programs for personal security, yet people survived, took economic risks, and even got past major illnesses and other personal disasters. They bought health insurance, depended on family, borrowed money, and had help from local government and private charities.

Can we return to those days of limited federal help? Maybe, maybe not, but it is certain that we cannot do it quickly. What we can do is start cutting back on federal involvement and moving funding and decision-making to local authorities and private citizens. If the federal government were to shrink, that would leave more resources available elsewhere. As discussed in Chapter 6, local authorities are more careful with local tax money than they are with federal grants.

But what about major problems, such as the Great Depression? Surely we need federal help to resolve that kind of nightmare, do we not? Actually, no. That belief is based on two assumptions, both false:

> First, the belief that the federal government has more resources than do state and local governments. Not true, all those governments get their resources from the same source: the taxpayers. If the federal government takes less, there will be more available for state and local governments, and even for private charities.

> Second, the "conventional wisdom" that federal involvement solved the Great Depression. Not true. Economists and others have found that the "New Deal" and Hoover's similar measures actually worsened and extended the Great Depression, though there is still some controversy about that.[249]

Government not only consumes resources. Taxes and over-regulation discourage private investment. That diminishes the resources available to fight

---

249   Folsom, Burton W. *New Deal or Raw Deal? How FDR's Economic Legacy has Damaged America,* op cit. Available from various sources. The whole book is dedicated to this subject.

any problem. And many politicians and others rail against the successful, thus further discouraging growth.

The Denigration of Success

Suppose you have an idea for an invention, a new business or something of that nature. You are not 100% confident it will work, but you try anyway. You quit your job, withdraw most of your savings, sell any stock you own, and borrow against your retirement. You go out on a limb – and you are not sure how strong that limb is. If this is a normal enterprise, you will have dry years for a while, maybe barely making it and wondering if it was really such a good idea.

Then finally! Customers realize how useful your product is and you begin to prosper. Soon you employ hundreds directly, plus many more people who work for your suppliers and distributors. You become wealthy, even more wealthy than you hoped, and you enjoy using your money for good causes. Life is good, not only because of your own success, but because you have helped several hundred people get good jobs.

Better enjoy that feeling while you can. There are plenty of people who will hold your success against you. The president of the United States may well accuse you of being among the 1% who exploit the poor. He may say that you do not need the money you have, that you should be ashamed to have accumulated so much. He will talk about the gap between CEO pay and that of the workers. Others will join him.

What have you done to earn such opprobrium? Is anyone worse off because of your success? Well, maybe your competitors are worse off, but your customers and employees are all better off than before. Yet among the "elites" many think that anyone earning a lot of money is automatically an exploiter (with some exceptions, like politicians and big political donors of their own persuasion).

Now your neighbor asks you for advice. He has a great idea and is considering taking the same risk you took. What will you tell him? You both know that success is uncertain; most new ventures fail. And you now know how people have reacted to your success. If his idea works, he will become a pariah in much of society. Maybe he wants to avoid the opprobrium so he stays in his current job. He creates no new jobs and serves no customers. He has security of a sort, but not freedom.

The search for absolute security is doomed from the start, but it does cause problems.

Categorical Thinking

"But if there's even one thing we can do, if there's just one life we can save, we've got an obligation to try." So spoke President Obama in February 2013.[250] We've all heard that and similar statements, some even stronger. I've even heard people claim that saving one child is worth any cost. The sentiment is understandable, especially when someone speaks of his or her own child. However there are problems when we look at the bigger picture. Whenever someone makes that type of statement we can be sure of three things.

> First, he has thought out neither the cost nor the fact that resources are limited. We could spend lots of money to save one terminally ill child, but how many other children do we not save and what other problems do we cause when we divert resources to a nearly hopeless case?

---

250   http://www.whitehouse.gov/blog/2013/02/04/preventing-violence-president-obama-asks-americans-stand-and-say-time-its-different

Second, he has not thought of the trade-off between length of life and quality of life. We might extend the life of that child by a few months, but is it really worth it if that time is spent in painful therapy?

Third, he has not thought of the side effects of that "rescue." We could, for example, save more than one child by banning trains, including subways. Just before I wrote this I heard of a child in Oregon hit and killed by a train. So we ban trains but then what? We have more trucks and cars that kill even more children.

The claim that some outcome is worth any cost is categorical thinking. It puts that one objective above anything and everything else; that objective becomes a tyrant. By concentrating on only one issue we divert attention from a myriad of other aspects of life, often even from the damage we do pursuing that one objective. For example, having adequate economic resources allows us to save the lives of many children. If we concentrate those resources on a few difficult but newsworthy cases, we may not have enough to help the vast majority of children with less severe problems, or even to provide adequate nutrition to millions of children.

In neither private nor public life do we want a single goal to the exclusion of all others. In private life, people want food, clothing, housing, recreation, often spouses and children. Nobody spends all his time seeking food while ignoring housing and clothing. Nor should we ask government to concentrate totally on something like child safety at the expense of infrastructure, law enforcement, and national defense. Multiple wants are just a part of this life.

Indeed, the very act of concentrating society on a single purpose destroys freedom. We cannot make individual choices if the state demands dedication to the government decreed goal.

Chapter 26 It Can't Happen Here – Can It?

Probably it is true that the very magnitude of the outrages committed by the totalitarian governments, instead of increasing the fear that such a system might one day arise in more enlightened countries, has rather strengthened the assurance that it cannot happen here. (Hayek)

Never Say Never

"Don't worry; if he comes to a road, he won't cross it, he'll stay right there."

We were looking for a lost hunter whose companions gave us that assurance. That narrowed our search area tremendously; we just had to search the area bounded by roads while someone patrolled those roads. Great, except for one little problem: the man was not in the area. He crossed two roads, finally reached the highway, and hitchhiked to town. Had he gone a different direction he would have missed the highway and continued to wander while we looked in the wrong place.

It ain't what you don't know that gets you in trouble; it's what you know for sure that just ain't so.[251]

We've all been blindsided by things we knew just couldn't happen. The great job turns sour; the wonderful stock loses money; the trustworthy friend hands our secret to the rumor mill. It happens. Likewise with tyranny. I would love to believe that tyranny cannot happen here. Sadly, I cannot be so optimistic.

As discussed in Chapter 1, freedom is an unstable state, an egg balanced on a fence. Unless we actively defend it, we will lose our freedom. It is easy, and tempting, to believe that it just it can't happen here, but such apathy is a greater danger than enemy missiles. In fact we have already had tyrannical laws. During

---

251   Attributed to Mark Twain

Roosevelt's New Deal big companies were allowed to effectively make law, even sending small business owners to jail for charging low prices. Jacob Maged of Jersey City, New Jersey was fined $100 and thrown in jail for charging 35 cents instead of 40 cents to press a suit. Pharis Tire and Rubber Company in Newark, Ohio was not allowed to compete on price, Firestone, Goodyear, and Goodrich made the law about how the tire business should be conducted. That drove small companies out of business and drove up the price of both tires and cars. Car sales, both domestic and for export, slumped, prolonging the Great Depression.[252] It was the old guild system writ large.

There are three primary routes from freedom to statist tyranny. The first, conquest from outside, need not greatly concern us. As I write this, there is no foreign enemy with the power and will to conquer and rule the United States of America. Not only does our military remain formidable, but we still have a people individualistic enough that a foreign conqueror would find us an indigestible meal. We need to maintain our strength, but foreign conquest is not an immediate concern.

The second danger is revolution from within. I doubt the U.S. will go that route; I know of no case of armed revolution taking over a truly free country. In fact, Solzhenitsyn describes a fellow prisoner, a committed communist and who had spent time in Canada and in the U.S. After observing life here, "he concluded that they would never have a proletarian revolution and even that they hardly needed one."[253] Even that committed statist saw that freedom eliminated the motivation for rebellion.

---

252   Folsom, op cit, pp53-55
253   Solzhenitsyn, op cit, pp37-38

The third route to tyranny, the one that does threaten us, is gradual abdication of freedom in exchange for statist promises. We slowly give up our freedoms for supposed security or financial benefits.

The Fable of the Feathers

The mighty eagle soared over mountain and valley, king of the air and feared on the ground. Foxes, coyotes, even wolves preferred to avoid him.

One day he spotted a rabbit and dove for the tasty lunch, but the rabbit escaped into the brush – right into the jaws of a waiting fox. The fox said, "I'm not very hungry today, but I would like one of your wing feathers for my babies to play with. How about if I give you half the rabbit and you give me one feather?"

The eagle had plenty of feathers, so he pulled one from his left wing and gave it to the fox. It was worth the pain.

The next day the eagle saw the fox again, this time with a chicken she had stolen from a nearby farm. "Would you like half of this chicken?" asked the fox. "If you give me another feather maybe my babies won't fight over the only one they have."

The eagle pulled a feather from his right wing and then enjoyed his half of the chicken.

The next day the eagle traded another feather for half a prairie dog. Then it was a whole mole for another feather. The eagle couldn't soar quite as high as before, but that didn't really matter as long as the fox gave him food.

Mice, rabbits, moles, chickens, anything he could eat. The eagle bought them all, paying with feathers. He got fat; and with fewer feathers he could no longer soar over the mountains. He just stayed down in the lower valley, but that meant he was closer to the fox and the food she sold him.

Finally the fox said that her sisters wanted feathers for their babies. She gave the eagle a whole rabbit for four feathers. Oh how good it tasted, and how full he felt! He flapped his wings but what was happening? He was so fat, and had so few feathers, that he could not fly at all!

The fox and her family yanked out the rest of his feathers.

Like the eagle, our danger lies not in sudden changes, but in gradual movement toward more and more government power. We will not lose all our "feathers of freedom" at once. Rather, we risk trading them away little by little.

"You Americans are so gullible. No, you won't accept communism outright, but we'll keep feeding you small doses of socialism until you'll finally wake up and find you already have communism. We won't have to fight you. We'll so weaken your economy until you'll fall like over-ripe fruit into our hands." So, in substance, spoke Nikita Khrushchev, premier of the USSR.[254] That is our danger. Not military conquest, but gradual acceptance of statist control.

So what forces are strangling our freedoms?

Executive Orders

"All legislative Powers herein granted shall be vested in a Congress of the United States, which shall consist of a Senate and House of Representatives."[255]

"he [The president] shall take Care that the Laws be faithfully executed."[256]

---

254   Ezra Taft Benson, *An Enemy Hath Done This,* Parliament Publishers, Inc. 1969, p320
255   Constitution of the United States of America, Article I, Section 1

Our founders wisely included those clauses in the constitution. If we allow one person to unilaterally change the law, we have at best an elected dictator. That is exactly the power Hitler acquired with his "Enabling Act." Passed in 1933, that act allowed Hitler "to issue decrees independently of the Reichstag (the German parliament) and the presidency.[257] He could claim to have won an election, but in fact he became a dictator. Our system of government is designed to prevent such a dictatorship by dispersing legislative power among 435 representatives and 100 senators. That means that no one person, indeed no small group of people, should be able to modify our laws. It was a great idea while it lasted.

We have destroyed that division of power. Bureaucracies effectively have power to write laws. Worse, we have a president who openly promises to act by executive order if Congress fails to do his bidding. "I've got a pen and I've got a phone, and I can use that pen to sign executive orders... I'll act on my own."[258] That president lacks, at least at present, the total power Hitler enjoyed. However, he has acquired power over our lives far beyond what the Constitution allows. He claims power to decide what Congress should do.

He acquired that power because of a gutless Congress. Some in Congress undoubtedly support his dictatorial actions, while others are simply afraid to stand up to him. For the time being at least, Congress has power to control the purse strings – if our representatives will use that power. Yet even the current Republican controlled Congress seems afraid to oppose the president. At least one

---

256   Ibid, Article II, Section 3
257   http://www.britannica.com/EBchecked/topic/186351/Enabling-Act
258   http://washington.cbslocal.com/2014/01/14/obama-on-executive-actions-ive-got-a-pen-and-ive-got-a-phone/

senator is taking legal action, but that will take time and the courts have shown no more courage in such matters than has Congress.

Nor is Obama the first president to use such power, though he probably is the first to use it so blatantly. Nixon issued a decree freezing wages and prices, though at least he could claim that Congress had delegated that power to him with the Economic Stabilization Act of 1970, constitutionally questionable though that act was. Obama has gone much farther, unilaterally changing his own signature health care law and even threatening to veto congressional changes that would do exactly what he is doing. He has also, without congressional approval, changed the Clinton era welfare reform and our immigration laws, among others.

The excuse, supported by many statists, is that if Congress won't act the president must do it for them. Can you think of a more dictatorial attitude? The president alone is the final arbiter of what the law should say. He claims that gives him the right to violate the Constitution and his oath of office. Big Brother knows best, and if we know what's good for us we will accept his decrees.

If this does not stop, it will create a dictatorship. The president will amass more and more power until his word becomes law. Only presidential integrity will stand between us and serfdom – if the president has any integrity.

We must insist that our representatives fight this concentration of power in the hands of one man, lest we regress toward the equivalent of serfdom.

And there are other forces driving us toward statism.

No Contrary Information Allowed

Berlin, Germany, 1971: I stood looking at the wall, its ugly appearance surpassed by an even uglier purpose. It stood four meters (13 feet) high, topped in places by razor wire. However Russian and East German authorities were replacing the razor wire with smooth concrete pipe, large enough in diameter to offer no hand or foot holds. Razor wire is no deterrent to people fleeing machine gun bullets.

The infamous Berlin wall was built to keep people in and ideas out, typical statist objectives. I saw firsthand the measures those statists took to control the people. To the best of their ability, they blocked all information from the west. (The West Berliners partially circumvented that with informational billboards, high enough to be seen over the wall.)

Nazi Germany likewise controlled information available to the people. "The prime mover in censorship was the Minister of Propaganda, Joseph Goebbels. It was his responsibility to see that the German people were fed with material acceptable to the Nazi state. Newspapers, radio and all forms of media were put under the control of the Nazis. Even the film industry became controlled by the Nazis."[259] Control of information provides near total control of people. If the ruler controls what people believe, he also controls their actions.

Censorship in the United States

Surely that can't happen here; we have the first amendment after all. Our government will not censor our information, will it? Sadly, we cannot count on our government defending freedom of the press; rather the opposite is true. People in power try to block information they don't like.

This started early in our history with the Alien and Sedition Acts of 1798. There were four laws that, among other things, restricted criticism of the federal

---

259   http://www.historylearningsite.co.uk/censorship_in_nazi_germany.htm

government. Thankfully, those laws were repealed in 1802; the sedition part clearly violated the first amendment.

Politicians have made various other attempts to control the information available to the public, ranging from heaping scorn on their enemies to the use of federal power to intimidate and punish anyone with the temerity to criticize people in power. When Bill Clinton's womanizing problems came to light, Hillary Clinton defended him, not with facts, but by claiming that it was just part of a "vast right-wing conspiracy."[260] It didn't work. Except for a few Clinton true believers, most of the country recognized that there was much truth in the accusations. So much truth that Clinton was eventually impeached and disbarred for lying (though the Senate did not convict him so he stayed in office).

The Obama administration has taken this much farther. As I write this, Reporters Without Borders has just released its study of press freedom throughout the world. The United States, during the last 12 months, fell from number 33 to number 46. The administration has gone after whistle-blowers with a vengeance. Worse, it has tapped phones of reporters and even confiscated the records of one reporter.[261]

We have already discussed the organization True the Vote and its troubles with the IRS, OSHA, FBI, and the BATF, all happening after that organization went contrary to what the administration wanted. We also have the famous cases of the IRS blocking tax-exempt status for organizations supporting freedom while statist groups had no trouble. Some of those freedom-supporting groups simply

---

260   http://www.washingtonpost.com/wp-srv/politics/special/clinton/stories/hillary012898.htm
261   http://www.bizpacreview.com/2014/02/18/under-obama-us-tumbles-to-46th-place-for-freedom-of-the-press-101532

changed their names to eliminate words like "constitution" or "freedom," and were quickly approved.[262]

Blatant Censorship Threatened

Undoubtedly the most frightening measure proposed, and that quite seriously, came from the Federal Communications Commission. They proposed putting "observers" in editorial rooms of broadcasters, and even newspapers.[263] Can anyone seriously believe that such "observers" would not have an effect on editorial decisions? The stated reason is "to seek their 'voluntary' compliance about how news stories are covered, as well as 'wade into office politics' looking for angry reporters whose story ideas were rejected as evidence of a shutout of minority views."[264]

Suppose you are managing editor of a broadcast news organization. You have, sitting in your newsroom, a representative of the bureaucracy that will determine if your license will be renewed. Maybe he even expresses his preference about which stories you should and should not feature on the evening news. Maybe he says nothing, but you suspect that he prefers that some stories be given banner headlines, others not broadcast at all. Will you ignore those preferences and proceed with business as usual? Or will you modify your broadcast to fit his preferences? You know which course enhances your chances of license renewal.

---

262   cf http://www.breitbart.com/Big-Government/2014/06/17/Judicial-Watch-Smoking-Gun-Busts-Open-IRS-Scandal-Again

263   http://news.investors.com/ibd-editorials/021314-690050-fcc-newsroom-plan-all-about-controlling-the-free-press.htm

264   Ibid

And why should the FCC pay any attention at all to the print media? That agency has no jurisdiction over newspapers or magazines. The "only" thing they could do would be to publicly announce that you do or do not give fair treatment to different stories or that you discriminate against some people. That announcement will go to the public and you will have no realistic legal recourse should it be false.

The unfortunate fact is that we now have a system that allows repression of the press. Agencies from the BATF to the IRS have power to investigate whoever they want to investigate. Those investigations are intrusive, time-consuming and expensive for the investigated. That is true even if investigators find no violations. However the rules are so many and so complicated that inadvertent violation is nearly certain. And for broadcast news organizations, the FCC has the power to withhold licenses and literally bankrupt the company.

The tools for repression are there. Unless we, the citizens, insist on changes, the only protection we have is the integrity of the officials charged with those investigations. If those officials decide to persecute news people, they have the power to do so. That is another step on the road to serfdom. It puts us closer to the situation of our John I who had limited access to information.

When officials control information they control our lives – and they are gaining more and more control over the information we can get. That bodes ill for independent thinking and freedom. Are we moving gradually (or maybe not so gradually) toward one-man control of our law? Yes, there are alternative news sources on the internet. However, most people still get their news from the major networks, the very organizations the FCC threatened to monitor. Only if citizens stand up against government control of information will we remain free. We will discuss this further after we look at another tool for the demagogue.

Scapegoats

Scapegoats are wonderfully useful to any demagogue. In Germany it was the Jews. We have other scapegoats today, scapegoats the demagogues use to draw our attention away from the real issues. It is instructive to look at how Hitler used his favorite scapegoat.

The Jews were outcasts in Germany (and many other countries) long before the Nazis came to power. Hitler did not create that bigotry, but he did use it to facilitate his rise to dictatorship. The unthinking accepted his claims and his promise of prosperity, if they would only give him power to deal with those pesky Jews. The early Nazis had twenty-five "points," demands they made of government. Two were specifically anti-Jewish, one of which demanded that Jews not be citizens. Five other points would restrict the rights of non-citizens which obviously included Jews.[265] That distracted the people from the real causes of their problems and helped the Nazis win power. If the Jews were the problem, then government must deal with that problem, and only the Nazis promised to do that.

So what scapegoats have we today in the United States? There are many, a situation that provides a perverse advantage to the citizens. Multiple targets for bigotry make it difficult for a demagogue to unite a majority against a single scapegoat. It would be preferable to have no scapegoats at all, but if we must have

---

265   http://www.historyplace.com/worldwar2/riseofhitler/25points.htm

them, let them at least be diverse; let them divide the efforts of the demagogues. Some of the scapegoats that various demagogues in the U.S. use today are:

The Rich It is common for collectivists to blame the rich for everything from the "wealth gap" to international unrest. In third-world countries the wealth gap is indeed a problem, the poor there often have essentially nothing as we have discussed elsewhere. In many cases the wealthy and powerful in the third-world do keep the poor down. However, in the United States the poor usually have more than even many in the middle class in other countries. It harms nobody if Warren Buffet has his billions. In fact his companies employ literally millions of people, helping those employees avoid poverty.

Politicians and others find that they can bend people to their will by railing against that "wealthiest 1%," in spite of the fact that most of those politicians are themselves among the 1%.

White People. We have all seen some of this. Crimes, or supposed crimes, against minorities, can get attention all out of proportion to their seriousness – and the demagogues automatically assume that some white person is guilty. Then the major news media piles on, in many cases blaming all Whites for the supposed crimes of a few. When some members of the Duke Lacrosse team were accused of raping a black woman, both the media and some high profile "civil rights" leaders "convicted" them before the evidence was in.[266] They even excoriated the black taxi driver who provided an alibi.[267] Racist assumptions trumped truth. And when George Zimmerman was accused of deliberately setting out to kill a black

---

266   http://today.duke.edu/showcase/lacrosseincident/
267   http://abcnews.go.com/GMA/LegalCenter/story?id=1858806&page=1&
       singlePage=true

teenager, MSNBC edited the 911 tape to make it sound like he was making a racist comment.[268]

This is an inversion of the older bias in which Blacks were often automatically presumed guilty. Both attitudes are bigoted and dangerous. Both harm our freedom.

Bankers. From accusations of racism when minorities did not qualify for mortgages at the same rate as whites, to later charges that bankers were sitting on money instead of loaning it to businesses, statists have blamed bankers for a good chunk of our ills. Starting especially with the Clinton Administration, banks were forced to reduce loan qualifications for the inner city borrowers, and many of those loans went into default.[269] That not only harmed the credit rating of those borrowers, but also played a big part in the economic crash of the early 21st century. Of course those accusing bankers of sitting on money neglect to mention that banks might be holding money instead of loaning it out because of uncertainty about government regulations and how that would affect borrowers' ability to repay. Banks have no incentive to sit on their money; they gain their profits by making loans that will be repaid. While some bankers have caused problems, we should not tar them all with the same brush.

"Conservatives." No surprise, statists excoriate anyone who would dare oppose big government. They call "conservatives" selfish, as though they were the only selfish people in the world. That in spite of the fact that a major study found so-called conservatives to be actually more generous than the

---

268   http://www.mediaite.com/online/nbc-news-admits-error-in-editing-george-zimmermans-911-call-apologizes/

269   http://spectator.org/articles/42211/true-origins-financial-crisis

collectivists.[270] "Conservatives" are also accused of being obstructionists as though that were automatically a bad thing. We could have used some good obstructionists to prevent things like our war in Iraq and our support of the Muslim Brotherhood in Egypt.

Immigrants. The accusations against immigrants, especially illegal aliens, do have some basis in fact. Those people do take jobs otherwise available to citizens. Some of them do bring in illegal drugs and organized crime. However others become good citizens. This is another case where we ought not tar them all with the same brush.

Our domestic demagogues use those scapegoats to acquire power and money, and to divide and conquer the citizens.

Clearly there is lots of blame to go around in our country today. However we should use care to place the blame where it belongs, not on people we just happen to dislike. Our skepticism should go on high alert when a demagogue starts blaming one group for our troubles.

And beyond scapegoats, there are other problems paving the road to totalitarianism.

Personality Cults

"Heil Hitler!"

Almost any movie about World War II shows that servile salute, with the arm raised to the approved angle. Everything revolved around Hitler, and it was

---

270   For more on the value of obstructionists, see my blog at
http://hallillywhite.blogspot.com/search?q=obstructionist

treason to speak against him. Today we regard such unthinking homage to a dictator as sickening, but are we the pot calling the kettle black?

Look at some of the idols receiving cult-like worship in our society today. Of course there are musicians and movie stars. That does little harm in itself, though it does cause problems when that celebrity worship gets in the way of clear thinking. Celebrities are no smarter than the rest of us and can make dangerous political recommendations.

More dangerous are political idols, placed on their pedestals for the wrong reasons. There was even at least one case of a school teaching students to sing the praises of the current president as though he were a demigod.[271] Good looks, speaking ability, or even just current fads create unthinking followers. The idols may be wise and good leaders, or they may be demagogues. However, those cult-attracting characteristics can cause idols to become overconfident, even narcissistic. Such people, unless they are wise, become self-absorbed and make decisions based on their self-image and the flattery of those around them. As discussed in Chapter 22, this too often allows the worst to rise to the top.

We need to evaluate candidates on the basis of wisdom, integrity, and commitment to constitutional government. We should ignore charisma and concentrate on what is important. Adolph Hitler, Jim Jones, David Koresh and others were all charismatic – and deadly. We must avoid such leaders. And we must not allow such leaders to indoctrinate us or our children.

---

271   http://www.foxnews.com/politics/2009/09/24/review-ordered-video-showing-students-singing-praises-president-obama/

State Control of Children

"We have to break through our private idea that kids belong to their parents or kids belong to their families." So says Professor Melissa Harris-Perry of Tulane. She claims that kids belong to whole communities.[272] Not many statists would say that out loud, but if you talk with many of them, you will find that Harris-Perry's belief is common. It is obvious why. Once they gain power over the children, they can indoctrinate them as they please. The next generation will be completely in their power. What children learn, true or false, usually stays with them. That is especially true if contrary information is not available.

Might our children be indoctrinated instead of educated? It's already happening, right here in the U.S.A. Most parents have heard of such indoctrination, but now there are even special schools that teach, at taxpayer expense, how to agitate for statist causes. In such institutions as Crescent Heights Social Justice Magnet School in Los Angeles and Chicago's Social Justice High School, the curriculum centers around teaching students to be "agents of change," that is to work for more government power and even UN control. "Activist teachers openly foster identity politics and systematically undermine individualism."[273] That should be no surprise for any school with "social justice" in its name.

At least the U.S. does not yet assign government agents to each child as Scotland proposed to do. That country "plans to give every child a 'named person', who could theoretically be anyone but their mother or father, from birth to the age

---

272   http://www.infowars.com/your-kids-belong-to-the-collective/ (The link includes video of the professor making that claim.)

273   http://townhall.com/columnists/michellemalkin/2014/08/08/readin-writin-and-social-justice-agitatin-n1876238

of 18. The individual, who would most likely be a social worker or head teacher, would have the legal right to ensure the child is raised in a government-approved manner and report any issues about their upbringing to the authorities."[274] While the intent is undoubtedly good, the opportunity for mischief is unlimited. That "named person" could decide just what parents may teach the child about everything from the alphabet to zygotes. Teach your child that the authorities are imperfect? Better be careful if the "named person" disagrees.

Of course that is what collectivists of all stripes have done, Nazis, Communists and others. As described elsewhere in this chapter, both Germany and Italy, during and before World War II, had their youth organizations. Stalin actually imprisoned parents for teaching religion to their children.[275] The clear intent was to create a people committed to their system, a people who would not even consider other options. The Germans and Italians failed only because they lost the war. The Russians largely succeeded because, until recently, they were able to keep opposing ideas out.

At present the statists have three primary tools of childhood indoctrination. Those are the news media, the entertainment business, and the education system. As discussed in Chapter 27, statists dominate in those businesses so we must fight them to maintain our freedom. That chapter also discusses how we can effectively oppose those forces.

While we might think that interfering with children is unethical, that is only the start of the ethical convolutions statists concoct to destroy our freedom.

---

274   http://www.telegraph.co.uk/news/uknews/scotland/10214975/Lawyers-warn-against-Big-Brother-plans-to-give-every-Scottish-child-a-state-guardian.html

275   Solzhenitsyn, op cit, p192

Twisted Ethics

26 December 2004. An earthquake, 9.0 on the Richter scale, struck off the coast of the Indonesian island of Sumatra. The resulting tsunami devastated not only Sumatra but coastal areas of Thailand, Sri Lanka and India. Hundreds of thousands were killed, more lost their livelihoods, and millions were left homeless, in unspeakable misery.[276]

The one good thing that comes from such disasters is an outpouring of human kindness. Literally billions of dollars worth of aid appeared as quickly as people could organize to deliver it. Germany donated $674 million, Australia $380 million, Japan $500 million. The United States Government? Only $350 million. What does that say about U.S. generosity? Nothing. Donations extracted from taxpayers were less than in other countries, but voluntary contributions exceeded $135 *billion*. Voluntary giving in the United States nearly matched the total of government aid from Germany, Australia, and Japan combined! Meanwhile voluntary giving in Europe was nearly zero.

And how did the statists react to that? They excoriated the U.S. for being stingy. In their minds, only government aid counts as charity.[277] To the statist, individual initiative is irrelevant, maybe worse if it overshadows state action.

During the European Parliament debate over helping those unfortunates, each MEP (Member of the European Parliament) would outdo the last in "generosity." One suggested a million Euros. The next, at least five million, then up to at least 50 million. All felt warm and charitable – until an Italian suggested

---

276   http://www.newscientist.com/article/dn9931-facts-and-figures-asian-tsunami-disaster.html#.VDhuJBbp-qk

277   Brooks, op cit, pp113-122

something radical. Why not be personally involved? Why didn't each MEP donate one day's attendance allowance (about 290 Euros or 360 U.S dollars) of his own money to the cause? The cheers quieted and the Italian sat down to a hostile silence.[278] For those parliamentarians, giving away their constituents money was wonderful. Giving their own was unthinkable.

That turns the definition of charity upside down. They are claiming that it does not count unless government takes the "charitable donation" from the people, whether the people agree or not. The people, the taxpayers, are not to act of their own free will. Those constituents are mere tools, providing resources to carry out decisions made by government functionaries.

That does not fit. Tools are not charitable; at best they fulfill a worthy function in the hands of someone else who makes the real decisions. Involuntary donors are no more charitable than is the airplane that carries their "donations" to the stricken area.

This attitude is consistent in collectivist countries. As Brooks explains in his book, *Who Really Cares*, collectivism leads people to expect government to take care of everything. Not only should the collective provide jobs and manage the economy, but it should also take charge of charity. Why should the individuals donate to tsunami relief when that is the government's duty, and when they have already paid taxes for that purpose?

True charity requires voluntary sacrifice of something we value personally. Unless we give of our own free will, and give something of value to us, it is no gift at all.

---

278   Hannan, *The New Road to Serfdom*, op cit p131

Too often, instead of urging voluntary sacrifice to help others, our "morality" involves forced "giving" coupled with the "right" to receive that largesse. Let government help the poor. Let it provide "free" contraception and even abortion. In no case should the recipients be held responsible for their own decisions. Just as serfs had no responsibility for anything but serving the master, so today many want no responsibility beyond obeying the government.

Collectivism breeds an attitude of dependence. Freedom breeds responsibility, for oneself and often for those in need. True ethics rejects dependence and insists on self-reliance and voluntary charity.

Collectivist "charity" and the other forces mentioned are pulling us toward statism, toward a serf-like existence.

A Real Danger

Will we wake up and see the danger from the greater and greater power we keep handing to our government? The Germans did not set out to create a totalitarian state, but create one they did. They acquiesced to each increase in government power as it came along. Each new measure appeared attractive. Then they woke up to find that they were living in a dictatorship.

The critical time in Germany was not when Hitler got his Enabling Law. It was long before that, even before voters reacted to economic and other problems by giving support to the Nazi party. It was when those voters started looking for a government savior instead of solving their own problems. Once that ball started rolling, the country was on the road to statist power. Hitler used that dependence to become chancellor. That put him in a position to take power after the burning of the Reichstag. He may or may not have ordered the fire; that is still controversial. However he had maneuvered himself into position to take advantage of the turmoil thus created.

How could Hitler get enough voter support to become chancellor? The answer is that the Germans were desperate, and desperate people may grasp at any straw. The Treaty of Versailles imposed onerous reparations on the country. That and other problems devastated the economy. Formerly prosperous families found themselves with little or nothing. As Hayek puts it, "It should never be forgotten that the one decisive factor in the rise of totalitarianism on the Continent, which is yet absent in England and America, is the existence of a large recently dispossessed middle class."[279]

As I write this, the American middle class is under siege. Should much of that middle class fall on hard times, that could open the way for a demagogue to take power. Indeed such hard times did open the way for the intrusive measures of the "New Deal" of the 1930s and 1940s. The conventional belief is that the New Deal ended the Great Depression. That belief is increasingly discredited.[280] However one thing the New Deal did accomplish was a concentration of power in the hands of the federal government, with even the courts accepting unconstitutional laws. The results are with us to this day. For example, the federal power to regulate interstate commerce has expanded to the regulation of all commerce, even some activities not involving commerce at all. If we want to manufacture something that never gets sold and never even crosses a state line, we may still have to follow federal regulations. That is clearly beyond the powers the Constitution grants the federal government.

---

279   Hayek, op cit, p215
280   Folsom, op cit. The whole book is dedicated to this subject.

Hitler did not create the economic problems that enabled his rise to power; they were mostly caused by the Treaty of tari. He did, however, use those problems to amass power. As documented in Chapter 20, many Germans detested Hitler personally but thought him the only person strong enough to solve their problems. Nor is it likely that anybody intentionally caused the problems of the middle class in the U.S. today,[281] but that matters little. What is important is the ultimate effect of a declining middle class. It may open the way for a demagogue, whether that decline was intentional or not.

Deliberate Economic Sabotage

We should not, however, neglect the possibility of intentionally created economic problems. Some statists have seriously proposed deliberate sabotage of the economic system in the belief that desperate people will then turn to collectivism. The prime proponents of that method were Richard Cloward and Frances Piven of Columbia University. They proposed deliberately overloading the welfare system to the point that it would effectively crash. They believed that such turmoil would cause desperate voters to turn to socialism.[282] Any deliberate effort to crash our economy will probably be based on their publications, though of course it will differ in detail from what they suggested. For that reason, measures aimed at destroying good government or otherwise creating turmoil are called Cloward-Piven strategies.

---

281   The U.S. middle class is declining in recent years, cf.
    http://www.businessinsider.com/decline-of-theus-middle-class-2013-10
282   http://www.discoverthenetworks.org/
Articles/theclowardpivenstrategypoe.html

There is, however, a fundamental problem with Cloward-Piven strategies. The whole idea is to show that existing government is incapable of doing the job it has undertaken. Why then should we trust it with an even bigger and more complicated job? If the welfare state doesn't work, why would we expect that a complete takeover of the economy will function any better? The statists who support that strategy prefer that we not think about that little detail.

There are accusations that Obamacare is a Cloward-Piven effort. The theory is that Obamacare is designed to fail and force people to move more toward collectivism by voting for full-blown socialized medicine. That is possible; such conspiracies can be difficult to detect.

Whether its failure is planned or not, I and many of my acquaintance believe Obamacare will fail. It is just too complicated and too poorly managed. It is already a mess and promises to get worse. We also believe that, after it fails, its proponents will try to use that failure to go farther toward government control of health care. They will probably claim that the only solution is to go all the way to socialized medicine (though they will use the euphemism "single payer health care"). In chapter 8 we discussed a good response to that.

Running a socialized medicine system, and doing it right, would require superhuman ability and unquestionable integrity. Do we think our politicians (or anyone else) capable of that?

Can we Trust our Politicians?

So what about our politicians today? Are they more moral and capable than the average citizen? We have already discussed how that profession attracts the power-hungry. Many, probably most, are honorable people, but certainly not all are. What would happen if a few real power-seekers were to obtain critical positions in our government? Only two things could prevent them from taking over and imposing their will on us. First their integrity, but that is always suspect. The only other protection would be if we maintain a system that denies such people the ability to overthrow our system. That means that we must vote for politicians who support our limited government and we must continually urge them to oppose bigger government.

Unless we do that, it can happen here. Nay, unless we do that it *will* happen here. Again, freedom is an unstable state. Without constant vigilance, we will regress to statism. The signs are there.

Chapter 27 Monopoly of Information and Opinion

There are only two sources of news more dangerous than a free press. Those are a controlled press and no press at all.

I am not ashamed to say it: The United States of America is the most successful country in history. Our economy has led the world for decades, and even our poor have material goods that are the envy of most of the world. We lead the world in invention and medical advances. Decades ago we put men on the moon, a feat no other country has achieved to this day. The technical and scientific departments of our universities attract students from all over the world. Immigrants, legal and illegal, flock to our shores seeking a better life. Our economy has allowed us to provide unprecedented aid to other countries, and to shield other countries from communist aggression.

With that success, you would think that everybody would want to keep moving in the same direction. You would be wrong. Many of the self-appointed elites, the news media, politicians, and others denigrate our system and want to copy other, less successful countries. Some even urge our courts to apply laws from other countries. They regard our constitutional freedoms as obsolete. Instead they want a government that meddles more and more in our lives.

One of the mysteries of human nature is how those people can simultaneously believe that citizens cannot manage their own lives, but that government officials, selected from those same citizens, can manage their lives for them. Yet that belief is not only popular but unquestioned in many circles today. Its adherents want to include their beliefs in our code of law.

With all our history of success while we were a free country, how did the statists manage to advance as they have? How did they convince so many citizens that we should change the system that served us so well? I am convinced that it is because they have taken near total control of four powerful and very influential institutions, what we might call the four horsemen of the political apocalypse: the news media, education, minority organizations, and the entertainment business. Those institutions now heavily support statism. They also feed on one another, each helping keep the others in the statist fold. Like the biblical four horsemen, they threaten everything we hold dear.

I am old enough to remember when those institutions generally supported our freedoms. Movies and music glorified (perhaps a bit too much) our country and those who fought to defend our freedoms. Today they often glorify our enemies and vilify the businesses that drive our economy. The news used to report on the heroism of our soldiers. Today they often ignore heroism and emphasize a few bad actors. Our schools once taught the reasons for our constitutional government; now they ignore that and often promote collectivism. Minority organizations, once the champions of equal rights, today openly support statism and special rights.

Deception and Groupthink

How did the statists take over those institutions? I am convinced that it was a combination of groupthink and deliberate, planned action. Yes, that means conspiracy.

Conspiracy? That is a strong word, but many statists have been quite open about their intent to deceive. The first hint can be found in the original coat of arms of the Fabian Society, a society devoted to the spread of socialism. That coat of arms was, believe it or not, a wolf in sheep's clothing.[283] Why would any organization chose to be represented by such a symbol? I can think of no other reason than that they planned to use deception to reach their goals. Want more evidence? One of their founders, George Bernard Shaw, instructed them to use "methods of stealth, intrigue, subversion, and the deception of never calling socialism by its right name."[284] Nor does it stop there. As we shall shortly see, many educational programs hide statist indoctrination under innocuous sounding names.

Of course, successful conspiracies are hard to follow; it is probably impossible to trace exactly how the Fabians advanced their cause. What is certain is that they planned to deceive, to hide what they were doing. In that they have been successful. Part of that success is undoubtedly the statist take-over of our news, education, entertainment, and minority institutions.

Beyond conspiracy, what created the near unanimity in those groups? Groupthink. Humans like to feel accepted by other humans. That often means accepting what other humans believe, especially if it appears that a large majority shares that belief.[285] Once an idea becomes conventional wisdom, those who disagree may be regarded as cranks, stupid, or otherwise just not worth paying attention to.

---

283   http://www.americanthinker.com/2012/05/never_call_socialism_by_its_right
    _name.html. The original Fabian coat of arms can also be found in many
    places on the internet. A simple search will find it.
284   Ibid
285   Irving Janis, *Victims of Groupthink*, Houghton Mifflin, 1972

While the majority of U.S. citizens probably don't swallow the statist line, many of the influential clearly do. That causes many of the sheeple to follow; Groupthink feeds on itself and militates against critical thinking. With groupthink, deliberate deception, and perhaps other means, the statists took over those four influential groups. Let's look at the statist four horsemen.

Gatekeepers of Information

What would you call a group of people in which 93% vote for the same party in presidential elections? The facts call that group the Washington, D.C. news correspondents. In a typical presidential election, 93% of news correspondents in that city voted for the democratic candidate.[286] Of course, not all news outlets are as biased as those in Washington, D.C., but statist bias is quite pervasive. That bias threatens our freedom. Any democratic government depends on informed citizens, and those citizens depend on the news media for information. We cannot vote wisely in ignorance, nor if misled by partial information. Misinformation is even worse. As citizens we should inform ourselves to the best of our ability, and that includes knowing how far we can trust news sources. If we understand their problems and biases, we will be better able to separate truth from misinformation, and to vote wisely.

That is why the First Amendment to the U.S. Constitution is so important. "Congress shall make no law …. abridging freedom of speech or of the press." That was written at a time when most newspapers made no pretense of neutrality;

---

286   Tim Groseclose, *Left Turn, How Liberal Media Bias Distorts the American Mind,* St Martins's Press, 2011, p99

instead they openly supported one political side or another.[287] However, different news sources provide diverse information. If all are allowed to publish, all viewpoints are likely to be aired. That does not mean that any, or even all, will be accurate. It just means that, with multiple news sources, the citizens at least have a chance of learning the truth. The problem today is that the major news outlets all dance to the same tune. That self-censorship is quite as dangerous as if the government were doing the censoring – which it tries to do with more success than we might want to believe.

Sharyl Attkisson describes this de facto censorship in her book, *Stonewalled:*

> In many cases, editors reject stories that reflect poorly on advertisers or on politicians they favor.[288]

> Government facilities and equipment are made available to for-profit film-makers and news people, but only if they support the government position. Anyone opposing that position need not apply.[289]

> Broadcast news managers carefully choose and edit some stories because they serve a specific set of agendas.[290] For example, in a story about minimum wage protests, a producer was not allowed to say that most protestors were not minimum wage workers, but were paid to protest. Nor was that producer allowed to include the fact that ten out of ten minimum

---

287   http://www.boston.com/ae/books/articles/2006/06/14/an_objective_and_
        colorful_look_at_colonial_news_bias/

288   Sharyl Attkisson, *Stonewalled, My Fight for Truth Against the Forces of Obstruction, Intimidation, and Harassment in Obama's Washington,* HarperCollins, 2014, p30

289   ˇ Ibid, pp44-45

290   Ibid, p47

336

wage workers interviewed had refused to accept offered raises because they did not want the added responsibility that came with the pay raise.[291]

News people who insist on publishing stories that oppose the current administration may be pressured, even harassed if they refuse to toe the government line. Attkisson's computers were hacked, with the hacking signal traced to a federally owned server. Her home phone would not ring when called, cut off calls, and shifted incoming calls to a strange number. The phone company was unable to fix the problem.[292]

Government public information officers, rather than provide information to the public, often spend their tax-paid time fighting to keep the public from learning the truth and pressuring news people to slant their reports.[293]

"The fact is, many of us in the media are more comfortable when we're on the right side of the government and corporations that guide us. When we are, there's less stress. Life is simpler. We can go home at night without work nagging at us. Nobody threatens to sue us. No one writes nasty emails or calls our bosses to complain. In fact the powers that be, prominent government leaders or corporate entities that we cover may even pat us on the head."[294]

Major TV news organizations tend to stick to "safe" stories, especially stories already published elsewhere or stories that praise advertisers. *CBS This Morning* featured a four and a half minute interview with the Taco Bell CEO about its new nacho cheese Dorito taco shells.[295] However the networks "had no time for" stories about waste of taxpayer money on green energy companies, many of which were known to be poor risks and ultimately failed.[296] This copy-cat "journalism" deprives the public of needed information.

---

291   Ibid, p83
292   Ibid, pp1-13, 282-343
293   Ibid, p73-76 and many other places in the book.
294   Ibid, p28
295   Ibid, pp54-55
296   Ibid, p155-157

The above only scratches the surface of the news problems described in Attkisson's book, which I strongly recommend – at least to those who have the stomach for it.

Forces of Bias

There are several reasons that the news is less reliable than we would like. Some are due to the nature of the business, some due to the nature of people working there.

> 1. Most news people are on the statist end of the political spectrum. One study found two of twenty major news organizations to be slightly less statist than the average U.S. voter, but more statist than the average Republican. All the rest, even the Drudge Report, were more statist than average, many significantly more statist.[297] That same study found that the news articles from various outlets closely mirror the bias of their reporters.[298]

> 2. News organizations work for advertisers. Those advertisers pay for the number of people exposed to their ads. That forces a bias toward the spectacular. They are tempted to "spin" stories to emphasize the spectacular at the expense of the important.

> 3. Some stories, by their very nature, are easier to present than others, as we shall see below.

> 4. News people live with a tyrant called the deadline. Miss the deadline and you don't make the next issue. Competitors take your readers or viewers and eventually your advertisers. That gives the news a bias toward speed over accuracy.

---

297   Groseclose, op cit, p16-17
298   Ibid, p154-155

5. Demagogues and others manipulate the news to their advantage. Talented public relations people earn large sums of money for the one-sided stories they get published. Worse, as discussed above, politicians pressure news people to avoid stories that would present them in a bad light.

6. With few exceptions, news people are not experts on the subjects they cover. They report on economics, technology, businesses, nuclear energy, etc. However they seldom have real expertise in those subjects. Even when they interview experts, time constraints or policy may not allow those experts to review the story for factual errors.

7.   News, especially TV news, shows only a small slice of the entire situation. Since the objective is to attract viewers, that small slice will emphasize the abnormal.

For all those reasons, we must be careful not only about how much of the news we believe, but about how much information is likely to be left out. I have participated in several events that made the news, both as a soldier and as a search and rescue volunteer. Most of the news articles had the main facts generally correct, but the details were often scrambled. Some of those stories were reasonably accurate, some as bad as the following:

A Non-political Example

It was a dramatic rescue. The victim fell off a cliff, coming to rest near the Sandy River. Rescuers rappelled 200 feet down a cliff to reach him. It was nearly impossible to get him out with ground teams alone, so they called in a helicopter. The good news was that he was expected to make a full recovery. So said the news.

As one of the rescuers, I saw a different event. The subject got drunk and fell, hitting his head on a stump in camp. Nobody got near any cliff; we walked down a good trail. We called the helicopter only because we thought he might need an emergency room in a hurry.

I do not know why the news got that particular story so wrong; I suspect it had to do with a deadline. The reporter may have known that there were steep slopes in the area, then just guessed what happened in order to get the story in on time. His guessing emphasized the spectacular. And of course that is only one example of errors in the news. Others are mentioned below.

Deceit by Selective Reporting

To be sure, news reports seldom tell deliberate lies. In fact most of what they publish is true, but they too often mislead by what they leave out. For example, on 3 June 2006 the *Los Angeles Times* had a front page article headlined "A Startling Statistic at UCLA." The facts presented were entirely correct, and if we look only at those facts, it appears that there was discrimination in admissions to the university. The article pointed out that:

1. Only 2% of incoming freshmen were black, the lowest since 1973.

2. UCLA is in a county that is 9.8% Black.

That looks bad, does it not? Similar to our sole blue taxi in town in Chapter 4, the evidence appears overwhelming. However, the article leaves out a few facts, facts that shed important light on the subject:

1. At UCLA, almost half of entering undergraduates are transfers, not freshmen. During that year, the number of Black transfer students

increased, so much that the total number of black undergraduates was *higher* than the year before.

2. The university has a separate admission process for star athletes. Because of an NCAA rule change, coaches requested a change to athletic admission standards. Only 20 black athletes were admitted that year, compared to 27 the year before.

3. Though 9.8% of the neighboring population was Black, only 4.6% of UCLA applicants were black. While they were still rejected at a higher rate than were non-Blacks, that is not nearly as bad as it appeared in the article.

4.   Only 31% of students expected to enroll were white, just short of a record low. (This fact was not mentioned in the article but could be deduced be examining an accompanying pie chart.)

The result was an article that told no outright lies, but gave a false impression by what was left out. Also left out was the author's bias. She and most of the people she quoted strongly supported affirmative action in college admissions.[299]

Did it Affect Electoral Outcome?

Another example: 16 October 2012. The second debate between Mitt Romney and Barrack Obama is underway. Obama, having lost the first debate, cannot afford to look bad in this one. Romney bores in, hammering the president about the recent murder of U.S. diplomatic personnel in Benghazi, Libya.[300] He

---

299   Groseclose, op cit, pp64-73
300   cf. Op Cit, Attkisson, pp159-225 On 11 September 2012 Islamic fanatics overran a diplomatic post in Benghazi, Libya, killing the ambassador and other personnel. The Obama Administration initially blamed the attack on a mob

questions why the president refused to call it Islamic terrorism during his Rose Garden news conference. Obama, during the debate, claimed that he had called it terrorism. Thus he made Romney appear uninformed and scored points with voters. That lie went undetected, at least by the public, with the result that Obama gained and Romney looked ignorant. The news media, at least CBS, covered up the truth.

On 12 September, right after the Rose Garden press conference, Steve Kroft of CBS's *60 Minutes* interviewed the president. That interview was recorded and available to CBS News management. They refused to allow reporters access. Finally, long after the debate, one reporter somehow got a transcript of the interview. That gave the lie to claims that the president had, in the news conference, called the Libya attacks terrorism.

> Kroft: Mr. President, this morning you went out of your way to avoid the use of the word *terrorism* in connection with the Libya attack.
>
> Obama: Right.
>
> …
>
> Kroft: Do you believe that this was a terrorist attack?
>
> Obama: Well, it's too early to know exactly how this came about, what group was involved, but obviously it was an attack on Americans.301

---

reaction to a video that showed Islam in a bad light. Later they admitted that it was a preplanned attack by organized insurgents. CIA and State Department knew the truth almost immediately but administration officials removed that information from the reports.

301   Op Cit, Attkisson, pp 278-280

A flat out admission that Obama deliberately avoided calling the Benghazi attack a terrorist action and claimed that it was too early to say what it was. The president was lying, both in the debate and in his interview with Kroft. It was known from the outset that the Libyan murders were an Islamic terrorist attack. The attempt to blame an internet video was total fabrication. For some reason CBS News management withheld that information from the public.

It is, of course, impossible to know what would have happened had that interview been publicized immediately. It is certain that Obama would have lost much of what he gained in that debate and Romney would have gained instead of appearing uninformed. Would that have changed the outcome of the election? We cannot know. We can and do know that CBS was protecting the president by selective reporting.

News Problems, the Nature of the Beast

Some problems make it easier to present one side than the other. Consider for example stories about families in need and how much they will be hurt unless we provide tax money to feed their children. Such families are easy to find, and often anxious to tell their sob stories. That tugs at our heart strings; nobody wants to see children go hungry. Those stories attract readers or viewers and bring in advertising money. Unfortunately, the emotional aspect discourages digging deeper. Some of those families did meet with job loss, high medical bills, serious accidents, or other unforeseeable disaster. Others are dealing with problems they caused themselves.

The press seldom asks the important questions. Did the parents acquire marketable skills before having children? How much do the parents spend on alcohol, cigarettes, illegal drugs, gambling etc? Does the father make a real effort to support his family, or did he just abandon them? Are the children the result of temporary liaisons with men who cannot or will not support their offspring? Did either parent think about the responsibility of parenthood before they started making babies?

A different example is the death row inmate. It is easy to get quotes from a friend, family or girlfriend about how he just could not commit the crime for which he was convicted, and how awful and unfair it is for him to be put to death. Or that he is now a changed man and absolutely will not do it again. It is impossible to show the terror and pain of his victim as he raped, tortured, and murdered her. Nor can we get inside the head of the criminal to learn if he really has changed, or if he is just a good actor. There is simply no way the news can show both sides with equal impact.

And what about national defense? There are plenty of people anxious to provide stories of atrocities committed by our troops. The crimes of a few of our soldiers at Abu Ghraib quickly became international news.[302] A false report that our guards in Guantanamo had flushed a Koran down the toilet caused riots in much of the Islamic world.[303] The fact that those incidents were few, and one totally fabricated, did not diminish their impact. No such stories come from the prisons of tyrants. Reporters, if they are allowed in at all, see only a sanitized side of those prisons. We had an example of that during the Vietnam War. Antiwar

---

[302]   http://www.cbsnews.com/news/exposing-the-truth-of-abu-ghraib/ Abu Ghraib was a U.S. prison in Iraq, used during the second war there. Some military police sadistically tortured prisoners and caused an international scandal.

[303]   http://www.washingtonpost.com/wp-dyn/content/article/2005/05/15/AR2005051500605.html

activists who went to North Vietnam reported that prisoners were treated well. Only when those prisoners were released at the end of the war did we learn how big a lie that was. The North Vietnamese, like statists today, knew how to manipulate the press.

U.S. Government Manipulation of the Press

And the statists in our government today do manipulate the press. As Attkisson shows, this has long been a problem, but the Obama Administration raised it to a high art. Any reporter or news organization with the temerity to show the administration in a bad light can expect pressure to change the story. Officials will demand to know who the reporter was, how he got the information, just what information he or she has. They will lobby and pressure the news organization's management. They will stall and withhold information that should be public. They will launch a propaganda campaign through their surrogates and sympathizers, attempting to divert attention from the facts. They will try to discredit the reporter or whistleblower. They will accuse the reporter of just being partisan.[304] In fact, their methods are reminiscent of the Soviet disinformation campaigns we discussed in Chapter 23.

The upshot of all this is that we should be very careful about trusting the news. We need to think critically and ask questions. It is also wise to get our news from several different, independent, sources. The problem with "independent" sources, however, is that many quote and copy each other. It requires extra care to find truly independent reporting. Fortunately, today we have the internet which provides news from many viewpoints.

---

304   Attkinsson, Op Cit, throughout the book, especially p232

Internet News

But, even as helpful as the internet is, its reporters face the same obstacles as their "mainstream" brethren. They deal with deadlines, the need to satisfy advertisers etc. In addition, the internet is the world's biggest, fastest, and most persistent rumor mill. It has independent reporters who do a good job. It also has people who send out anything they hear, especially if it supports their biases. And internet rumors seem to have eternal life. For example, there is a persistent claim that Madalyn Murray O'Hair is urging laws against religion. She did plenty of that in the past, but she might find it difficult to continue that effort today. She died in 1995.

We must be as careful with on-line news as we are with the main-stream media.

Emotion vs. Facts

The tearjerker, the sob story, the miscarriage of justice. All those play on our emotions and get attention. They attract readers, listeners and viewers along with advertising dollars. However such stories, by their very nature, distort our picture of reality. They emphasize the emotional at the expense of the factual.

When a news story tugs at our heartstrings, we must be extra careful. Are there real facts behind the story, or just guesses and feelings? Do the facts support the emotions that story creates? Are there possibly other facts that would change the story? Do the people quoted provide solid information? Or only emotional claims?

What Can We Do About It?

We must have news and other information if we are to vote wisely. However we must carefully segregate real information from the spin and outright error, and to get all sides of the stories. There are two good ways that we can better inform ourselves.

First, as mentioned, we should seek information from a variety of sources. Every citizen should find at least one news outlet with a statist outlook, and one with a bias toward less government, then regularly consult both. That may be difficult with the media being heavily biased toward statism, but we should try our best.

Second, we should look beyond the news media. Fortunately, the internet makes many original sources easily available. If a news story refers to some study, we can often find the study itself on line. We should, however, be skeptical. There are biased researchers as well as biased as news reporters. A good method of evaluation is:

> First, look at the authors of any research or other information. Are they competent? Do they have any identifiable biases?
>
> Second, is the report in a recognized, peer reviewed journal? That does not guarantee accuracy, but it helps.
>
> Third, ask the following questions:
>
> > What is the assertion?
> >
> > If true, would you care?
> >
> > Who stands to benefit from the assertion?

How good is the evidence? Does it come from multiple independent studies? How good are they?

What are the key elements of the study? (Population, exposure, outcome, effect size.)

Are the data supporting the assertion *relevant?* Is it the right population, the right exposure, an important outcome, and a big effect?

Are the data supporting the assertion *valid?* Is there a comparison group? Is the comparison fair? Is the outcome measured properly? Might the effect be due to chance?

Are there other studies with similar findings to support the assertion?[305]

That caution should apply to all information sources, news, education and anything else.

Education

Plant an idea firmly in the minds of children and you will create a generation of adults who regard that idea as unquestionable. As obvious as that is, we have allowed the statists access to our most precious population. We should have seen it coming. From the first days of socialism they set out, quite deliberately, to indoctrinate the children.

"It was not the Fascists but the socialists who began to collect children from the tenderest age into political organizations to make sure that they grew up as

---

305   The quoted questions are from the Center for the Evaluative Clinical Sciences at Dartmouth University. That institution kindly provided a reference card listing those criteria.

good proletarians. It was not the Fascists but the socialists who first thought of organizing sports and games, football and hiking, in party clubs where the members would not be infected by other views.... *Balilla* and Hitlerjugent, *Dopolavoro* and *Kraft durch Freude*, political uniforms and military party formations, are all little more than imitations of older socialist institutions."[306]

The statists, whatever else we say about them, do find effective ways to spread their gospel of bondage. Winning the next generation to their side is an obvious goal, schools an obvious target. They count on teachers to help destroy our freedom.

Where do we get teachers for our primary and secondary schools? From universities of course, but what values do those teachers acquire there? Various studies have shown that university faculties are overwhelmingly statist/collectivist.[307][308] And on many campuses, diverse ideas may be called hate speech.

Want to go on campus and give a speech in praise of freedom? Better be certain that the word doesn't get out. On most campuses you will be shouted down, assuming you can schedule your speech in the first place. Campus "speech cops" are ever vigilant. Even independent student newspapers that support

---

[306]   Hayek, op cit, p143 *Balilla* was the Italian Fascist organization for boys, *Hitlerjugent* the "Hitler Youth supporting Hitler, *Dopolavoro* the Italian Fascist recreation program, and *Kraft durch Freude(Strength through Joy)* the German recreation counterpart of *Dopolavaro.*

[307]   See for example, Yancey, George, *Compromising Scholarship, Religious and Political Bias in American Higher Education,* Baylor University Press, 2011

[308]   David B. Klein and Charlotta Stern, http://www.criticalreview.com/2004/pdfs/klein_stern.pdf

freedom are routinely destroyed – with the tacit approval of university administrators.[309] One study found that for 2012 and 2013 statist (liberal) commencement speakers outnumbered freedom supporters (conservatives) six to one. Student and faculty objections, even threats of riot, forced several potential speakers on the freedom side to withdraw.[310] That included such luminaries as Dr. Ben Carson. Neither faculty nor students would tolerate viewpoints contrary to statism. Fortunately, there is opposition to that monopoly of opinion. FIRE, the Foundation for Individual Rights in Education, regularly battles restrictive policies on university campuses.[311]

It is no surprise that the primary and secondary teachers that those universities "educate" follow their ideology, often teaching against our way of life. Many claim to teach about our history and political system "warts and all," but too often, they concentrate on the warts and forget the "all." For example, a new advanced placement history program fails to mention John Winthrop, or Thomas Jefferson, or even Martin Luther King, Jr. Instead, it pushes a revisionist view of American history that deletes heroic individuals and emphasizes oppression and conflict. The course denigrates the Constitution as a product of old white men,[312] as though there is something wrong with being old, white, or male. An advanced history review book contains the same racist, sexist implication.[313]

---

309   http://www.uvm.edu/~dguber/POLS21/articles/leo.htm

310   http://articles.latimes.com/2013/may/19/opinion/la-oe-hassett-colleges-muzzle-conservatives-20130519 Note that though this is an op-ed it describes the authors study of the data.

311   http://www.thefire.org/

312   http://www.newsweek.com/whats-driving-conservatives-mad-about-new-history-course-264592

313   Tom Meltzer and Jean Hofheimer (updated by Susan Babkes), *Cracking*

They are judging the Constitution, not by its content or results, but by racist, sexist criteria. The writers of the Constitution did not meet their criteria for diversity, so they imply that it cannot be useful.

Another book, previously referenced and recommended by the federal "Common Core" educational standards, claims that, though slavery had existed throughout human history, it was in America that it "was established as a permanent and inheritable legal condition, defined by the color of a person's skin.[314] Hardly! Slavery was an inherited condition at least as early as the biblical account in the book of Exodus. Nor did skin color define slavery in the United States; there were many free Blacks throughout our history, even Blacks who owned slaves.[315] That claim is just not true, but they are teaching the lie to our children.

Of course we do have warts, as does every other country. Perfection is as uncommon as unicorns in this world. However, total concentration on our warts, while ignoring the good in this country and the warts elsewhere, gives an impression that is both false and dangerous.

Even one generally excellent textbook cannot resist the comment that, during the writing of the Constitution, "The sorry truth is that the fledgling idealism of the Founding Fathers was sacrificed to political expediency. A fight over slavery would have fractured the fragile national unity that was so desperately needed."[316] The comment about "political expediency" is excessive.

the AP U.S. History Exam 2013, The Princeton Review, 2012, p87

314   Monk, Op Cit, p206

315   http://www.theroot.com/articles/history/2013/03/ black_slave_owners_did_they_exist.html

316   David M. Kennedy, Lizabeth Cohen, Thomas A. Bailey, The American

As the following sentence in that book indicates, it was not only expedient, it was necessary. Madison said, "Great as the evil [of slavery] is, a dismemberment of the union would be worse.[317] "In the short term, slavery was bound to continue, with the Constitution or without. If liberty *for anyone* was to have a future in America, the indispensable first step was a stronger national government on a democratic basis."[318] (Emphasis in the original)

Had the north insisted on abolition of slavery in 1787, the south would have left the union. Slavery would undoubtedly have persisted even longer than it did. Yet even the authors of *The American Pageant* cannot resist calling allowance of slavery merely "politically expedient."

How the statist educational system developed is a question beyond the scope of this book. What is important is that it did happen and what we can do about it. Let's look what too often happens in education today.

Fads displace important subjects. Self esteem, multiculturalism, bilingual education, diversity, environmental commitment, and on and on and on. Educators are no more immune to fad and fashion than any other group. Thomas Sowell describes some of these fads in his book, *Inside American Education.* Fads have changed since he wrote that book, but the problem of fashion remains. As the book documents, this creates several problems:

Pageant, A History of the Republic, Advanced Placement Edition, Houghton Mifflin Company, 2009, p167. The high school near my home uses this text for Advanced Placement American History.

317   Ibid

318   Thomas G. West, *Vindicating the Founders, Race, Sex, Class, and Justice in the Origins of America,* Rowman & Littlefield Publishers, Inc. 1997, p15

1. Schools have the power to force the latest fashion on students, often over the objections of parents. We can refuse to buy the latest silly fad in clothing, but we are stuck with what the school authorities dictate.

2. The fads and fashions become dogma, unquestionable and sacrosanct. Parents and others who object are excoriated, considered reactionary or unqualified.

3. As with all fads, the driving force is popularity rather than truth or effectiveness. Indeed, many of them appear to be counterproductive to their stated goals. Bilingual education educates in neither language, multiculturalism is associated with increased ethnic strife, diversity encourages dependence on ethnicity rather than an expectation that students will learn.

4. The fads displace the teaching of basic skills. We have students with good self esteem, but who are unable to write a coherent sentence or to do simple math problems.[319]

Antipathy to critical thinking. Anyone who thinks critically will be naturally immune to fads and groupthink. Too many educators not only fail to think critically, they also fail to teach critical thinking to students. Many even discourage such thinking. That is to be expected; the student who thinks critically just might ask unpleasant questions about the teacher's favorite political beliefs. There are some teachers who encourage critical thinking, but not nearly as many as we need. Indeed, some teachers tell me that they are forced to do the best they can in a system hostile to critical thinking and other effective teaching tools. For fear of repercussions, they dare not speak out publicly.

---

319   Thomas Sowell, *Inside American Education, The Decline, The Deception, The Dogmas*, The Free Press, 1993. Chapter 4 discusses educational fads and dogmas.

Group Pressure. Peer pressure is a problem for all humanity, but especially for young people. They crave acceptance and are especially susceptible to peer pressure. Unfortunately some teachers have been known to use this to pressure students to accept the teachers' beliefs.[320]

The result of these and other problems is too many students with good self esteem, indoctrinated in the latest fads, but lacking basic skills and knowledge. I remember asking a co-worker, graduate of what was considered a good high school, to use her calculator to divide five by seven. She claimed that it was not possible to divide a number by a larger number, and was amazed when I demonstrated otherwise.

What can we do about it?

What should we do? First, we can hold our local education systems accountable. We can examine the textbooks our children use. When we find bias or errors, we can start by making suggestion to the publisher and school. In many cases they will act on good suggestions. If they do not, we should complain - publicly. We can also look at the homework and other assignments to see if they represent both sides of the story, or if grading is biased. If the school emphasizes some non-academic program such as multiculturalism or bilingual education, we can demand solid proof that the program actually works. The squeaky wheel gets the grease so let's squeak – loudly!

We should also pressure schools to teach the basics before they wander off into pretty sounding detours. Elementary students need to learn reading, writing, and basic mathematics. Starting usually around middle school age, the mind

---

320   Ibid, chapter 3

develops enough that critical thinking becomes important and should be part of education. All students need a store of basic facts from which to reason. Those facts should include the basic history of our country, why the Constitution says what it does, and how we can participate in our government.

Next, if we are in position to donate to our alma mater or some other university, let's be wise about who gets our money. Why should we support any institution that works to support statism? If a school has regulations about things like "hate speech" that is a red flag; most such regulations amount to prohibition against freedom. While real hate speech does exist, the term is too often used to restrict free speech. Only certain viewpoints were allowed. For example, one university punished a student for posting an invitation to a speech by writer who opposed government welfare.[321] If a university appears to support statism or to restrict defense of liberty, we should withhold our donations and tell them why.

Those who have time and ability should also get involved in things like the school board. Attend board meetings and maybe even run for that board. Complain loudly about bias in the school system. On the state level, we can complain to the legislature about bias. We might even audit classes, especially from statist professors, and ask some pertinent (or impertinent) questions. Those professors are our employees, after all. We have the right to expect them to allow diversity of opinion.

There is, however, one mistake we must not make. We must never, ever, take the word of teachers, principals, school board members, professors, university presidents or anyone else in the educational establishment. They have an obvious incentive to show their system in the best light. Too often they have

---

321   http://articles.latimes.com/2004/may/06/local/me-calpoly06

even deceived the public about what they are doing to our precious children. In fact, programs such as sex education have gone so far as to instruct teachers not to show materials to parents.[322] Check the claims your school system makes, find out if they are really true.

I must warn you however. If you publicly oppose statism in the schools you can expect opposition – nasty opposition. Statists will call you anti-education even though your program would help education. They will call you racist even if you want to improve inner city schools. They will take your statements out of context and probably twist them into something you never said. It is even possible that your property will be vandalized. Some statists will stop at nothing to smear you and to prevent improvement and balance in education. Be prepared for opposition.

Oppose statist indoctrination in schools we must. We must encourage schools to teach without bias and to reward critical thinking. Only thus can we avoid a generation of sheep trained up in collectivism.

Entertainment

Ever hear of "Friends of Abe"? It is a group of freedom lovers (conservatives) who don't want their political beliefs known for fear of job loss.[323] No, they don't work for the Democratic Party, nor for any politician. They work in Hollywood, where the great majority supports statism/collectivism. Sadly, their fears are well-founded. Big name entertainers such as Clint Eastwood can get

---

322   Sowell, op cit , *The Vision of the Anointed,* p 20
323   http://www.washingtontimes.com/news/2008/jul/23/hollywoods-conservative-underground/?page=all

away with opposing statism, most cannot. For example, actress Maria Conchita Alonso was pressured to resign from a job in San Francisco after she publicly supported a Tea Party candidate for governor.[324] Freedom lovers were not allowed in that job. That is ironic; entertainment, more than almost any other business, depends on freedom of expression. Yet few businesses are more repressive when it comes to political belief.

Of course, entertainers are entitled to their opinions. The problem comes when they deny others the right to differing opinions and, even worse, when people accept what they say just because they are celebrities. Actors are good at acting, at pretending to be what they are not. They earn their living in a fantasy world, and I fear that many of them lose touch with reality. Their talent does not include any particular wisdom; if it did we would see fewer Hollywood stars in the news for all the wrong reasons.

For example, during the Alar scare,[325] actress Meryl Streep testified before Congress about how that chemical was dangerous.[326] Streep is a fine actress, but if she has any special knowledge about carcinogens, that knowledge remains hidden. Yet she got a national audience and was able to sway our legal system.

Too many people "go gaga" over celebrities. It does little harm when teenage girls swoon over some entertainer, but it is dangerous when voters blindly

---

324   http://sanfrancisco.cbslocal.com/2014/01/18/actress-out-of-san-francisco-production-after-endorsing-tea-party-candidate/

325   Alar, a trade name for Daminozide, was used to control ripening of fruit, especially apples. Huge doses of the chemical led to cancer in test animals, though, as far as I know, reasonable amounts were never shown to harm either animals or humans. It was banned in 1989.

326   Daniel Kahneman, *Thinking Fast and Slow,* Farrar, Straus and Giroux, 2011, p143

accept celebrity pontifications. That turns thinking over to people who live in Fantasy-land. How being an actor or singer gives one special political wisdom remains unexplained. Yet many celebrities got lots of attention and have too much influence on voters.[327]

We are unlikely to change the beliefs of most movie stars or other entertainers; they live in a world far removed from the rest of us. A few use their free time to learn about things other than acting or music, sometimes even about economics and free government, but they are the exceptions. We should be wary when someone who earns a living playing make-believe talks about the real world. We must study the issues ourselves and make up our own minds as wisely as we are able.

Minorities

"Oreo." "Uncle Tom." "House Nigger." "Not authentic Black." All those slurs and more will be thrown at any black politician who fails to support the statist agenda. It is no secret that minorities, especially Blacks, vote overwhelmingly for big government. Any black politician who fails to support the democratic, statist position will find himself excoriated, no independent thinking allowed. How did it happen? More importantly, what is that groupthink doing to the black community and to our country? After all, it was Republicans who freed the slaves and who were the major supporters of the Civil Rights Act of 1965. Though other minorities also tend to vote statist, Blacks are the major ethnic group in the statist camp, so we shall use them as our prime example.

---

327   http://www.celebuzz.com/2012-11-04/election-2012-celebrities-who-support-barack-obama-gallery/

One black member of Congress said, "one of the advantages, and disadvantages of representing blacks is their shameless loyalty ... You can almost get away with raping babies and be forgiven. You don't have *any* vigilance about your performance." (Emphasis in the original)[328]

And what happens should a black politician step out of line? Some did just that and were reprimanded for their temerity. They complained that black unemployment under Obama had increased, more than had white unemployment. Obama's response? He told the Congressional Black Caucus, "I expect all of you to march with me and press on."[329] A presidential imperative to engage in groupthink!

More Groupthink Devastation

Groupthink creates chaos beyond the political arena, especially among our black fellow citizens. As black writers such as Thomas Sowell and Walter Williams tell us, it keeps millions of those people in bondage to a warped idea of what it means to be black. Young Blacks, even children of middle and some upper class families, fear the accusation that they are "acting white." Success in school? Best avoided, that is acting white. Speak normal English, the language that helps get good jobs? Don't do it! That is acting white. Have good manners? Again, acting white. Fail to commit mayhem at any suggestion that someone is "dissing" you? Ditto. Work hard at a productive job? More evidence of acting white.[330]

---

328   Jason L. Riley, *Please Stop Helping Us, How Liberals Make it Harder for Blacks to Succeed,* Encounter Books, 2014, p10
329   Ibid, pp14-15
330   Thomas Sowell, *Black Rednecks and White Liberals*, Encounter Books, 2005. The first and fifth chapters discuss this.

All too many Blacks celebrate a culture of lawlessness, crudity, and poor communication skills, thinking that such is a requirement to be an "authentic Black." That militates against occupational success and safe communities.[331] The result is Blacks kept down by crime and lack of skills, living in ghettos where all too many young black men die at the hands of other young black men.

The irony is that what that counterproductive black subculture lionizes is really acting white, following a particular low-class white subculture. That developed from the southern redneck culture imported from the lawless regions on the frontiers of England and Scotland. Many immigrants to the southern U.S. came from those border areas, bringing with them their redneck/cracker culture. It was a culture that opposed to work but glorified violence, a culture where any perceived offense would likely lead to a "no holds barred" fight to preserve the honor of anyone who fancied himself offended. It was the equivalent of today's "he was dissing me" excuse for mayhem. That chip-on-the-shoulder attitude was not only accepted, but demanded. Southern Blacks, some of them, absorbed that culture and took it along as they moved to inner cities.[332]

On the other hand, what would it take to really act Black, to follow the example of the Blacks who escaped slavery and fought Jim Crow? Many of those people worked hard and sought education, even at the risk of beatings and sometimes of their lives. In many places it was illegal to teach slaves to read and write, but they learned anyway.[333] Many of those black people saw the problems with the redneck/cracker culture and deliberately sought a different culture, a

---

331   Ibid, pp 1-63, especially p59
332   Ibid, p3-27
333   http://www.historyisaweapon.com/defcon1/slaveprohibit.html

culture that worked rather than the culture that produced so many problems. Former slave Booker T. Washington worked hard to bring literacy and a functional culture to the more disadvantaged former slaves. Freeborn W.E.B. Du Bois worked similarly for those Blacks who were not as disadvantaged. Both saw the advantages that literacy and marketable skills offered their people.[334]

Yet today many in the inner cities follow the redneck/cracker culture, thinking that only thus can they "act black." They excoriate any Black who really seeks an education while they support black criminals, even criminals that prey upon other Blacks. That groupthink harms our entire country, especially Blacks. And it is one reason Blacks tend to support statist politicians. Those are the politicians who support keeping them in their counterproductive culture. That is a particularly damaging form of co-dependence.

Fortunately, some Blacks have the courage to stand up to that groupthink. I've referenced both Thomas Sowell and Jason Riley here. There are others as well, a look at a "conservative" web site such as townhall.com/columnists will show several black faces. We need more; we need to break the near monopoly of statist support in the black community.

Poverty, Minorities, and Voting

How did Blacks come to vote so heavily for the statists? Partly because of welfare programs. Lyndon Johnson's "Great Society" was intended to reduce poverty, and did in fact increase hand-outs to the poor. Though no real fan of

---

334   Sowell, Op Cit, *Black Rednecks and White Liberals,* pp231-235. Contrary to some legends, Du Bois and Washington were not enemies but supported one another. They just had different, complementary, emphases in their work.

Blacks, he was politically astute enough to make sure that Democrats got the credit. He apparently said, ""I'll have those Niggers voting Democratic for the next 200 years."[335] Then, with the help of a heavily democratic Congress, he sent checks worth tens of billions of dollars to the poor. That was the most ambitious income redistribution attempt in U.S. history.[336] That tax-funded bribe worked, for almost 50 years his prediction has come true. Though Blacks had been edging away from the Republicans for decades, since Johnson they have voted democratic in droves. Black leaders hold as an article of faith that Democrats are their friends. Blacks, especially in the inner cities, still vote nearly 100% for Democrats – with decidedly unhappy results as their cities deteriorate.

The Black Family

A disproportionate number of Blacks are poor and living in inner cities, which provides motivation to want government assistance. There are many reasons for that, but one important cause is that many black children come from single-parent homes. Until about 1965 black women age 35 and older were more likely than their white counterparts to have married. However, in about 1950, the percentage of never-married black women started increasing, and in about 1980 it began increasing precipitously. That was just when daughters of welfare mothers reached child-bearing age. By 2010, one quarter of black women 35 and older had never married.[337] In addition, black men are eight times as likely to be

---

335   http://canadafreepress.com/index.php/article/some-of-the-lost-history-in-the-civil-rights-movement.

336   Riley, op cit, p2

337   http://www.census.gov/hhes/socdemo/marriage/data/acs/ElliottetalPAA2012paper.pdf Figure 5

incarcerated as are white men.[338] That means that many black children are being raised in single parent homes. Single parenthood is a major cause of poverty, poor health, and crime,[339] though the health problems may be the result of poverty rather than being directly caused by single parenthood.

Because of poverty and crime, many Blacks were looking for any help they could get. Johnson promised help, and that help included aid to single parents, but not to mothers married to and living with the fathers of their children. The War on Poverty subsidized single parenthood. If you want more of something, just subsidize it – and that is what happened with single black women. Since Blacks started out with a higher poverty rate than whites, they got the most "advantage" from the War on Poverty – and suffered the greatest destruction of families. That program did not reduce poverty, but it has been effective in accomplishing what Johnson wanted. The welfare benefits swung the black vote to the Democrats.

Unquestionably, the welfare state provided largesse disproportionately to Blacks. It is less certain that welfare helped those people in the long run; the destruction of the family wreaked havoc. How much of that destruction was caused by welfare and how much by the general counterculture movement of the 1960s? That is not certain, but it is certain that both contributed. It is fair to say that a government dole fosters dependence, and that dependence in turn fosters poverty.

Another reason for this block voting is that for some reason the Republicans have failed to articulate why they are better for black people than the Democrats. (Of course since Reagan they seldom articulate much of anything very well, so

338   Ibid, p6-7
339   http://www3.uakron.edu/schulze/401/readings/singleparfam.htm

that should be no surprise,) Republicans are more likely to support such things as charter schools and school vouchers that would help inner-city blacks.[340] They are also more likely to support good law enforcement which could help protect inner-city Blacks from the high crime rates they face. Yet they fail to make the case for those measures.

One-party Damage

Democrats just assume that they will get the Black vote, and usually they are right. Maybe the Republicans have just given up on them. That is a mistake. One-party rule in many of our cities has done unspeakable damage to Blacks and others.

What have the Democrats done for their black voters? It is not pretty. Cities like Chicago and Detroit, long democratic strongholds, have become hell-holes. The Democrats have defended black criminals, resulting in high crime rates. Statist controls from Washington, D.C. make classroom discipline difficult and contribute to making most inner city schools downright atrocious. Then Democrats usually oppose the charter schools and school vouchers that would allow students to attend real schools where they might actually get an education.

All that is the natural result of statist policy (though abetted by the Democrats dependence on union votes, since teachers' unions fight tooth and nail against charter schools and school vouchers). Democrats have long worked to give the federal government complete control of everything and to stop holding

---

340   https://nonprofitquarterly.org/policysocial-context/23577-republican-gubernatorial-campaigns-play-the-charter-school-card.html

people accountable for their own actions. That affects inner cities more than it does the suburbs.

After the statists have created all those problems, it is no surprise that black unemployment is much higher than that for other ethnicities. Who would want to set up a business in a neighborhood with the high crime and poor education those policies created?

Turning this around will be difficult and time consuming. We need to help our minority friends understand the benefits of freedom. That could include everything from letters to the editor to talking with friends and neighbors, especially if we have black friends or neighbors. We should help them understand the damage that dependence does to their race. We should help them understand our system of government and how checks and balances are supposed to keep any one person from becoming too powerful. We should help them understand that every government welfare payment comes out of the pocket of the widow, the family trying to pay medical bills, and others of their friends and neighbors. Most of all, we should help them understand the human dignity that free people have and which can never be part of a collectivist society.

Opposing the Influential

Educators, minority leaders, entertainers, the news media. All present dangerous viewpoints with pretended wisdom. We must fight them with our own wisdom, pointing out where they are wrong and tolerating the invective they will inevitably throw at us. Failure to effectively fight their deception will sentence us to statism.

Chapter 28 World Government?

In North Korea, the people are held in bondage, not allowed to leave what amounts to a nation-wide prison; and speaking against their "dear leader" can bring a prison sentence or worse. In many Muslim countries women are not allowed to drive cars, or to leave their homes unless accompanied by a male relative. Resource-rich Venezuela has shortages of everything from toilet paper to food. The list of human misery goes on and on. What should we do about it?

One World

Should we create a one-world government, something to overcome all the national differences? Some well-meaning people seriously propose that, claiming it would stop war, poverty and other ills. Even President Harry Truman suggested turning the United Nations into what amounts to a world government.[341] This one doesn't just bump up against the shoals of reality, it crashes full speed onto the reefs of the real world.

The first question to ask about world government is, "Just who is going to run this gargantuan state?" Now the questions integrity and ability of the rulers return – with a vengeance. Why would anyone believe that the rulers of a world-wide government would have any particular wisdom or integrity?

If you want an example, just look at the United Nations. That organization has two authorities, the Security Council and the General Assembly. In neither do free, democratic countries have real power except for vetoes in the Security

---

341   http://news.google.com/newspapers?nid=1338&dat=19460125&id=
    m9hXAAAAIBAJ&sjid=efUDAAAAIBAJ&pg=4077,4801132 (A link to an article in
    the *Spokane Daily Chronical*, Jan 25, 1946)

Council. In fact, third world tyrannies are the major voice in the General Assembly.

The UN Human Rights Council is an example of how a future world government might work. That council, which ostensibly promotes human rights worldwide, instead gives voice to tyrannies including China, Argentina, Cuba and Saudi Arabia.[342] Those tyrannies condemn the U.S. for things like having the death penalty, but give a pass to collectivist governments that imprison their opponents. An example of what UN rule would be like comes from the Convention on Rights of the Child, an international law applicable to every country that signed it. The Roman Catholic Church made the mistake of signing and is now ordered to reconsider its stance on abortion and pre-marital sex.[343] So much for freedom of religion under a world government.

Why would anyone expect a full world government to behave differently? When a tyrant rules in a place like Cuba, there is hope for eventual change, and that tyrant lacks a world-wide monopoly. If tyrants take over a world government, there is little hope that the tyranny will ever change.

The UN has also become a center for corruption, from cheating on Iraqi oil[344] to corruption and rape in peace-keeping operations.[345] Of course government corruption is not unusual in this world, but the difference here is that the UN is world-wide and accountable to no-one. If the corruptocrats gain the

342   http://www.ohchr.org/EN/HRBodies/HRC/Pages/CurrentMembers.aspx
343   www.breitbart.com/national-security/2014/02/05/un-committee-catholic-church-report
344   http://international.ucla.edu/media/files/heaton.pdf
345   http://news.bbc.co.uk/2/hi/7420798.stm

total control of a world-wide government, it will be impossible to stop their corruption.

How could we oppose the oppressive measures such a world-wide state would inevitably impose? There will be nowhere to flee, no way to escape. With the technology available today, officials would be able to monitor us nearly everywhere. Even if we disconnect from cell phones and web access, they will have satellites, roadside monitors, and probably other technologies not yet invented. A society such as that described in Orwell's *1984* becomes not only possible bit probable. We can only hope that such a government will be incompetent, incapable of enforcing its oppressive laws. And we would lack the advantages of seeing how different systems work.

International Diversity

The one-world advocates want a single government, the same power ruling in China, Malaysia, the United States, and everywhere else. If they get their way, different countries will cease to exist. Have they considered the advantages of competition, not only between businesses but between countries? What happens if only a single model of government is available?

Currently we have various forms of collectivism, all too many tyrannies, and at least two major forms of representative government. People can see the difference; they can look at which type of government they prefer. They can then try to establish that form of government in their own countries. In fact many of them "vote with their feet," moving to the country they think will serve them best (usually the United States of America).[346]

Should world government become a reality, the U.S. would be forced to follow the rest of the world. Those who now flee to our shores would have nowhere to go; they would remain prisoners in whatever system holds them. Those who want to copy our freedoms would have no example to follow. The United States is an ideal as well as a country. That ideal, if we hold true to it, is a shining city on a hill, providing an example to the world. World government would destroy that example.

One-world government is a terrible idea until such time as we have perfect people to run such a government. Rather than bring the rest of the world up to our standard of freedom, we would more likely impose on the entire world a tyranny such as rules in third-world dictatorships.

I close this chapter with the last paragraph of Hannan's book. After pointing out the disadvantages of the current European system and decrying the U.S. tendency to copy the worst aspects thereof, he concludes,

> So let me close with a heartfelt imprecation, from a Briton who loves his country to Americans who still believe in theirs. Honor the genius of your founders. Respect the most sublime constitution devised by human intelligence. Keep the faith with the design that has made you independent. Preserve the freedom of the nation to which, by good fortune and God's grace, you are privileged to belong.[347]

---

346   http://247wallst.com/special-report/2013/09/25/countries-with-the-most-immigrants/3/

347   Hannan, *The New Road to Serfdom,* op cit p187

Chapter 29 Conclusion

The tyranny of a prince in an oligarchy is not so dangerous to the public welfare as the apathy of a citizen in a democracy. (Montesquieu)

Freedom and statism remain locked in battle. Statism fights with deception and attractive promises, promises it cannot keep. Freedom must attack with the weapon of truth, widely distributed. Each of us can and must do our part. The spread of truth is our task, liberty our reward. Will we revert to the serfdom of John I or move toward the freedom of John II? Liberty, ours and that of unborn generations, depends on us.

Of course freedom has problems, as do all systems. Indeed, the problems of freedom afflict collectivism as well. Inequality, shortages, inaccessible medical treatment, all those and more are at least as widespread in the collectivist world as they are in the free world. The only real advantage we would have in a collectivist country is that we need not worry about making important decisions. That would be done for us.

Statism/collectivism advances, not because of actual results delivered, but because it presents such an attractive promise. Unfortunately we live not in the theoretical world of promises, but in the world of reality. In that real world, statism delivers not freedom but government control, not equality but rulers who are "more equal than others," not plenty for everyone but dearth of necessities of life. Yet its proponents continue to make their case, often using Saul Alinsky's four methods: polarization, demonization, organization, and deception. That we must oppose.

Reprise

After wading through the gory details, let us return to the problems of statism described in Chapter 1. The statists, mostly with good intentions, are working hard to advance their cause. If intentions sufficed we would have a wonderful world. Sadly, intention and reality are often strangers to one another. What the statists actually deliver is closer to serfdom than to freedom.

Statism assumes that our leaders will be wise and moral enough to do what is best for everybody. In practice, those leaders are self-selected from the citizens and neither wiser nor more moral than the average citizen.

Statism assumes that the central planner, hundreds of miles away from the action, can decide more wisely than the person on the scene. In practice, that results in one-size-fits-all regulations that really fit nowhere.

Statism assumes that government functionaries can effectively manage the entire economy. In practice, that economy is so complex that effective central management is impossible.

Statism constructs wonderful, self-consistent theories and applies them to the people, be those people in agreement or not. In practice, those theories make shipwreck on the rocks of reality – but statists ignore that and insist that their theories are still good.

Statism demands unlimited power to do what it claims will help us. In practice, that power is turned against the citizens for the benefit of the powerful.

Statism requires experts in the bureaucracy, empowered to make regulations for the rest of us. In practice, that creates conflicting and burdensome rules, harmful to both freedom and the economy.

Statism promises security for everyone. Food, clothing, medical care, housing etc. In practice, someone must create those things and government must take from the productive for the benefit of the recipients. The productive then lack incentive and become less productive.

Statism promises democracy – until that democracy goes against the wishes of the powerful, whereupon it finds a way around democratic decisions.

Statism promises freedom. In practice, bureaucrats and others force their decisions on the people.

Statism promises benign rulers who will act in the best interest of the people. In practice, it provides opportunity for the power-hungry, even psychopaths, to rule.

Statism promises that government-controlled property will provide for all. In practice, that common property is either allowed to deteriorate or is exploited for the benefit of the ruling class.

Statism promises security, but delivers the security of the serf or slave. And even that can be revoked at the will of the rulers.

The promises of statism/collectivism are myriad – and only marginally related to what it actually delivers. It does, however, deliver bondage similar to that of serfdom.

We, all of us, will suffer under statism and benefit under freedom. We, all of us, have a part in the battle to defend freedom. If we learn the facts and how to present them, we can be effective. We can convince voters to support freedom. We will never convince everybody, but we can convince enough people that the statists cannot win, even if they cheat.

I hereby issue a call to battle to all freedom lovers. Take up the arms of truth and liberty. Resist tyranny and demagoguery wherever we find them. Let us regain the freedom that made this country great.

I shall now violate one of the prime rules of writing. I am supposed to provide a satisfying ending to my book. That I cannot do. We have reached the end of the book, but the battle is not won and the story goes on. You are one of the characters, hero, bystander, or villain.

The path of freedom passes through the confusing terrain of statism/collectivism. The temptations to deviate from the path are as attractive as a worm to a fish and as frequent as the morning news. That temptation we must resist – continually. Therefore this is

NOT REALLY THE END

Appendix: Constitutional Amendments

For decades, politicians and courts have twisted meaning of the U.S. Constitution to their taste. For example, they used the interstate commerce clause to make it illegal for a farmer to raise wheat to feed his animals. That wheat never crossed any state line; indeed it was not traded in commerce and never even left his farm. That type of anti-constitutional corruption has destroyed many of our freedoms. In addition, professional politicians have found ways to shirk responsibility and to allow the bureaucracy to become the de facto government of the United States. Congressional representatives claim that they are not responsible for bureaucratic decisions, after all those decisions never went through Congress. They ignore the little fact that Congress created those bureaucracies and that Congress can rein them in. If we expect to regain our freedom, we must change that.

Meanwhile, laws and regulations have accumulated, many now obsolete and even contradictory to one another. It is effectively impossible to know every law that applies to us, much less obey all those laws. We cannot expect Congress to fix this; the current situation gives senators and representatives cushy positions while making it difficult in the extreme for any opponent to unseat them. That will not change unless we, the people, force a change. Only by amending the Constitution do we have any hope of fixing the underlying problems.

Nor is it likely that Congress will propose the amendments we need, though we should pressure our representatives to do so. More likely, we will have to resort to the other option Article V of the Constitution offers, "on the Application of the Legislatures of two thirds of the several States, [Congress] shall call a Convention for proposing Amendments." Calling such a convention will be difficult, but almost certainly necessary.

I submit that we must add the following seven amendments to our Constitution:

First, we must eliminate the professional politicians who use the power of their office to make it difficult for any opponent to win an election, and who have little or no first-hand experience with the life of ordinary citizens.

Washington D.C.: 300 square miles totally surrounded by reality. (Based on a Tom Clancy quote)

New Amendment 1

Section 1: No person shall be eligible to serve in Congress without having first been employed for a minimum of three years in work not directly connected with government activities and not in any way connected with attempts to affect government action.

Section 2: Any person who has served in Congress for a total of six years shall be ineligible to continue such service until employed for a minimum of three years in work not directly connected with government activities and not in any way connected with attempts to affect government action. After three years of such employment, he shall be eligible to serve a maximum of six years in Congress until again having spent a minimum of three years in such employment.

Section 3: Representatives and senators serving at the time this amendment is approved may finish their terms, but shall then be ineligible to serve until they meet the requirement of Section 2.

Second, we must devolve power back to the states and local jurisdictions; it is just plain silly to think that federal officials, hundreds of miles from the situation, can make better decisions than can those closer to the problem. Though the tenth amendment specifies this, it is largely ignored so we need something more specific.

New amendment 2

Section 1: No federal law or regulation may have any effect on anything completely internal to any state. The exceptions shall be taxes constitutionally approved, commerce and roadways that cross state lines, national defense, laws for federally owned lands and facilities, the national Social Security Program, and disasters so great that state authorities request federal aid.

Section 2: Notwithstanding Section 1, the federal government and the states shall be bound by Amendments 1 through 10, 13 through 15, 19, and 24 except that birth to a non-citizen mother shall not automatically confer citizenship.

Section 3: Any federal laws that contradict each other shall all be null and void.

Section 4: Congress shall be allowed a maximum of five years from the date of approval of this amendment to bring the Federal Code into compliance. After that time, any laws or regulations violating this amendment shall be null and void.

Third, we have a growing problem of "anchor babies" and other children born to non-citizens who then use their children to claim the right to stay in the country. The 14th amendment was intended to guarantee citizenship to freed slaves, but was written in such a way that any child born in the country, be the parents here legally or not, is automatically a citizen. Some politicians are trying to allow indiscriminate immigration and expect those immigrants and their children to become citizens and automatically vote for one party. That is a danger to our democratic process; unthinking voting helps the demagogues and destroys freedom.

New amendment 3

Section 1: No child born to a mother who is illegally or temporarily in the United States shall be a citizen except through the normal naturalization process.

Section 2: Congress may not create any special route to citizenship for children born to mothers not legally in the United States or her territories.

Section 3: This amendment shall not apply to any child born in the United States before the year 1997 AD. [Exact date to be determined. The purpose of this section is to prevent a flood of anchor babies as the amendment nears ratification.]

Forth, We must tame the bureaucracy and restore government to our elected representatives. I propose two versions of this amendment, the first what we really should have, the second a fall-back position in case we cannot get the first version. Regarding the second version, if either house of Congress can prevent a bill from becoming law, either house should be able to prevent a bureaucratic rule from taking effect.

New Amendment 4a

Section 1: Only Congress, by the constitutionally specified procedure, can make law or regulation. Agencies in the executive branch may propose laws which Congress may at its discretion enact or fail to enact by the normal legislative process.

Section 2: No judicial power shall exist outside the judicial branch, and all judicial proceedings shall allow the accused the protections specified in this Constitution.

Section 3: Congress shall be allowed a maximum of five years from the date of approval of this amendment to bring the Federal Code into compliance. After that time, all laws and rules not made in conformance with this amendment shall be null and void and all administrative judges dismissed.

New Amendment 4b (in case we cannot get 4a passed)

Section 1: All administrative rules shall be presented to Congress and shall not take effect until Congress has been in session for sixty congressional working days after such presentation. Either house of Congress may, by majority vote, prevent such rules from taking effect.

Section 2: In either house of Congress, a vote on such rules shall be taken within ten days of a request by twenty percent of the voting members of said house.

Section 3: No administrative proceeding may deny any citizen the rights guaranteed by this Constitution, to include but not be limited to the rights listed in the fourth, fifth, sixth, and seventh amendments.

Section 4: Any appeal of administrative ruling to district or higher court shall be treated without prejudice. No evidential value shall be assigned to the verdict of the administrative court.

Fifth, Laws get made, they almost never get unmade, no matter how ineffective or counterproductive they turn out to be. Congress finds no glory in repealing laws so such repeal almost never happens. The only solution is mandatory sunset clauses and mandatory review of obsolete laws.

New Amendment 5

Section 1: No law, new or existing, shall remain effective for more than ten years unless:

(a) The bill is passed by 60% of the voting members of each house of Congress, and

(b) The bill includes a clause specifying the duration of its effectiveness, and

(c) Either the president signs the bill, or Congress overrides any veto by vote of three quarters of the voting members of each house. However, Congress may override the veto by a vote of two thirds of each house, whereupon the ten year limit shall apply.

Section 2: Congress shall, within five years of passage of this amendment, review all existing laws. At that time, approval by majority vote of both houses shall be required for any previously existing law to remain in effect. Laws not so reviewed shall be null and void. Laws reviewed and passed shall remain effective for no more than ten years unless they meet the requirements of Section 1 for more extensive duration.

Section 3: Any law nullified by Section 2 shall remain in effect for up to two years to allow time for Congress to create a path for orderly change. A 60% majority vote of both houses shall be required to extend this time beyond two years.

Sixth, At present we have government programs suspended but still funded. Nor can anyone fire civil service employees for any but the most extreme reasons. While the president should not be a dictator, he must have authority to manage the executive branch in a reasonable manner.

New Amendment 6

Section 1: The president shall have authority to impound funding for any federal program no longer active, except that Congress may continue such funding by a majority vote of both houses. Impounded funds shall be returned to the general fund of the Treasury.

Section 3: The president shall have delegatable authority over personnel decisions in the executive branch, including authority to terminate public employees, within budgetary guidelines and neutral hiring protocols established by Congress.[348]

Seventh, Our courts are clogged, and lawsuits often obstruct even obviously worthwhile projects. Meanwhile, frivolous suits damage our economy as companies settle rather than face the cost of going to court. While the courts must remain available to those genuinely damaged, we must stop to the practice of treating them as a lottery, or as a method to delay construction projects that are legal.

New Amendment 7

Section 1: Notwithstanding the provisions of the Seventh Amendment and any state law or constitution, in any federal lawsuit or lawsuit involving entities from more than one state, judges shall draw boundaries of reasonable claims and defenses, and dismiss claims and defenses falling outside those boundaries. No person or entity shall be required to respond to any lawsuit unless a judge shall determine that the claims are reasonable and that there is reasonable evidence to support the allegations.[349]

---

348   Howard, op cit p181.Section 3 of this amendment is taken verbatim from that source.
349   Ibid, p182. Section 1 of this amendment is mostly a partial quote from that source.

Section 2: Should any tort case be found groundless during trial, defendants shall have the right to sue the plaintiffs to recover all costs of defense plus reasonable remuneration for damage to reputation and other ill effects caused by such a suit. Liability shall be imposed on both the plaintiffs and their attorneys as the court shall determine.

Section 3: An attorney, faced with a client desiring to initiate a groundless lawsuit, may inform both the client and the court that, in his judgment, there are no grounds for the suit. Should the client insist on continuing after both client and court are so informed, the attorney shall not be liable.

Annotated Bibliography

(Selected references only)

Books

Alinsky, Saul D. *Rules for Radicals,* Vintage Books, 1989, original copyright 1971. Alinsky was a leading rebel against the American way. While some of his ideas were good (for example, stopping racial discrimination), he was clearly out to impose his statist ideas on the citizens. This book is his plan of action, telling statists how to advance their cause. From this book we can learn about the tactics statists might use against freedom.

Attkisson, Sharyl *Stonewalled, My Fight for Truth Against the Forces of Obstruction, Intimidation, and Harassment in Obama's Washington,* HarperCollins, 2014. Describes just how controlled our press is. The author, winner of five Emmy Awards and an Edward R. Murrow Award for investigative reporting, describes her difficulties getting stories on the air. In many cases, network managers blocked a broadcast because it did not fit the viewpoint they wanted to push. Government officials also tried to block her stories and those of other reporters, sometimes successfully. Someone, probably from government, also harassed her through her phone line and apparently hacked into her computers. This book describes her reporting on several major scandals, along with the push-back she received. A frightening book, but one every U.S. citizen should read.

Babiak, Paul PhD and Hare, Robert D. PhD, *Snakes in Suits, When Psychopaths go to Work,* Harper 2006. This is an excellent book by two experts in the subject. It is oriented toward the business world, but much of the information is also applicable elsewhere, including in government. We can hope that the authors will write a follow-up specific to government and politics.

Brooks, Arthur C. *Who Really Cares,* Basic Books, New York, 2006. At a time when statists and much of the news media assume that "conservatives" are selfish and that "liberals" are generous, this book shows that so-called "conservatives" are more generous than those calling themselves "liberals."

D'Souza, Dinesh, *America, Imagine a World Without Her,* Regenery Publishing, 2014 an excellent description of the changes the statists want to impose on the United States and why their reasoning is flawed.

Folsom, Burton W. *New Deal or Raw Deal? How FDR's Economic Legacy has Damaged America,* Available from various sources. This book describes, with copious references, how the New Deal did not in fact end the Great Depression but in fact extended it. It also describes statist abuses during that time.

Friedman, Milton and Rose, *Free to Choose,* Avon Books, 1980, 1979. This is an excellent book, with one of the authors having received the Nobel Memorial Prize for Economics. The authors explain, in very readable style, the advantages of a free economic system and the problems with collectivism.

Groseclose, Tim, *Left Turn, How Liberal Media Bias Distorts the American Mind.*, St. Martin's Press, 2011. Based on a peer-reviewed article published in the *Quarterly Journal of Economics,* this book describes a statistical measure of "conservative" vs. "liberal" for politicians and applies that measure to news outlets. Not surprisingly, it finds most news outlets are statist/liberal.

Hamburger, Philip, *Is Administrative Law Unlawful?,* The University of Chicago Press, 2014. Describes how the Bureaucracy has grown into administrative law. Bureaucrats effectively not only make law but provide "judges" who owe allegiance to the bureaucracy rather than to the people. Describes how this developed, how it is similar to "prerogative rule" under kings. Also describes how it violates the Constitution and how the courts have neglected their duty regarding this near absolute rule.

Hannan, Daniel, *Inventing Freedom*, Broadside (Imprint of Harper-Collins Publishers), 2013. The author, a trained historian now a member of the European Parliament, describes how freedom developed first in the British Isles and then in the United States, with ample theory about why it did not develop elsewhere. The biggest flaw is its lack of standard citations.

Hannan, Daniel, *The New Road to Serfdom,* Broadside (Imprint of Harper-Collins Publishers), 2010. This is a modern follow-up to Hayek's book listed below. It describes the lack of freedom and other problems of the European Union. The author contrasts the EU with the U.S.A. and warns against following the European path. This is a valuable description of how democratic governments can move toward statism and lack of freedom.

Hayek, F.A., *The Road to Serfdom.* My copy is *The Definitive Edition,* edited by Bruce Caldwell, University of Chicago Press, 2007. However there are several printings available from different sources and pagination differs. This is one of the seminal works of freedom, showing that collectivist economies lead inevitably to totalitarianism. The difficulty for the modern English speaking reader is that the author's background in German-Austrian scholarship shows through in his writing style. Another difficulty for our age is that the book was written during World War II and of course is not up to date. Nevertheless, this is one of the most important books in the literature of freedom.

Head Start Impact Study, Final Report, Executive Summary, January 2010. and *Third Grade Follow Up to the Impact Study, OPRE Report 2012-45*, October 2010 are both available on line and document the fact that preschool programs have essentially no long-term effect on student success.

Howard, Philip K. *The Rule of Nobody, Saving America from Dead Laws and Broken Government,* W. W. Norton and Company, 2014. This book does a good job of describing many problems created by bureaucracies and rigid government rules. He proposes several constitutional amendments to solve the problem, most of which would be effective though I think some should be modified and the last proposed amendment not implemented. However he neglects the most important method of dealing with bureaucratic gridlock: reduce government to the areas where it really belongs. As long as government intrudes into so much of our lives, it will cause the problems he describes.

Janis, Irving, *Victims of Groupthink,* Houghton Mifflin, 1972. This is an excellent book, one that has withstood the test of time. The author describes groupthink and provides several examples. He also describes how to avoid the problem.

Lee, Senator Mike, *Our Lost Constitution, The Willful Subversion of America's Founding Document,* Sentinel, 2015 Describes how our Constitution has been subverted and the damage it does to ordinary citizens as well as to businesses.

Levitt, Steven D. and Dubner, Stephen J. *Freakonomics, a Rogue Economist Explores the Hidden Side of Everything,* William Morrow, 2005. A fun book that addresses a wide range of topics. Though only a few topics bear on our subject here, it is a good example of how to think about various questions.

Pacepa, Lt General Ion Mihai and Professor Rychalk, Ronald J., *Disinformation, Former Spy Chief Reveals Secret Strategies for Undermining Freedom, Attacking Religion, and Promoting Terrorism,* 2013, WND Books, 355pp plus 58 pages of references and bibliography. General Pacepa is the highest ranking eastern bloc intelligence officer ever to defect to the west. Rychalk is the Mississippi Defense Lawyers Association Professor at the University of Mississippi School of Law. This book is written in Pacepa's voice, using his personal experience from years in the Romanian intelligence organization, said organization being essentially controlled by the Russian KGB and its predecessor/successor organizations. Rychalk appears to have mostly provided the references to back up what Pacepa remembered. The book describes how the Soviet bloc spread false information that harms the free countries of the West. While lying and skullduggery are nothing new in international relations, this book documents how communist Russia raised that to a whole new level.

Riley, Jason L. *Please Stop Helping Us, How Liberals Make It Harder for Blacks to Succeed,* Encounter Books, 2014. Describes how mostly well-intentioned measures such as affirmative action, poor school discipline, and welfare have kept Blacks from getting out of poverty. Also describes a Black sub-culture that denigrates education and promotes the very actions that keep them in poverty.

Shaffer, Lt Col Anthony, *Operation Dark Heart,* Thomas Dunne Books. This book describes Lt. Col. Shaffer's time in Afghanistan as well as work with Operation Able Danger and the bureaucratic wrangling that interfered with effective fighting against Al Qaeda and the Taliban.

Silvergate, Harvey A. *Three Felonies a Day, How the Feds Target the Innocent,* Encounter Books, 2009. Describes how the U.S. Justice Department forces people to testify against employers, friends and family, even at times constraining them to testify falsely. Plea bargaining often encourages people to avoid the risk of long prison terms by providing testimony that may or may not be true. The Justice Department also brings charges for actions that are not clearly illegal.

Solzhenitsyn, Aleksandr, *The Gulag Archipelago,* available from various sources in various printings. It was originally in three volumes though different printings may combine them. This is a literary description of the author's experience, from his arrest for daring to criticize Stalin in private letters, until he was eventually released after Stalin's death. It describes the horrors of Soviet prison camps, the arbitrary power authorities possessed, and the degradation and deprivation they forced on anyone unfortunate enough to be accused. It even describes how accusation alone was enough to "prove" guilt. This is not a pleasant read, the evils described are appalling. However it is important that free people everywhere know what statist evils can do. For that reason I recommend that everyone read at least enough of this work to get a understanding of what the USSR hid behind its closed doors, and what is undoubtedly still going on in places like North Korea.

Sowell, Thomas, *A Conflict of Visions, Ideological Origins of Political Struggles,* available from various sources. Though this author's numerous writings generally come down squarely on the side of freedom, in this book he makes a great effort to be neutral. In my opinion he is successful in that. The author describes two different mind-sets which he calls the constrained and unconstrained visions. People with the unconstrained vision tend to believe in essentially unlimited ability of the human mind, at least for those they regard as the elite. This leads to belief that unlimited government by those elites will solve the ills of the world. The constrained vision, on the other hand, is that people are neither perfectly wise nor perfectly moral. This vision values the experience of the ages and the abilities of individuals in their own specialties over any elitist ideas. Those with the constrained vision tend to want limited government and to allow individual freedom. I highly recommend this book. While it may not cause the statists and free men to agree, it can at least move the discussion to a more productive level.

Sowell, Thomas, *Affirmative Action Around the World, An Empirical Study,* Yale University Press, 2004. This book looks at various countries that have tried "affirmative action," the idea of giving preferences to certain classes. It shows the bad results of those well-intentioned programs. A prime example is India which not only has the probably the oldest modern affirmative action programs in the world, but which keeps the best data. India breaks the data down much finer than other countries. This allows the researcher to see that even the people from the preferred groups who are helped most are not those most in need, but those already doing well.

Sowell, Thomas, *Basic Economics, a Commonsense Guide to the Economy,* First published in 2000. Not directly referenced in this book but a good basic introduction to the subject, available in both hard cover and paperback as well as pdf and sound recording. A bit dated now, but the basics of economics don't really change. If you read only one book on economics, this should be it. If you like this book, a good follow-up by the same author is *Applied Economics, Thinking Beyond Stage One.*

Sowell, Thomas, *The Vision of the Anointed, Self-Congratulation as a Basis for Social Policy,* Basic Books, 1995, also available in .pdf. In this follow-up to *A Conflict of Visions,* Sowell drops all pretense of neutrality and points out the damages done by the self-proclaimed elitists that he calls "the anointed." It is an excellent book, not only for the information it contains but as a reference to his sources which are numerous and useful.

Yancey, George, *Compromising Scholarship, Religious and Political Bias in American Higher Education,* Baylor University Press, 2011. Shows how our universities support statism and discriminate against information that would support freedom.

Magazine Article

U.S. News and World Report, November 2009, p26 . Describes leadership styles and advantages, including the dangers of charismatic leaders. Available on line.

Selected Web Sites

http://www.weeklystandard.com/blogs/senate-aide-gun-law-wouldnt-have-stopped-newtown-massacre_716215.html. Documents some of the gun control controversy, especially the fact that some proponents know their proposed measures will not be helpful, but they want the appearance of doing something.

http://www.historyplace.com/worldwar2/riseofhitler/25points.htm. Gives a description of the tricks Hitler used to become dictator of Germany.

http://www.historyplace.com/worldwar2/riseofhitler/25points.htm. Lists Hitler's 25 points that he formulated before taking power.

http://www.researchgate.net/publication/4768694_Italian_city-states_and_financial_evolution. Describes how much of our modern financial system got started, including the part played by the Italian cities of Genoa, Venice, and Florence in developing banking, maritime commerce, and manufacturing.

http://www.theobjectivestandard.com/issues/2008-summer/standard-oil-company.asp. Gives much history of the Standard Oil Company, including the means that company used to improve efficiency, cut costs, and make kerosene much more available to the masses.

http://www.thefire.org/cases/university-of-kansas-anti-nra-tweet-results-in-professors-suspension/, and http://www.thefire.org/ Web site of FIRE, the Foundation for Individual Rights in Education. That foundation combats campus rules against free speech and other statist measures on campus. Lists many campus rules that prohibit free speech.

http://www.nationalreview.com/article/348756/true-scandal-jillian-kay-melchior, and http://canadafreepress.com/index.php/article/61052. Articles about federal pressure on the founders of True the Vote. These sites document the pressure brought to bear on them when they fought against election fraud.

http://www.infowars.com/your-kids-belong-to-the-collective/ (The link includes video of the professor making that claim.) Documents that at least one statist wants the "community," not parents to be responsible for children.

http://www.historylearningsite.co.uk/censorship_in_nazi_germany.htm. A description of how Nazi Germany controlled information available to the people.

http://news.investors.com/ibd-editorials/021314-690050-fcc-newsroom-plan-all-about-controlling-the-free-press.htm Documents the FCC giving consideration to putting "researchers" in newsrooms.

http://www.discoverthenetworks.org/Articles/theclowardpivenstrategypoe.html This web site describes the Cloward-Piven strategy in all its gory detail. Everybody should know about this statist technique.

http://www.theatlantic.com/health/archive/2012/07/the-startling-accuracy-of-referring-to-politicians-as-psychopaths/260517/ Describes some commonalities between psychopathy and what we see in many politicians. Although this is a popular treatment, it does draw on some research. However, as far as I can determine, research in this area is still in its infancy.

About the Author

Hal Lillywhite was raised on a dairy farm in New Mexico, then escaped the cows by studying physics and engineering. He has master's degrees in solid state physics and in electronic science. That education taught him the value of logical and critical thinking, something he believes is lacking in our political world today.

Hal has been a mountain rescue volunteer for nearly 30 years. He has also been a paratrooper, missionary, teacher, and project manager.

In the army and as a missionary he lived in and visited statist countries and saw the difficulties such governments cause. He has been knocking around this world long enough to see the increasing power of the federal government and the damage that power does.

Hal now lives with his wife in Oregon while their grown children are scattered all over the country, and even out of the country.

Index

www.ingramcontent.com/pod-product-compliance
Lightning Source LLC
Chambersburg PA
CBHW081057290526
45795CB00006B/1893